THE HIGH
PROBABILITY
OPTIONS
TRADER

THE HIGH
PROBABILITY
OPTIONS
TRADER

*Winning Strategies to
Take You to the Next Level*

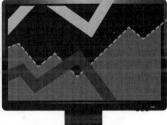

MARCEL LINK

New York   Chicago   San Francisco   Athens   London   Madrid
Mexico City   Milan   New Delhi   Singapore   Sydney   Toronto

1 2 3 4 5 6 7 8 9   LCR   28 27 26 25 24 23

ISBN   978-1-264-90576-8
MHID   1-264-90576-9

e-ISBN   978-1-264-90911-7
e-MHID   1-264-90911-X

This publication is designed to provide accurate and authoritative information in regard to the subject matter covered. It is sold with the understanding that neither the author nor the publisher is engaged in rendering legal, accounting, securities trading, or other professional services. If legal advice or other expert assistance is required, the services of a competent professional person should be sought.
—*From a Declaration of Principles Jointly Adopted by a Committee of the American Bar Association and a Committee of Publishers and Associations*

McGraw Hill books are available at special quantity discounts to use as premiums and sales promotions or for use in corporate training programs. To contact a representative, please visit the Contact Us pages at www.mhprofessional.com.

McGraw Hill is committed to making our products accessible to all learners. To learn more about the available support and accommodations we offer, please contact us at accessibility@mheducation.com. We also participate in the Access Text Network (www.accesstext.org), and ATN members may submit requests through ATN.

Dedicated to Sally, whom I ignored more than a bit during the last few months of writing this book.

Contents

Acknowledgments

In the course of writing this book, I used many online sources for information or refreshers. These are the ones I have found most helpful:

tastylive.com

OptionsPlay.com

MarketChameleon.com

EarningsWhispers.com

OptionAlpha.com

OptionsEducation.org

Cboe.com

eDeltaPro.com (for back testing)

I would like to thank Stephen Isaacs, formerly from McGraw Hill, who gave me a shot 20 years ago and published my first book, *High Probability Trading*, without which I wouldn't be writing this one, and also to whomever has the task of fixing my grammar and some of the excessively long run-on sentences I tend to write, kinda like this one.

There is also Luna the annoying cat, who didn't think I could write this book without her help as she walked on my keyboard or sat in front of my monitors every night as I tried to write.

Introduction

When I first started writing this book in 2021, the stock market was in the midst of one of the most incredible bull markets I have ever seen. Then the Federal Reserve started a program of massive interest rate hikes throughout 2022 to combat high inflation, and for the following year we were in one of the worst bear markets I have seen. Many of the stocks that had ridiculous gains in 2021 plummeted in 2022; I saw stocks go from to $20 to $400 to $10. Stocks that were $500 a share went to $40; even the old faithful ones like Amazon, Apple, Google, Netflix, and Facebook (now Meta) saw huge losses, some losing more than half their values in months. Many aggressive traders who weren't alert nor flexible saw a year's worth of profits disappear in a couple of months. Hopefully this book can help you avoid those wild equity swings of an unpredictable market.

INTRO TO THE INTRO

Twenty years ago, I submitted the 512 page manuscript of my first book, *High Probability Trading*, to my editor. His immediate reaction upon reading it was, "It's a good book, but it's way too long, you need to cut out at least 100 pages." My immediate reaction is probably unprintable, but I painstakingly set about to tackle this, eventually removing a 40 page chapter on options that, while good, didn't flow with the rest of the book. Now here I am, 20 odd years later, watching the popularity of options trading go through the roof, revisiting that chapter and giving it its fair due by turning it into a book of its own.

GROWING POPULARITY OF OPTIONS

In the last few years, trading volume has increased dramatically for both stocks and options, with the Covid-19 pandemic helping even more. According to data compiled by CBOE (Chicago Board Option Exchange), the volume in single-stock options averaged 17.3 million contracts during 2020, up 68% from the 10.3 million daily average for 2019. Options trading has continued to accelerate, and now in early 2023, the average daily volume of equity options is between 40 and 50 million. I don't see that trend slowing down, so if you are going to join the option's trading bandwagon, why not learn to do it with the highest probability of success you can.

One reason for the growing popularity, I believe, is that because of Covid, there was an explosion of locked-down, bored-at-home people with nothing better to do. Coupled with quite a bit of extra money from the government's stimulus checks, a slew of new traders emerged. Many of these new traders start with small accounts, and in order to get the most bang for their money are lured in by the low barriers of entry and high potential rewards of option trading. These traders cannot afford to buy Tesla outright, but they can buy cheap out of the money calls on it. Adding fuel to the fire is the recent capability of nearly zero cost commissions. Even more experienced traders are finding it easier to trade more frequently, and put on spreads and four-sided trades that they may not have done when they had to worry about commissions eating potential profit.

WHY READ THIS BOOK?

Whether you have no knowledge of what an option is or have been trading them for a while, this book will put you on the path of becoming an options expert. First, this book is not just about understanding how to trade options, but also for developing the basic foundation every trader should have both before and after making a trade. Great traders rely on those building blocks, combined with the proper trader's mindset to achieve success.

If you are new to options, you will learn the basics before advancing to the next level of trading. For advanced traders, you will leave with new ideas to take advantage of a wide range of high probability trading opportunities, with many personal examples past and present under different market environments. This book will cover topics like knowing how far out to go in time, which strike prices are best, when is the best time to exit, how to take advantage of earnings, how to manage your trades, and how to value risk. You should finish this book with a thorough understanding of option pricing, how to use different trading strategies, how to think like a professional, how to manage your portfolio, and even how to understand Gamma risk.

THE BEAUTY OF OPTIONS

I love trading options because they are a versatile tool for trading that can be used in multiple ways in different market environments. They offer a trader much more flexibility than the traditional buying of stocks, and if used properly, lower risks. One of the great things about trading options is that you can be slightly wrong in market direction and still make money—unless of course you are just buying calls, for which you need to be very right, and in a set amount of time. You can use options as a defensive hedge, like having an insurance policy protecting your investments in case of a market downturn. Options can be used to capture extra money from stocks you may be long or can be used to buy stocks a little cheaper. Another great reason to trade options is that unlike trading futures or stocks, you don't need to be glued to a screen all day. Regardless of experience or risk tolerance, options can and should be a tool a trader has in their toolbelt to help take advantage of multiple market situations.

GOALS OF THE BOOK

My goal in writing this book is to help traders who want to expand their trading arsenal and move to the next level of trading. This book is not just about how to put on a great trade, but also how to manage that trade, as well as a whole portfolio—which in my opinion is even more important than being able to spot a good trade. The ultimate goal of a great trader should not be making great trades and maximizing profits; instead, it should be to maximize potential profits while limiting risks. Without proper risk and money management, it takes very little to wipe out an account; this book will constantly drive that point home, to make you an all-around better trader and to have you thinking like a professional.

WHO WILL BENEFIT FROM THIS BOOK?

The simple answer is: you. Many traders do not fully understand the power of options, and the different ways to use them. Many start by just buying out of the money calls, because they are a cheap way to play a stock. While this worked great in 2021, as the markets kept moving higher and higher, giving many new "traders" the sense that they were great traders, in reality it's not hard to make money in a runaway bull market.

If you view options as too complicated, something that should be left only to hedge fund managers and floor traders; if the terms iron butterfly, credit spread, Delta, or Theta leave you scratching your head, then this book should provide you clarity. You may think options are too risky for you; yet, if used properly, the opposite is true. Yes, while improper use of options can lead to a lot of risk, they can also be used to set up trades with high probabilities of making money or to lower portfolio risk.

WHAT NOT TO EXPECT

This book is not a get rich quick scheme. My methods do not look for homerun trades that make thousands on a $50 option; rather it's about the steady growth of income with higher probability trades while protecting what you have. Though when conditions are right it sometimes makes sense to put on a huge potential trade, for the most part, these are a very small part of my trading; instead, I will focus on ways to make small but steady gains.

This book stays away from complex formulas, advanced pricing modules, that may bore you senseless. Instead, I will attempt to make understanding and analyzing options common sense with easy-to-follow straight talk. You will still get a thorough understanding of option Greeks and valuation, and I will try to make it entertaining.

WHY LISTEN TO ME?

After a short stint as a stockbroker in 1987, I started working on the floor of New York Mercantile Exchange as a Crude Oil options clerk, where I first started gaining invaluable option experience. It was here that I learned the intricacy of option trading, far beyond the typical speculative buying of puts and calls. Though it wasn't till years later that I took full advantage of that learning experience, things like Delta hedging and volatility trading became ingrained in me. In 1989, I got a seat on the floor, trading NYFE, Dollar Index, and Cotton futures. I'm not sure why they call it a seat; I never once saw a chair, and stood almost seven hour a day. I must have gotten tired of all the standing after a while; I decided to go graduate school in 1994 and started trading out of my clearinghouse's office in my free time, where I finally got to sit.

> The NYFE was a futures contract traded on the NY Cotton Exchange in New York. It was an affordable version of the S&P futures contract, trading at about half the speed with much smaller margin requirements. With the popularization of the E-minis in 1997, it has become obsolete over the years.

After completing graduate school in 1996, I started an online commodities discount brokerage firm, which I sold two years later. I moved away from futures and began day trading stocks on a trading desk, and over the years I opened up a couple of bars in NYC. Along the way I wrote two trading books, *High Probability Trading* in 2003 and *Trading Without Gambling* in 2009. In 2010, I sold my last bar, moved away from the city, and returned to trading futures and futures options for myself. In 2012 I opened a restaurant in the Hamptons, which took up a good chunk of my time, and found it easiest to trade equity options, as I didn't have to monitor them as much as futures. I, luckily, sold my restaurant six months before the beginning of Covid-19 shutdowns, and began trading full-time again; nowadays option trading comprises the majority of what I trade.

With my 35+ years of trading experience, including years surrounded by both great and bad traders, I have either seen or made just about every mistake a trader can make—which I don't mind sharing so hopefully you don't need to make them yourself. More importantly, I have also been able to observe the winning qualities a good trader possesses. One favorite lesson became the concept for my book *High Probability Trading*: you can make a lot more money by simply not making the same stupid mistakes over and over again.

I hope this book helps you get to the next level of options trading, and you tell everyone you know to buy a copy. Feel free to email me at Marcel@MarcelLink.com with any questions.

CHAPTER 1

10,000 Hours

"How to Turn $2,000 into $1 Million Trading Options Without the Use of a Time Machine."

That would be a great book, but unfortunately, I can't make that kind of promise. It can happen, as it might have if you were lucky enough to buy GameStop calls the week before the WallStreetBets subreddit pushed it from $18 to $450, and managed to get out before it dropped down to $45 a couple of weeks later. In reality, it is unlikely that someone will do this (and keep their profits if they do), yet there are folks out there with the grand delusion that this is normal. The strategies I talk about are not these home run types of trades; instead, you will learn how to build an account in a steady fashion while reducing risk and developing as an all-around trader.

FIRST DISCLAIMER

Don't worry if I mention something you may not understand or if I use a term you haven't heard before; it's not important yet. I do promise that by the end of book everything I mention will be thoroughly explained and should become part of your vernacular.

QUESTIONS THIS BOOK ANSWERS

Some of the questions you should be able to answer after reading this book include:

What are the factors that will make my option move in price?

How do option prices erode over time, and how can I benefit from it?

Is an option's volatility relatively cheap or expensive?

What is the trade's probability of profit if held to expiration?

How far out in time of an expiration should I use?

What's the best strike price for my trade?

How can I reduce risk on my option portfolio?

When should I exit to minimize risk?

WHY TRADE OPTIONS?

To make money of course—or could it be to protect your money? Or maybe to expand your trading capabilities? Though most people get their exposure to trading by buying stocks, options have the allure of the ability to make a lot more money with a lot less money than you can with stocks. Though this is a good way to start—and it's how I started—it's not the best way.

Some investors who own stock get their exposure to options by selling covered calls to make extra income. This is a better method of using options, but it's just scratching the surface of your capabilities. As you learn the many ways to trade and use options, it will open up many more advantages over trading stocks.

First, when you trade stocks there are really only two ways to make money: you can go long by buying a stock hoping it goes up, or you can go short by selling a stock if you believe it's going down. With options trading, on the other hand, you can also make money if the market doesn't move, or even if the market moves slightly against you. You don't even need to trade for price moves; you can try to capture time decay or discrepancies in the speed of volatility in two offsetting options.

THE BUSINESS OF TRADING

Prior to discussing options and actual trading, these first two chapters will get you to think like a professional trader. Not so much like hedge fund managers and the market makers who have millions of dollars behind them, but as the person who can eventually make a living trading options for themselves. Whether you are a total newbie or have experience behind you and are looking to move up the trading ladder, you need to put in the time learning and getting your hands dirty to get there.

Being a successful trader is a wonderful thing that beats a full-time job any day, but it's not easy; it can be stressful and often leaves you with self-doubt. If you do plan to make a living from trading, you should take it as seriously as the guy who opens up a pizzeria or as the woman who trades at Goldman Sachs. These are people working their butts off, putting in 12-hour days trying to make their businesses thrive, not looking for shortcuts. As someone trying to make a living trading, you should have your full attention on the market, your positions, checking your risks, looking for trades, and learning. Even if you can only be a part-time trader, treat trading as a business; spend time when you get home, after your real job, to do the proper research looking for trading ideas, reviewing your portfolio of positions, and never stop learning.

STAGES OF A BUSINESS

As with any other business, trading success doesn't happen overnight. A business can have several stages it goes through before success finally comes.

Startup Phase: Year One and Before
This is where the business gets established. Most new businesses take time to turn a profit, during which the business owners are learning the ropes. Professionals will take the time to learn a business and then make a plan before spending all of their capital. You would never start a pizzeria without good knowledge of pizza making, and ideally you would have worked in a pizzeria before. The first year is when you need to absorb as much information as you can and gain as much expertise as possible, not just about making pizza, but about

your customers as well. The goal here should be to manage your funds to ensure you still have some at the end of the year, when you will hopefully have a better idea of how to manage the business. An options trader, even one who has traded stocks for years, also needs to take this time to master their trade.

Growing Stage: The Next Few Years

Your pizza joint is starting to turn a steady profit. You have made your share of mistakes along the way, but you are figuring out how to succeed. You have figured out how to manage your inventory and expenses, and you know how to staff properly and cost effectively. You've learned what dishes work and have reluctantly eliminated the chopped liver and pickles pizza you really thought would be a winner, that never worked out.

It can be a struggle getting though this stage; these are the make-or-break years. During this stage it's important to stick to the business plan that got you here, but it's also important to review and update it. An options trader will go through the same process; these years are the most critical, and many traders don't survive. You will start to learn what strategies and parameters work and those that don't. You will either have learned risk and money management, or simply put, you will no longer be trading.

Mature Stage: Beyond

As the pizzeria matures and brings in more steady income you can relax; maybe you can expand and buy four more pizzerias and a car dealership at once, or if rich enough even buy Twitter. Of course, I am kidding: the amount of work and discipline required to run a successful business will not diminish, nor should you grow your risks beyond those you have calculated well. Don't be like some business owners who after a good run start throwing away money on risky decisions and purchases that could ruin them, instead of sticking to the plan that got them to success.

The options trader likewise should not start taking on more risk than they can handle just because they are now more successful and more confident. As your equity increases, so does the need for greater risk management; you do not want to watch the fruits of your hard work disappear. It's OK to expand

and use multiple strategies to make money, but keep within your plan's risk parameters. Lastly, never stop learning and perfecting your skills; markets change, and you need to be able to adapt with them.

Learning the Business

So, how do you go about learning the business of trading options? The real answer is to put in the time. There is a lot to learn, like option valuation, how to lower risk, how to evaluate implied volatility, how to use technical analysis, which strategies to use, and what time frames to look at. Learning the business of trading options is not just learning to look at charts and putting on a directional trade. It also includes basic things such as how to enter an order, how to use your broker's trading platform, the different order types (market, limit, stop, etc.), how to use margin, and what to do if you get assigned.

The 10,000 Hour Rule

Have you heard of the 10,000 hour rule? It was popularized by Malcolm Gladwell in his book *Outliers: The Story of Success.*[*] It's not an exact science, but it more or less states that in order to achieve mastery of complex skills and materials and reach elite levels in a field, it takes 10,000 hours of intensive practice.

This can apply to playing the violin, becoming a chess master, being a gold medal Olympic athlete, or just being great at whatever field you choose.

For 45 years I have been playing guitar and piano, and I consider myself a pretty good musician, but I never devoted the hours to get truly great. My 17-year-old son, however, plays for what seems like four hours a day and has become much better than I am on both instruments, as he puts in his 10,000 hours to achieve his goal of being a professional musician. Though I would prefer it if he spent more time doing schoolwork over learning every note of every Led Zeppelin, Beatles, Grateful Dead, and Jimi Hendrix song on guitar, piano, bass, and drums. (As I go over the edits of the book a year later he is now studying at Berklee College of Music. Hopefully I don't have

---

[*] Malcolm Gladwell, *Outliers: The Story of Success* (Back Bay Books, Little, Brown and Company, 2008).

to open another restaurant so he can become a waiter, if his dream of being a rock star doesn't pan out.)

I would apply this dedicated time to trading as well. If you want to get good, and I mean really good, you need to devote those 10,000 hours of practice, learning, and experience to become a real master of the field. Plumbers, electricians, doctors, lawyers, and pizza makers do it; so should a trader. Ten thousand hours to master the art of trading would take seven years if you traded every tradable hour every day; five years if you spent quite a bit of time doing research and homework every night. That is not an unreasonable amount to master something—it's no different than going to college and then getting a master's degree.

Though it's always encouraged to paper trade to get a feel for things, you can't paper trade for seven years. It is also a lot easier to follow rules when real money is not on the line, because when you are trading real money it can be harder, mentally, to take a loss. Paper trading does not help you with the emotional side of trading, and it's from this side that poor money management and excessive risk creeps in, making it easy to lose money.

Instead, I suggest learning by trading one contract in small moving, low-cost options, with strategies that won't kill you. You need to devote money to learning the business. This is what I call the *tuition of trading*. It's the money you will lose as your learn the business and make mistakes. There is no college degree for trading; if you are good, you will learn from mistakes; if you are not good you will make these mistakes repeatedly and with an Ivy League–like tuition but without the knowledge.

Learning to trade is more than just learning by trading, of course; read as much as possible and watch tutorials, take classes, and listen to better traders. One word of advice: when listening to others, always be skeptical of what you hear and read, especially when listening to CNBC, and do your own research. Sometimes people are pushing their own trades when they recommend something; other times they are just dead wrong. I do get a lot of ideas from watching CNBC or tastylive.com, but I never blindly jump in: I make my own analysis first. If do you follow someone's advice and lose money, don't blame them—it's still your fault for putting on the trade, especially if you didn't do your homework first. If I tell you strangles are one of the best profit making trades you can make, and you decide to put one on a very volatile stock, losing $4,000 because you were wrong and didn't get out, that's on you, not me.

THE BEATLES' 10,000 HOURS

The Beatles weren't just a band that got a lucky break and made it big. One main reason they became the phenomenon they were was that they put in the hours to be great. According to the BeatlesBible.com, between 1960 and 1962, the Beatles performed 281 times in Hamburg, playing a total of between five and seven hours a day. They also did another 292 shows at the Cavern in Liverpool around this time and a 199-show tour of England in 1963. In their spare time they practiced and worked on their songwriting skills.

This doesn't add up to 10,000 hours, but they had already been playing and writing music together day and night, eating, breathing, and sleeping rock 'n' roll, since July 1957. Those countless hours had their rewards. By the time they reached America in 1964, their songwriting had evolved and they were such a well-oiled machine that they could play live in a stadium without being able to hear each other over the screams of the crowd. Ringo, not being able to hear the rest of the band, said he knew where they were in a song by the way Paul shook his head.

Without those long hours they put in, they might never have gotten a record deal, been invited on *The Ed Sullivan Show*, or written some everlasting songs. Instead they would have been more like the Merseybeats. Who, you ask, are the Merseybeats? They were another Liverpudlian band that didn't put in their 10,000 hours and blamed and fired Brian Epstein (the manager they shared with the Beatles) for their lack of success and for not buying them fancy suits like he did for the Beatles.

My advice: Be like the Beatles and put your time in.

Advice #2: Don't blame others for your lack of skills.

HAVE A PLAN

If you were to start a business and try to get financing, anyone would ask for a business plan. The same is true for trading. Have such a solid plan that it could convince someone to give you money to trade with, even if that someone you are convincing is yourself. Convince yourself that you have what it takes to put down real money. Even as a part-time trader, you should treat trading with the same respect. You don't need to show your plan to anyone, but take a few minutes and start working on one for yourself.

Though it should be the one of first things you do, you won't have the knowledge to make a plan right away. While you are reading, start thinking about your goals, what strategies you will use, how much available capital you have, and what your risk levels are. As you progress through the book, it will be easier to put together a trading plan.

THE TRADING PLAN

I had written a few chapters that wound up on the cutting room floor as the book ended up being too long, but more about that in the final chapter. One of these was about making a trading plan. You can find the trading plan chapter along with a few other gems on my website, MarcelLink.com.

ADOPT THE PROPER MINDSET

Being a top trader is not just about making great trades; there are many little activities that add up to get you to that point. One of those is having a winner's mindset. You can know everything there is to know about options and have the greatest strategy, but that doesn't mean you will succeed. The traders who constantly make money have developed the proper psychological mindset, enabling them to be consistent winners. They believe they will be successful, and a few bad trades won't shake their confidence. They understand that no matter how good they think a trade will be, it can go sour for many reasons. They know how to take a loss and move on, instead of trying to make back double the next time. They do not believe they can outsmart the market and will accept it when the market tells them they are wrong. They also know when a trade is over on the winning side, and are not trying to squeeze every last penny out of a trade. Most importantly, these winning traders are not gamblers, and know how to respect risk.

In a scenario where a trade loses money, a trader with the wrong mindset will look at it as a bad trade, whereas one with the right mindset will look at it as a good trade that didn't work out. I make a lot of trades that lose money; however, if they are part of my trading strategy and I haven't overtraded, then I consider it a good trade, regardless of the outcome. You cannot control what a stock does after you are in. This can be discouraging when you have a few losing trades in a row, but if you follow your rules, making good high probability trades while controlling your risk, you will be on the right track to success. Don't let a bad trade get to you; review your trades, see if you did anything wrong, what you could do differently next time, and then move on to the next trade.

Elements of having the proper mindset include:

Being comfortable taking risks. You cannot make money if you never take risks. I've seen traders who are so concerned about risk that they either bypass many trades or never give trades a chance to work, losing money because their stops are too tight. Being able to take calculated risks within the parameters of a trading plan and knowing how to limit them is part of being a successful trader.

Being able to adapt to changing market conditions. If you fall in love with a position or direction, it can be easy to justify to yourself why your position is correct, as you continue to lose more and more money. A stock like Roku, for instance, that steadily rose from the $20s to almost $500 was a great stock to be long for a few years, but then it dropped rather quickly to around $200 (at time of writing, it has dropped to $41). The smart money knew this trade was over long ago, but some traders struggle to believe the uptrend is over, seeing every one-day rally as proof they are correct. The proper mindset acknowledges that you are wrong, not the stock.

Having the ability to view the markets with an unbiased opinion. Every night I review all my positions. When the reason I got into a trade no longer exists, I look to exit. If I sold a put spread because I thought the implied volatility was going to come down or the stock would rally, but neither has happened after two weeks, then I know I was wrong; I take my loss or very small profit and move on. I like to ask myself, "If I had no trade on, what would I do now?" Often when you are losing, you don't want to hear the answer, and can justify to yourself why you should give it one more day. You need to be able to constantly look at positions with a fresh perspective, to clear your head.

Being able to control emotions. Don't get overly excited when you are on a winning streak, because when you think you are invincible, you may throw your rules out the window, start overtrading, and end up losing a lot more than you just made. Trust me—it has happened to me more than once. Always be humble; never think you are better than the market. The same is true when losing; if you let it get to you, it can easily affect the way you trade. You may not pull the trigger on the next good trade, or you may end up taking profits too early just to have a winner, or let losses ride because you can't mentally absorb another loss.

KNOW YOUR TRADING STYLE

Traders are like snowflakes: no two are alike, and what may work for one trader may not work for another. It is impossible to give someone a fail-safe, off-the-rack trading plan that will work for all. One of the goals of this book is to give you the ingredients to succeed that you can tailor to your own style, so you can make a custom fit trading plan.

I know I can't scalp (trading in and out of stocks all day trying to make a few pennies per trade). I see no point in it, and yet if my friend Bruce holds a trade for more than 15 minutes he breaks out in a sweat and gets out. We both make money, but in two completely different ways. Some people love trading high-volatility and expensive options like Tesla, but a person with a lower risk tolerance may not be able to ride out a giant swing in those options and is better off trading options in Apple, which are less volatile with a much tighter spread. Before you can develop a trading plan, you need to know what type of a trader you are. Here are some questions to think about:

Are you a conservative or an aggressive investor?

Do you prefer big gains with more risk or slow, steady smaller gains?

Will you trade options that expire in a few days, or do you prefer options that have months to work out?

Are you looking to make quick in and out trades, or do you prefer holding for days, weeks, or months?

Do you prefer to focus on a large number of stocks, sectors, or indexes, or just a few select stocks?

Are you looking to buy options or to sell them?

How much risk can you take on?

Can you control your ego?

How much time can you dedicate to watching the markets?

How big is your account?

Are you a trend follower or always looking for reversals?

Do you like to buy cheap out of the money options or buy deep in the money ones instead?

Hopefully, after reading this book, you will make a trading plan that incorporates your strengths and be able to develop your own tailor-made trading style that you can follow.

TRADE DELUSIONS OF GRANDEUR FOR REALISTIC GOALS AND EXPECTATIONS

I have seen a lot of hype over the years about how much money can be made buying options, especially lately on YouTube ads. Some "gurus" promise 1,000% and even 10,000% returns each year. If you believe this, you are in for a surprise. Not a single person who can make that kind of money needs to sell you his entry and exit points or her trading course; these "gurus" do it because they need money. It is unrealistic to assume that everyone or anyone can start trading options and turn $5,000 into $100,000 in a year. Crazy returns should not be your goal—they are a delusion of grandeur. There is little chance that someone can sustain such returns over time. I used to hope it was possible, but I only started making money in options when I stopped chasing after the big-money "home run" trades and started writing spreads instead.

Professional money managers pray they can match the S&P and throw a party if they achieve 20% returns a year, so don't think because you read a few books you will grossly outperform them. Yes, it is possible, but it would mean (a) you got really lucky or (b) you found the once-in-a-lifetime trading market, like the rally after the initial Covid plummet, or (c) you are trading beyond your capital means and can easily blow out, or (d) you have the time machine I mentioned at the beginning.

Instead, I recommend that you have a realistic plan about the returns you can earn and how long it may take to achieve them. Your first realistic goal in year one should not be how much you can make, but how little you will lose, so you can still be trading after a year's time, when you have a lot more trading and option know-how. Goal number two might be to learn everything you possibly can about option trading. Goal three: develop a trading plan that works. Goal four: quit my job and trade full time in three years. Final goal: move out of my mom's basement.

FULL-TIME VERSUS PART-TIME TRADER

The advice and strategies I give throughout this book could apply to either a part-time or full-time trader. The only difference would be in how much time you have to devote to the markets. One of the great things about option trading is you don't have to be glued to a screen all day. I put on a lot of spreads, iron condors, and broken wing butterflies and will hold them for weeks. You don't need to babysit these types of positions, and most of your homework and position management can be done at night. You still do need to be able to enter orders and occasionally look at prices, so there are strategies I don't recommend to part-time traders, like trading naked options, trading on earning reports, or weekly options expiring in a few days. Overall, though, you can have a full-time job and have a successful time trading options. You just need to cater your plan to your trading style and work with what you are comfortable with.

IT TAKES MONEY TO MAKE MONEY

People don't want to hear this, but unfortunately, you do need money in order to make money. Trading is a zero sum game, and it's hard to compete with a few thousand dollars against people who have $2.3 billion behind them. So, how much money do you need to trade options? That depends on your goals, and whether you are looking to trade full time or not.

I will start with the full-time trader. Like any other business, it is crucial to start out properly capitalized. I would not even attempt to trade full time for a living without $100,000 that can be dedicated to trading. But even that is a bit low; people who make a living trading have accounts much larger than that. Of course, everyone has to start somewhere. You can trade full time with $25,000, but if you think that you can make a living with that, you are in for a shock. In time though, you should be able to steadily grow it, until you can make a living from trading.

Not even considering profits or losses, you need to take into account living expenses, unless you have extra capital or your mom or spouse is supporting you; if you need to worry about making $3,000 a month just to live on and you start trading with $100,000 in capital, you need to aim for 30% to 40% yearly gains just to break even, and this may be a stretch. This may result in you pushing to make less favorable trades or risking too much at any given time just to pay your bills. If you have to start dipping into your trading account to live on, it will slowly shrink to a level that can't sustain your trading full time. Another thing to keep in mind: there are no guarantees in trading, and there will be some lean months or years even after you have achieved success. You cannot depend on saying, "I will make $3,000 a month" and expect it to happen. You can make a fair amount of money seven months in a row and then lose for a few months, even though you are doing nothing different. It's a part of trading that should be taken into consideration.

If you are trading options but not looking to do so full time, you can technically start with any amount as long as you can meet the margin requirements. Most brokerage houses will let you trade on margin with a $2,000 minimum account balance, and that is enough to place spreads and few other trades that can give you a small but diverse options portfolio. I recommend having at least $5,000 to give yourself a chance and to make a few mistakes along the way. If you are looking to sell naked positions, $10,000 would be a good starting amount.

Regardless of your account size, in the early stages you should be making small in size, conservative trades that probably won't yield a tremendous profit. You may actually lose some money at the start. Remember to plan for your business's infrastructure costs, things like extra monitors, any informative websites you want to join, any paid software you may want to subscribe to, and any other costs that would cut into your capital.

WHY TRADERS FAIL

To make it as a trader, it's best to know why traders fail and avoid those traits and mistakes. There are many reasons why someone fails, but here are a few of the top ones, in no particular order. I will expand on some throughout the book.

Lack of preparation: Not doing homework before making a trade—every trade should have a reason for being made. It should have predetermined exit points in mind, not necessarily a price target, but can be based on other criteria such as time or volatility. Every trade should be planned out with best-and worst-case scenarios.

Following other people: You should be able to make your own trading decisions and not follow the advice of so-called experts. Listen for ideas, but make your own decisions.

Being undercapitalized: This doesn't mean you can't trade with a small account; it means you have to trade within your means. If you have $5,000, don't risk $3,000 on a trade.

Not knowing how to lose: I don't mean being a sore loser, but not knowing when to get out of a bad position. It's incredible how traders will refuse to take a $70 loss when they know a trade isn't working correctly, only to take a $2,000 loss a bit later. Being able to mentally take a loss is crucial. It also frees up capital for new trades that hopefully will work out better.

Revenge trading: In the same vein, trying to make up money after a loss or refusing to acknowledge you are wrong on a stock and doubling up or reentering a closed-out trade with larger volume to get your money back is another deadly sin of trading. Ego has no place in trading: when you are beat, you need to let it go, lick your wounds, and move on to new trading opportunities.

Chasing the market: This is one that I still struggle with at times, but if you are constantly chasing the market and paying top dollar for something, you will be buying at the top more often than you think. You are so much better off waiting for a pullback and getting a better entry point. You need to be able to say, "So what." If you completely miss something, there will be more opportunities down the road.

Not being able to pull the trigger: On the opposite side of chasing is never being able to enter a trade. You simply cannot make money if you never trade or you wait too long trying to get five indicators to line up.

Greed: Trying to make too much, holding out for every penny, or trading options too rich for your account size while looking for big, quick gains is deadly. Don't overtrade, and take what the market gives you without overstaying your welcome.

Misusing stops: There are a number of ways stops can hurt: (1) you don't use them, (2) you make them randomly, (3) you place them too close, or (4) you keep canceling stops as they get close. I don't believe in entering stops in most option trades because of the large bid and ask spreads, but you should have stop levels in mind and written down and actually follow them.

Ignoring money management: Though there are many reasons that people fail, I would have to say the number one reason is poor money management skills. I will devote a chapter to this later, but for now I want to emphasize one thing I was taught many years ago: "Be a money manager first, and a trader second." It simply does not matter how good you are at putting on great trades if you cannot manage your money and risk—it could only take one bad trade to blow you out. However, with proper money management skills, you could lose 15 times in a row and not have it impact you much.

Lack of discipline: And finally, you must have the discipline to follow your rules, do your homework, wait for trades, get out of trades, not overtrade, not trade out of boredom, basically not do all the above mistakes. Without discipline you are going to struggle.

A PROPERLY THOUGHT OUT TRADE

Here's an example of a trade with solid reasoning behind it. Looking at charts, I believe Microsoft, currently at $341 with an implied volatility (IV) of 27% and IV percentile (IV%) at 55%, will be going higher in the next six weeks, while volatility will be going down. If I turn out to be wrong, I don't believe it will drop below $320. Here $310 would be the lower level of a one standard deviation move in that time period, but the uptrend is strong, so I am comfortable with $320 as my support level. The strategy I want to use for this trade is to sell a 320/310 put spread, with 50 days before it expires. The spread is currently trading at $1.85. This strategy fits my game plan and risk levels, so it is safe to use. I will exit for a profit when the spread is trading at $0.75. If the price of Microsoft goes below $310 or the IV goes above 40%, I will exit even if I am losing money. Lastly, I will exit when there are 14 to 21 days left to expiration to avoid Gamma risk.

You may not understand any of this now, but don't worry—you will as you keep reading. The point though is that every trade should be properly thought out with as much detail as possible.

This is much better than a poorly evaluated trade of, "I am buying ten $350 calls that expire in three days, YOLO."

FINAL THOUGHTS

Put yourself in the mindset of a winning trader from the start. Do everything possible to make your trading business a success and get the hours and experience you need to become a next level high probability trader. If you can do it, it sure beats a nine-to-five job.

CHAPTER 2

The Versatility of Options

No other financial instrument can do the things that options can do. Their versatility, from multiple ways of making money, near-limitless strategies, and ways to protect your portfolio, is immense. This chapter looks into just a handful of the many ways you can use them.

WHY TRADE OPTIONS

Here are some of the many reasons to trade options.

Versatility

The versatility and flexibility of options tops my list of why trade options. Because of the many things one can do with options, they should be considered at every level of trading, from the trader with a small account looking for some leverage to the giant hedge fund manager protecting against a downfall in the market; from the retired teacher looking to generate a little extra income from his investment account to the savvy trader who makes a living selling spreads and strangles or shorting volatility. Options traders don't have to buy a stock and hope it goes up to make money; instead, they can put on a position where they hope the market goes up, and they can still profit even if it goes down a bit. Your odds of success are greater when you don't have to be as right every time. Plus, wouldn't it be great to want to buy a stock, and end up getting it at a cheaper price, like you could with a covered put?

Income Generation

One of the biggest reasons some investors trade options is to produce income. Much like a dividend on a stock, options can be used to help generate an income stream. There are some options strategies, as I will discuss in Chapter 13, that let you collect money on your existing or future stock positions. Many traders get their feet wet with options by writing covered calls against stocks they own, making a possible 5% to 10% a year extra return on their stocks. You can create a similar situation by selling diagonal spreads without owning the stock. You can also bring in some money when trying to buy a stock at a lower price by selling covered puts below the current price of the stock; if the stock goes up, you make some money—the premium you collected. If the stock goes down and you get exercised, then you must buy the stock at the cheaper price, and you get to keep that premium.

Leverage

Some traders use options for the leverage they afford, meaning you can commit much less money to profit from a stock's price move. For example, instead of buying 100 shares of Tesla for $100,000, you can buy a deep in money call for $7,000 and get almost the same results if it rallies. If you are wrong, though, and it drops, you could lose a good chunk of that $7,000, so use leverage wisely.

Speculators and small account holders love this aspect of options, which allows for strong potential returns with a relatively small amount of money. If you ever hear of someone making $200,000 on $1,000 options plays, it's this leverage and a fair amount of luck that made it happen. This book is not about that type of trading, though I will make these kind of long shot trades on occasion if everything lines ups. I have had a few amazing trades over the years, but when coupled with the many small losers the results tend to even out.

Hedging

Hedging is a way traders try to reduce risk on current positions in case things don't work out quite as planned. In this case, options aren't a source of making money but of protecting it. Since most people tend to buy stocks instead of shorting them, options can protect you from an unexpected move down in either your individual stocks or your portfolio. They can also be used to lock in profits, albeit you will give up a bit of your profit for this protection. It's the same as having insurance on your car; you hope never to see the benefit of the premiums you paid in, but if you are ever in a crash, you will be happy you had the insurance.

Options can be used when you may think the market may have a downturn, but you don't want to sell all of your stocks and later buy them back. Instead, you can buy puts to hedge against this downturn while keeping your portfolio intact. It's much easier to buy S&P puts to hedge your whole stock portfolio, rather than trying to hedge 25 different stocks.

Flexibility

There are so many ways one can trade options that I could write a 1,000-page book about it that no one in their right mind would buy. This book will stick to the best, most common strategies, or at least what I think are the best strategies, but there are almost endless ways one can trade and use options on many types of underlying securities like stocks, indexes, ETFs, and futures. Even within a simple strategy like a vertical spread, you have flexibility in picking different time frames and strike prices. You can have the flexibility to either buy a call spread or sell a put spread to create a similar market outlook. You can go for the big kill or the steady income, you can trade long or short term, be bullish, bearish, or neutral, or just think volatility will pick up or slow down. Beyond what I describe in this book, you can go on for quite a while learning strategies like Gamma hedging, Christmas trees, double diagonal spreads, jade lizards, risk reversals, and so forth—you could be entertained for life learning them all.

BERNIE MADOFF'S CAN'T LOSE OPTION STRATEGY

Bernie Madoff had a great method of consistently making 10% to 15% profits for years. He called it a split strike conversion, but it's normally called a collar, which is not an uncommon strategy and can be profitable. It's not important to understand what a collar is, but I give this example to show the versatility and different ways one can use options. His strategy was as follows:

Step 1: Buy the SPY ETF to track the S&P 500 index.

Step 2: Buy out of the money puts for downside protection.

Step 3: Sell out of the money calls to finance those puts.

Step 4: Ignore steps 1–3 and just put investors' money in your bank account and buy yourself yachts, real estate, and Rolexes; give investors phony statements showing 10% gains. If someone needs a cash out, give them someone else's money.

All of Madoff's clients were happy for years with their fake paper profits, until the market collapsed in 2008 and too many people started to withdraw their money at once and he couldn't cover it all. I was personally heavily affected by Bernie Madoff's scheme, as a lifelong NY Mets fan. The team's owners, the Wilpons, had many accounts with Madoff and financed their payroll with money they got from Madoff profits. The Mets' payroll had been the second highest in baseball, but after Madoff's arrest it quickly dropped to small-town status, bringing a decade-long disappointment for Mets fans as the team couldn't afford a winning lineup anymore. The funny thing is, the Wilpons actually made a lot of money with Madoff. Over the years they had recommended many people to him, but were eventually sued, as enablers, for a billion dollars in restoration efforts to Madoff's victims. They wound up "only" paying back $61 million in 2017, but had stopped spending money on payroll while the suit lingered for almost a decade. Luckily, they sold the team in 2020 to a billionaire spendthrift.

HAVE I MENTIONED VERSATILITY?

Option trading can get sophisticated and complicated, with many more uses than I can pretend to know. What follows is an inkling of just how versatile option trading can be—far beyond what can ever be achieved by trading stocks.

Speculating

Combined with the power of leverage, options make a great tool for speculating on a directional move in stocks, markets, or commodities. They can be used just as easily with a bearish or bullish outlook and require much less capital than buying or shorting a stock. Some people like to gamble, and options give them this thrill; taking a $150 position that lets you control 200 shares of a stock for a week and that turns into $3,000 is awesome and can be addictive. This type of trading, however, though occasionally rewarding, is not my preferred method.

Directionless Trading

By "directionless trading," I mean two things: first, with options you can put on positions that will prosper if the market stays within a given range. Selling a spread, butterfly, straddle, strangle, or iron condor will accomplish this. Second, if you expect a big move but are not sure in which direction, you can buy these trades that would take advantage of a big move in either direction. Neither of these scenarios can be accomplished when trading stocks, as stocks are always bets in one direction.

Selling Versus Buying

You may have heard that 90% of all options expire worthless, so why would anyone ever want to buy options, when the odds of winning are so much greater if you sell them? That's not a true fact, though at times it may feel like 90% of the options you personally buy expire worthless. What is much closer to the truth is that about 10% of options get exercised, 60% are closed out prior to expiration, and about 30% expire worthless. When expiration does comes around, the majority of those left expire worthless because their buyers are hoping for a miracle; the options that had value are already closed out.

If you have ever bought options, you know how hard it is to make money doing so, and it may seem like you are always throwing money away. It can seem like it's the seller of those options, the one who is collecting the premiums, who is raking it in. Selling options has a higher probability of making money than buying them, giving the seller an edge as they collect time premiums. This definitely comes with more risk, as you can collect premiums for 20 straight trades, and then one catastrophe can wipe you out, but as I will discuss there are ways to lower those risks.

Trading Volatility

Trading trends in volatility can be an alternative to trading trends in price movement. Stocks tend to have a historical volatility that they revert to. For example, currently as I am writing, the historical one-year volatility of Nvidia (NVDA) is 45%; however, the implied volatility (IV) based on option prices is 57%. This is high for the stock, and looking at how its current IV ranks compared to its yearly range, you would see it is at 83% of its normal range. If you believe the volatility will revert back from 57% to its normal 45%, then there are option strategies to take advantage of this.

Trading Spreads

Options don't have to be bought or sold outright. You can put on positions where you sell one option to collect a premium and sell another to protect yourself, or maybe you can buy one expiration while selling another. For me, this versatility is one of the beauties of option trading, because you can always protect yourself and limit your losses. When I first started trading options for myself, I would only buy puts or calls, hoping for an endless directional move; now I mostly put on trades with multiple options to them.

Controlling Your Risk

With the exception of selling naked options, many options positions have clearly defined maximum risk, which you will know when you put on the position, giving you peace of mind. You can adjust those risks to your liking. When you trade a stock, it can gap open and you can easily lose a few thousand dollars overnight. On an option spread you know up front the most you can lose, and you can control that amount, regardless of what happens.

Hedging Existing Positions

Options can be used as a risk management tool to lower the overall directional exposure of a stock or portfolio of positions and protect you against heavy losses. Say you have 10 open positions (stocks or options) and you are much longer than you want to be for the conditions the current market warrants. By putting on some options positions that lower your Delta, you can be more neutral, lowering your exposure to a one-sided move, while still keeping on the trades you like. You can view this as an insurance policy.

Estimating Market Moves

Option prices and their volatilities can be used to predict the expected range a stock or market may move in a given period in the future. They can also be used to estimate the probability that a stock will reach any particular price you pick. This is a great starting point to knowing where to place trades.

PROS AND CONS OF OPTION TRADING

There is no question that using options has many benefits, but they do have some deterrents to them as well. Some of these are self-explanatory, so they will be brief.

Advantages of Options

We'll start with some of the many advantages of options.

You Don't Have to Be a Market Guru

One of the great things about selling options strategies is you don't have to be as right when trying to pick a direction the market is going. Instead it's easier to try to figure out where it *won't* go and take advantage of that.

Leverage

Apart from the typical idea of leverage with buying cheap out of the money options and looking for a big gain, you can also buy deep in the money options that almost parallel the move of a stock while putting up a fraction of the money of buying the stock outright, thereby controlling the stock at a much lower cost.

High Rate of Return

I am not referring to the home run type of trades, but even a simple spread that risks $350 to make $150 in a month's time has a ridiculously high return on capital.

Probability of Success

Almost every time you put on an option trade you can see or figure out the chances that trade will make money. Many option strategies have a success rate of 65% to 80%.

Premium Collection and Time Decay

Unlike a stock that has a tangible value, options have a built-in premium that is made up of time value and the hopes that the stock will do something in the future. With every day that passes this premium will shrink. Option sellers can take advantage of that time decay and make money when a stock does nothing or stays within a range.

Low Barriers of Entry

You don't need a big account to get started trading options. Someone with a few thousand dollars can trade options. You can do it with less, but you won't be giving yourself any room for error. Larger accounts do have more choices available, like selling options outright or selling strangles, etc. But as long as you stay within your means you can trade options with a small account.

Volatility
When stocks get volatile you may consider trading them too risky, but options traders love volatility due to the potential gains from over-priced options and their rich premiums.

Minimal Commissions
As of a couple of years ago commissions made some option trades not worth making. Putting on a deep out of the money iron condor with commissions that ate up 25% of potential profits was impracticable. Now that commissions are next to nothing, some option strategies have become more favorable to trade, and you can better compete with the big guys who always had the advantage.

Less Risky Than Stocks
When traded correctly, option strategies can be less risky than trading stocks.

Insurance
Options allow investors to safeguard their positions from moves against their underlying position or portfolio.

Being the House
Being able to sell options is like being the casino: under the right conditions the odds will tend to favor you. With options, you don't need a million dollars for this privilege to act like a market maker. As long as you meet the margin requirements, you can do so.

Option Prices Can Predict the Future
When the volatility of an option starts going up and option premiums on a stock are suddenly very expensive, this may be a sign something is about to happen.

Easy to Short
For some reason many investors will never short a stock. With options, if you want to benefit from a stock going down you can buy a put. This tends to be a much easier mental process than shorting a stock.

Disadvantages of Options

Just when you thought options were the end-all answer to trading, be aware that they do come with risks if you are not careful.

A Lot to Take In

There is a long learning curve when it comes to mastering option trading. An advanced book on option pricing and modeling can take a PhD to understand and is a good alternative to melatonin and warm milk as a bedtime aid. This book will get you through to a level where you can be quite comfortable understanding and trading options. The few technical chapters I have included, especially those on volatility and option Greeks, are not nail-biting page-turners, but they shouldn't be too bad to get through and will definitely teach you a thing or two. Don't skim through them, as it is an important step in the learning process.

Lots of Homework

I am not referring to the learning process, but there is a lot more work involved in preparing and finding good option trades than you would normally put into trading a stock. A typical morning involves reviewing all open positions, looking for new trades by doing a scan of stocks with high implied volatility (IV) that have options with a fair amount of liquidity, and looking at charts to make an opinion on trends as well as the IV direction—then looking to see which stocks have earnings announcements coming up. Once you have a few trade ideas, you have to figure out which strategies to employ and what strikes and expirations to use. Once you have a portfolio of trades, then you need check them on a regular basis keeping them close to an overall Delta position you like, then make any adjustments necessary to be more long or short. You also have to monitor everything to make sure your Gamma risk is not too high, as well as managing your exits as your positions near expiration.

Risks

When buying options there is a good chance you will lose your entire investment, if the trade doesn't work out and you don't take a predetermined loss. If you buy 100 shares of a $150 stock and you guess wrong and it moves $5.00 against you, you will lose $500, or 3% of your investment. With options, if you bought an option for $500 and were wrong, you could easily lose 100% of that $500. The actual dollar amount may be less per trade, but percentagewise you can lose much more. You can even lose 100% of your investment if you get the direction correct but it doesn't move fast or far enough.

There is also the chance for unlimited losses when you short options, and yes that chance is there when trading stocks, but it is a lot more amplified when you shorted a put for $200 in premiums and you lose $10,000 because Facebook dropped $100 after earnings, as opposed to losing $10,000 on a $35,000 stock position.

Time Decay

While time decay is a bonus to option sellers, If you are an option buyer you will be fighting an uphill battle as time decays eats into your position's value a little every day.

Having a Deadline

Not only does your market move prediction have to be right, but it has to be correct in a specific time period as well. I can't begin to count the number of times I have bought short-term calls that I've watched expire worthless as the market reached just below my strike price, then the day after expiration the market made its move that would have made me money, which at that point was meaningless to me unless I had a new position.

Hard to Place Stops

Because some options aren't very liquid and there can be wide bid and ask spreads with little activity, placing a stop on an option can be a recipe for disaster, where you are sure to get filled regardless of what happens. Instead you need to be diligent about having predetermined exits strategies.

Too Many Choices

Looking at an options table and trying to figure out which is the best strike price and time to expiration can be daunting. If you want to buy 100 shares of IBM, you buy 100 shares of IBM. If you want to use options to capitalize on a move on IBM, you could be looking at 2,000 choices on which strategies to use, how many days to expiration to go out, and what strike price to use.

Leverage

Yes, leverage can be an advantage of trading options, but that same leverage can easily wipe you out if you are not careful. Options prices can fluctuate significantly from day to day, and price moves of more than 50% or 100% in a day are not uncommon. While this is great when you are on the right side of it, leverage can work against you just as fast. Be careful of leverage, as it can be a double-edged sword. What I can't figure out is why a double-edged sword is a bad thing. I would assume that those who used swords knew how to use them and weren't stupid enough to hurt themselves with one. If anything, I can see it as being an advantage as you have two sides to attack with.

FINAL THOUGHT

Every trader or investor should take advantage of the many facets of options. Once you understand the ins and outs of option trading, they can become a powerful moneymaking tool.

CHAPTER 3

The Nuts and Bolts

Some of these nuts and bolts may feel rudimentary if you are a more advanced trader, but I am sure something in here will be a useful review. It will especially be helpful for those of you who feel you have no clue what options are. Trading stocks or futures is fairly easy—though the making money part of it is hard. If you think something is going up, you buy; and if you think it's going down, you sell. There is not much more to it. Options, however, have many more moving parts to consider when putting on in a trade, like time frames, strike prices, volatility, Delta, time decay, Gamma risk, extrinsic value—just a few things that make them more difficult to grasp. When you do understand them, they can open up a whole new world of trading opportunities.

WHAT IS AN OPTION?

The clinical definition of an option is "a legally binding contract giving the buyer of the option the right or choice, but not the obligation, to do something in the future." To be more precise, it is a binding contract with defined terms giving the buyer the right to buy or sell 100 shares of a stock at a predetermined price (the strike price), on or before a specific expiration date. If the buyer wants to have more time to exercise this right, they pay extra for that extra time.

There are two types of options, *puts* and *calls*:

A *call* gives the owner the right to buy a stock at specific price by a certain date.

A *put* gives the owner the right to a sell a stock at specific price by a certain date.

DISCLAIMER #1

Options relate to an underlying asset that could be a stock, ETF, index, or futures contract. Whenever I refer to an option's underlying asset, it could be any of these. If I say a stock, or an ETF, or even generically the market, they are all interchangeable.

When you buy an option on a stock, it gives you the choice to buy or sell 100 shares of that stock to the person who wrote the option. The key here is that it's the right, and not the obligation, to buy or sell a stock. If conditions aren't favorable, you are not required to do anything. The seller of the option doesn't have a choice on what happens after he sells it, he must abide by the terms of the contract. The person who buys the option to do something in the future will pay up for that privilege, and the writer (seller) of that option, who has taken on future risk, collects a premium for being at the mercy of the option buyer.

JOHN'S SNOW PLOWING

I will make this clearer by not using stocks. This example is not much different than using calls on a stock: John's snow removal company normally charges $20 per inch of snowfall to plow a typical driveway. The normal snowstorm over the last few years was five inches of snow, so on average they charged $100 a plow, and when it snows a lot they get pretty busy and ignore people's calls. This winter they decide to offer binding coupons (options) where you can pick a set predetermined price at which they will guarantee to plow for you, regardless of how much it snows. These coupons also come with different expiration dates. Some will last a week, while others may last a month, and others up to four months. Each one is good for only one plow during that time frame.

TABLE 3.1 Snow Plowing Options

Today's Date: Jan 1	Days To Expiration		
Plowing Charge	**7 Days**	**30 Days**	**60 Days**
(Strike Price)	**Cost of Coupon (Options Price)**		
40	61	65	75
60	42	47	55
80	23	28	35
100	4	10	17
120	3	5	8
140	2	4	7
160	1	3	5
180	0.75	2.00	4
200	0.50	1.25	2
250	0.25	0.75	1.50
300	0.10	0.50	1

Looking at Table 3.1, the first column, "Plowing Charge," is what you agree to pay for a plowing—this would be equal to an option's strike price. Whichever option you bought is how much you would pay to get your driveway plowed, even if it snows eight feet in one day. The next three columns are what you pay (option price) for that coupon or right with 7 days, 30 days, and 60 days before that coupon expires. I've highlighted the $100 price as an example. This scenario assumes the seven-day weather forecast says four to six inches of snow is possible. If it had said "blizzard warning," or "record highs expected all week," the costs to buy an option would be different. These coupons are priced on the expected range of the forecast (this is similar to volatility).

Because there is a reasonable expectation that it may snow this week, you may be willing to pay $4 to guarantee you get plowed for a $100. If you don't use this option by the end of the week, it will expire worthless and you will lose that $4. However if it were to snow 10 inches this week, then you would be in luck as you cash in your coupon and pay just $100 to get plowed while your neighbors are paying $200 ($20/inch × 10 inches). John wouldn't be as happy plowing your driveway for only $104, but he took that risk.

If it were to snow only three inches, then you would not want to use your option, because you are better off paying the market price of

$60 for a plow. You can also decide you don't need a plow; in either case you lose your $4. If it doesn't snow at all, you also lose your $4, and John made a little money, though he's still unhappy as no one is getting their driveways plowed.

Keep in mind that all options have an *expiration date*: a date when the option expires and becomes worthless. If you wanted to have that option to be plowed, but instead of for just a week, for the next 30 days, then you will pay more for that privilege as there is a better chance that you will get an above-average snowstorm in the next month as opposed to just the next week. That $4 option would now cost you $10. If you went out 60 days before it expired, you would pay $17 for the right to pay $100 to be plowed if it were to snow in the next 60 days. As you can see, options lose value as the time to expiration shrinks. This is because the chances of something happening decrease as time decreases. This is called *time decay*, and it should make sense that the chance of a big storm hitting in the next 30 days is much greater than the chance of it happening tomorrow. The chance is even greater if you get 60 days to use your plowing option.

Looking at the different options for plowing charges (strike prices), you can start to see different benefits and risks. Looking just at the 30 days to expiration coupons, assume you want to guarantee you pay $40 for a plowing in the next 30 days; you would pay $65 for that privilege. Every winter over the last few years there has always been one decent snowstorm in your area, so you think it's a good bet. If you end up being right and use the plowing option, the total price would be cheaper than paying $10 for the 30-day $100 option plow. If it does snow six inches, it would end up being a total $105 cost with the $40 option, compared to $110 total with the $100 option ($65 option plus $40 coupon versus $100 option plus $10).

However, in the $65 scenario, should there be no snow, you are screwed. You just paid $65 for a coupon you never used. This may cause someone else to prefer to pay just $1 to lock in a $200 plow, and they will deal with the consequences if it snows normally in the next month—at least he's covered if it snows over 10 inches.

But Wait, There's More

You don't actually have to use your option; you can sell it to someone else. For example, if you had a 7-day $4 option, and suddenly a previous forecast calling for a 2-inch snowfall was upgraded to a 20-inch blizzard for tomorrow, many people would be willing to pay you much more than the $4 you paid to be plowed at $100, instead of the $400 it would cost them for a plowing. You can now say, "The hell with this snow, I'm going to Miami" and probably sell your option for around $300 to someone who wanted to ensure a plow. If demand is strong enough, somebody may end up paying you $320 to guarantee a $100 plow. Meanwhile John has to plow them for $100, and once again he is not happy. This is what often happens in the stock market, as most options are not held to expiration but sold off at some point prior. At the end of the season, John is happy; he priced his coupons perfectly and made enough money by selling coupons that were out of the normal range of snowfall that nobody ever got to use which expired worthless. In the end these worthless coupons more than covered the loss he had when it snowed too much, and he had a larger profit than he had made in the past. You could even become a snow speculator, buying options far out of the expected range of snowfall cheaply with no intention of ever getting plowed, but if there is a blizzard, you could sell them for a nice profit.

This is just the tip of the iceberg—there is much more involved with options. However, use this illustration to understand options by substituting a stock's price for plowing charges, and the price of a call for the cost of the coupon. As you can see, options have several features, like time and expected range, that determine their price. Now that you have a better understanding, I will stop talking about snow and move on to real options on stocks.

BREAKING DOWN AN OPTION TABLE: THE BASICS

In order to trade options, you first need to be able to navigate an option table, also referred to as an option chain. Most financial websites and brokers provide real-time option chains that include a wealth of information. Each platform will have little differences, but they all should have the same basic features. In its most primitive form, an option chain is a listing of an underlying stock's available options, both by strike price and by time to expiration. Depending on the platform you use, at the top will be the name of the underlying stock, its ticker symbol, its current market price, and its volume. Some platforms will have implied volatility and implied volatility rank up front. Option chains are where you will find all your Greeks, probabilities of things happening, and other informative features that help you understand how options are priced, which I will cover in the next few chapters.

Option Chain 3.1 is a condensed version of a typical option chain or option table. This is TradeStation's version. Each platform will vary a little, but they all have basically the same info. For now, the first few things that you absolutely must understand when you look at an option table are:

1. The underlying asset and its price
2. The expiration dates
3. The strike price
4. Puts and calls
5. Option price (bid and ask)
6. Volume and open interest
7. Delta
8. Expected move and implied volatility

I've numbered the above elements (1–8) on Option Chain 3.1 to match the eight headings for an easy-to-follow reference as I dig deeper into some of the basic components of an option chain.

OPTION CHAIN 3.1 Reading an Option's Table: Apple

Source: TradeStation

1. The Underlying Asset

Options can't exist on their own: they are a derivative instrument that needs an underlying asset that they are priced against. Think of it as a virus that can't survive without attaching itself to a host. The first and most obvious thing you need to know is what that underlying asset is. Here, it is Apple stock (AAPL), which is in the top left-hand corner, but it could be crude oil, SPY, or any other traded thing. Next to the underlying asset is its price, which is the most important piece of information you need to price an option; in this image, Apple is trading at $129.97.

Types of Underlying Assets

The following are underlying assets that have options:

Stocks: For the average investor, stocks need no introduction. Pretty much all stocks over $3.00 will have options that trade around them.

ETFs (exchange traded funds): ETFs are funds that trade on the exchange just like a stock, but typically represent a basket of assets. For example, XLE, which is Energy Select Sector SPDR Fund, is a fund that contains a basket of oil sector related stocks. An ETF can also track a commodity, like in the case of GLD, which tracks gold by holding gold bullion. Options on ETFs like SPY (S&P 500), QQQ (Nasdaq 100) and IWM (Russell 2000) are very popular, having some of the highest daily options volumes of all assets.

Indices: You can't trade indices like the SPX, which is the S&P 500 index or the VIX, but there are options based on these indices that you can trade.

Commodities: Futures contracts are things like gold, crude oil, cotton, and financial indices like the E-mini S&P futures.

2. The Expiration Dates

Options will have a chain of expiration dates that expire on the third Friday of every month. These are the monthly expirations. On the Apple table they are the 17 and 45 days to expiration (DTE) options (see box 2). There are a lot more months going out almost two years. I can't fit them all here, but if you were to look at any option table on your own, you would see pages worth. Different stocks will have a different number of active months' worth of options; some may have 4 months, then they may skip a few months and go out further in time, while others may have decent activity throughout the next 12 months. As months expire, new ones will begin trading. Securities with more actively traded options will also have five weeks of weekly options starting around 45 days to expiration. Some ETFs and indices have even more, like QQQ, SPY, and SPX, which now have daily expirations for the front two weeks. These short-term options have been steadily gaining in popularity and are very liquid close to expiration.

In Option Chain 3.1 you can see some of the different expirations for Apple. I only expanded the Jan 6 and Feb 17 expirations; the rest are collapsed. Apple as a very actively traded security will have more expirations than a lightly traded stock would. AutoNation (AN), for example, will not have weekly or as frequent monthly expirations. This is a result of supply and demand: if the demand is out there, market makers will find a way to make money and create more options. For thinly traded options, there is little point in having many expirations if they have no volume.

Options will get more expensive the further out in time you go, as they have more time to move. For example, looking at a call with a 130 strike price, you will see how the price changes from $2.50 to $7.65 (by looking at the ask price in the columns to the left of box 3) when you go from 3 to 45 days to expiration. This is simply because there is a greater chance of the price getting higher than $130 when you have an extra 42 days for it to do so.

3. The Strike Price

Next, you will want to look at strike prices or exercise price, which runs right down the middle of the option table (box 3). This is the action price that determines what an option's buyer will pay for the stock or sell the stock at. When buying options, the strike price is like the goal line you are hoping a stock crosses (or doesn't, if you are shorting). If you buy a 130 call with three days to go, then you want Apple to go above $130, plus the amount you paid for that option ($2.50), in order to make money. The strike price is a critical part of determining an option's price and its moneyness (defined later in this chapter).

Strike price intervals are not uniform: when you look at the further month the strike prices are more spread out, with $5 jumps in between them, but this range gets tighter as you get closer to expiration and the volume increases. Here you can see that the 3 DTE cycle has $1 intervals and the 45 DTE cycle has $5 jumps. If you were to look further in or out of the money, where there has been little activity, you would see $10 intervals as well. Apple starts to have $1 intervals as the weekly options start trading and more of the activity is concentrated around the current price. In the end it comes down to demand; there is no set pattern, and some lower-priced stocks like Ford, which is at $16.65, have options priced in 50-cent intervals. More expensive stocks may start with $10 intervals.

4. Puts and Calls

There are two kinds of options: puts and calls. As you will notice, the option table is divided down the middle, with the left side giving you information on calls and the right side on puts. My snow plowing example was like a call, because when you bought a plowing option you wanted to see lots of snow. In the most basic sense, if you buy a call on a stock, you want that stock to rally above the strike price of that call, and if you buy a put, you want it to go down below the strike price. The way I learned to remember this back in college was *to call someone up and put someone down.*

Calls

A call option gives the buyer the right (but not the obligation) to buy the underlying stock, bond, commodity, etc., at a specific price (the strike price) at or before expiration of the contract chosen. In other words, the owner has the option to exercise his right and buy the underlying stock at the exercise (strike) price. The seller of the call option has to sell the stock at the exercise price if the owner of the option elects to exercise it. In that case, the seller is required to sell the stock at the exercise price, regardless of how far above the exercise price the stock is currently trading. The seller's incentive for writing a call is the premium in the form of cash they get when they sell the option; this is theirs to keep regardless of what happens.

Puts

A put option is the opposite of a call option. It gives the owner the right (but not the obligation) to sell the underlying stock at a specified price (the strike price) within the specified time period. When people first get into trading, they are more likely to buy stocks instead of shorting them, as it feels more natural, and stocks tend to go up in the long run. This is also the case with options: people are more apt to understand buying a call over buying a put—some people I've met can't grasp the concept that you can make money if you think the market is going down. Puts can be a little more difficult to understand at first because of the buying only mentality of investing in stocks, but if you think a stock price is headed downward, you could buy a put option on that stock to benefit from the move down. Like calls, the owner of a put option gets to choose whether to exercise his right and sell the underlying stock at the exercise price before or at the option's expiration to the put's seller. If exercised, the seller of the put option is required to buy the stock at the exercise price, regardless of how far below the exercise price the stock is currently trading.

Puts and Calls in Action

This is how buying a put actually works: Assume you believe Apple will go down in price from its current $130 level to below $125 in the next few weeks. You buy a 125 put with 45 DTE for $5.15. Apple drops to $115; if you decide to exercise that put, someone who sold that option has to buy 100 shares of Apple from you at $125 a share. It doesn't matter that you don't own the stock yet; if you exercise, you will be short 100 shares of Apple at $125. You can keep that short position, hoping it goes lower, or buy 100 shares of the stock to close out the position. You would make a quick $1,000, minus the cost of the option ($515) on that trade.

Most of the time, people will not exercise options. Option prices will move with changes in the price of the stock, and you can easily sell them at any time for a profit or loss. In this case, as Apple dropped, the price of the put would rally, and it usually makes more sense to just sell the option for a profit.

If you are bullish on a stock, expecting it to rise in the near future or within a specific time frame, then you could buy a call option to capitalize on that scenario. If you were bullish for the next few days thinking Apple will jump to $140 in three days, you could buy the Jan 6 130 call with three DTE for $2.50; you would now need AAPL to rally above $132.50 to make money at expiration. If it does rally above $130, you can decide to keep the stock and buy it at $130, or sell your option before expiration. If Apple rallies to $140, your calls would be worth about $10, which is a nice 300% return in three days. Welcome to the power of leverage that options provide! You could have bought a call at a different strike price and expiration, with different results. Trying to pick the best combination of strike prices and expirations is one of the hurdles of trading options.

5. Option Price

Option price is pretty straightforward (box 5); it's what you pay as a buyer for an option, or what you get for it as a seller. This is the option's premium. It's important to understand that an option on a stock, ETF, or index corresponds to 100 shares of that underlying. If you see an option with a $2 price, you must multiply by 100 to get its real cost of $200 ($2 × 100 shares) to trade it. Keep in mind that if I talk about buying an option for $2 and then selling it at $6, what I mean is a profit of $400. Options on futures are different, however, as they are only worth one futures contract, not 100 shares; you would need to know the multiplier of that future to see its worth. For example, an option on E-mini S&P futures that is quoted at $10 is worth $500 as its multiplier is 50.

There is no column that says option price; you determine this by looking at the bid and ask prices. The *bid* is the current price that market makers and options buyers are willing to pay for the option. The *ask* is the current price that they are willing to sell it at. If you are buying an Apple 130 put with a bid/ask of $2.46 / $2.50, and you bought it at the market, you would buy it for $2.50 ($250 in real money).

This price that an option trades at is its premium. It's the price option buyers pay for the chance at something, and what the seller gets for the risk they take. The premium is what determines your breakeven price on a trade.

One piece of advice I will give you for now is to stay away from thinly traded markets with wide bid and ask spreads. A 4-penny spread is very tight, but when you start seeing $2.00 spreads, it makes it harder to break even.

6. Volume and Open Interest

Volume and open interest often go together (box 6), and you should pay attention to them. Like using the bid and ask spread to determine if a market is liquid or not, I recommend looking at volume and open interest as well. This will help to make sure you are trading active markets instead of thin markets where it may be difficult to get out of a position at a good price. I will repeat this a few time in the book, *do not trade illiquid markets.*

> *Volume* is the number of options contracts that have traded on a particular day. It can be found as a total for all the options for a particular stock, for all of the puts and calls, and for every individual option at every expiration. In general, the closer to expiration and the closer to the current price of the underlying asset, the higher the volume will be.

> *Open interest* shows the number of outstanding open contracts for each specific put and call, per strike, per expiration. It is calculated daily by the Options Clearing Corp, and whereas volume changes all day long, open interest is only updated at the end of the day. It includes all long positions held by investors that have been opened but haven't yet been exercised, closed out, or expired. In our snow plowing example, if the company sold a total of 1,000 plowing option contracts, the open interest would be 1,000 to start; as people used up the contracts or they expired, the open interest would decline.

Open interest and volume don't necessarily match up. If a stock was trading in the $100 range for a while, there would be a lot of open interest and volume for options trading in the $100 area. But if that stock eventually rallied to $150, the options volume would shift and be much higher, in the $150 range, with little activity in the $100 area; however, the open interest range might still be pretty strong in the $100 range of strike prices.

In general, the monthly expirations options will have much better liquidity than the weekly ones in between them. This means that the 17 and 45 DTE options are much more liquid than the 24, 31, and 38 DTE ones. The option expiring the soonest, three DTE, will have the highest liquidity of all.

7. Delta

Delta is a part of what is known as option Greeks, and I will discuss these further in Chapter 6. Delta is the Greek you will use the most, so here is a brief glimpse into it. Delta estimates how much an option will move based on a $1 move in the underlying. So an option with a Delta of 0.20 will move 20 cents when the stock moves a dollar.

Puts have a negative Delta, so they move in the opposite direction of price; a put with a Delta of –0.50 will drop 50 cents if the price of a stock increases a dollar. To clarify further: Stocks have no Deltas—only puts and calls do. If a stock rallies $1.00, then a 0.20 Delta call will rally 20 cents, while a –0.20 Delta put will lose 20 cents in value. I will go into Delta in more detail in Chapter 6, but one quick note is that many times the decimal (and minus sign for puts) will be omitted when you see Deltas. So you are more likely to see it referred to as a 20 Delta put as opposed to a –0.20 Delta put.

Delta has a few other uses, including keeping a hedged portfolio, but one especially helpful aspect of Delta is that it can be used to predict the probability that an option will finish in the money. An option with a 0.30 Delta has roughly a 30% chance of expiring with value.

8. Implied Volatility and Estimated Move

A good options platform will give you both implied volatility and an estimated move for the stock for every expiration. Implied volatility (IV) measures the current volatility assumed by an option's price and should play a big part in your trading. By the end of this book I will have discussed volatility to nauseam, but what I want to point out in this "basic" chapter is how it can be used to calculate a stock's expected move. Each option and each expiration will have its own IV. In the Apple option chain (Option Chain 3.1), look to the far right, just under where you see Open Int and Pos. The 49.56% is the IV and the shaded (+/–5.24) is the expected move for the expiration. This implies that Apple is expected to move up or down $5.24 in the next three days. You will see the same for other expirations in box 8 below it. Notice that the further you go out in time, the bigger that predicated move gets as the stock has more time to move. Now look down to the 45 DTE options, where I can show it clearer (bottom line in the same box 8). The expected move is now (+/–15.96), which corresponds to the shaded box around the strike prices that are $15.96 from the current $129.97 price (in box 8 in the lower middle of the option chain). This is a great little feature that you should pay attention to if your trading platform provides it. In the three DTE chain, the whole area of strike prices is shaded; this is because I am only showing 10 strikes. If I had the room, the shaded area would only have been between the 125 and 135 strikes. (Later on I will also be using tastytrade's option tables, where it will look like a shaded ruler.)

One Last Thing

One last thing for now: The option table is useful for seeing the relation between an option strike and the current price. We already know the current price is $129.97, but you can also get a rough idea of the current price by looking at the option table itself. You should notice that there is light shading that divides an expiration into four quadrants. The options in the darker shaded area are in the money (ITM), and lighter ones are out of the money (OTM). Where the calls are darker, the puts are light, and vice versa, because when a call is ITM, its counterpart put has to be OTM. The point where they are both at the money (ATM) is where a stock is currently trading. You can also see the ATM price by finding the options closest to the 50 Delta. The 51 Delta call and –49 Delta put at the 130 strike are pretty close to the current stock price of $129.97.

ONE LAST DISCLAIMER

Throughout the book I will use common abbreviations that as a trader you will see often. These terms will include DTE for days to expiration, IV for implied volatility, ITM, OTM, and ATM for describing moneyness, and a few others. I will go back and forth between the written out and abbreviated versions to reinforce them, as they should become part of your trading vernacular.

MONEYNESS

I just touched upon moneyness when I mentioned in, out, or at the money. These terms express the relation of an option's strike price to the current price of the stock. For all options, the strike that matches the underlying price is considered the at the money strike. For calls, an option is in the money when a stock is above the strike price, and out of the money when it is below the strike price. To expire with any value, an option must be in the money. A call that is out of the money will expire worthless unless the market rallies before the option expires.

In simple terms, with Apple at 130:

A call with a strike of 125 is $5 ITM.

A call with a strike of 130 is ATM.

A call with a strike of 135 is $5 OTM.

For puts it is the opposite: A put is in the money when a stock is below the strike, and out of the money when it is above the strike. A put that is out of the money needs the market to fall for it to expire with value.

A put with a strike of 135 is $5 ITM.

A put with a strike of 130 is ATM.

A put with a strike of 125 is $5 OTM.

You can visualize the moneyness of these strikes with Apple trading at $130 in Table 3.2. I will explain moneyness a little better when I discuss extrinsic and intrinsic value in the next chapter.

TABLE 3.2 Moneyness of Strike Prices with Apple at $130

Call	Strike Price	Put
ITM	125	OTM
ATM	130	ATM
OTM	135	ITM

OPTION PAYOFF DIAGRAMS

Payoff diagrams are something you will see often and will encounter later in the book. These diagrams show what you can expect to make or lose at expiration. They are based solely on price and are not dynamic in that they don't reflect things like time to expiration or changes in volatility. After reading this book you will know that holding to expiration is not ideal, but payoff diagrams are helpful in that they allow traders a chance to visualize how different option strategies work. Diagram 3.1 is a simple example of a long call payoff to get you started visualizing options. (On a side note, one of the hardest parts of writing this book was the eight hours it took to figure out how to make and format these diagrams.)

Long Call Payoff

Assume you buy a call with the following parameters:

Current stock price = $50

Call strike = 54

Premium paid = $2 ($2 × 100 shares = $200)

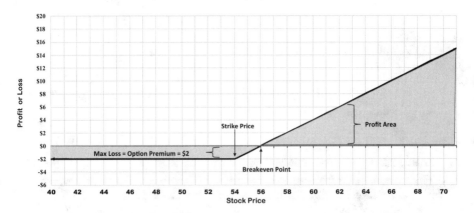

DIAGRAM 3.1 Long Call Payoff Diagram

The first thing to look for is the strike price (54); this is what you need the stock price to be above to avoid losing your whole option premium, which is $2.00, but don't forget, the trade cost you $200. Any price to the left of this point results in a loss of your entire premium as the option will have no value at expiration. Next, look for the breakeven point (56); this is the strike price plus the $2 you paid for the option. Everything to the right of it is a profit. As the price of a stock increases, the area between the strike price and the breakeven gradually becomes less of a loss until it reaches the breakeven point. Note that as the stock goes above the exercise price, the option gains one dollar in value for each dollar increase in the stock's price, and this is technically unlimited. On the losing side, the loss is capped at the $200 cost of the option if prices fall anywhere below the strike price.

FINAL THOUGHT

This is the first of a few chapters that build a good options knowledge foundation. Don't overlook them as you need to know this stuff inside and out to be a top trader. This chapter may be rudimentary, but it should help newer traders, while refreshing a more experienced trader's knowledge.

CHAPTER 4

Option Pricing 101

To understand how options work, this along with the next three chapters are the most important in the book, as they will explain how options are valued and what factors contribute to their pricing and moves. If you are someone who thinks "who cares, just show me the best strategies already"—I say, don't rush it, learn what makes an option tick first, and you will have a much clearer understanding of how and why you may make or lose money as you become a better overall trader. Being able to predict what an option may be worth in the future given certain changes in the market, and what makes certain strategies better than others, will give you an edge in making higher probability trades.

INTRINSIC VERSUS EXTRINSIC VALUE

Although there are several factors that make up an option's value, an option is really made up of two core components: *intrinsic value* and *extrinsic value*; everything else is accounted for by these two measures.

Intrinsic Value

Intrinsic value is pretty straightforward; it is what an option is actually worth if it expired now. It is the amount an option is in the money (ITM) compared to the current stock price. Only options that are in the money can have intrinsic value, because if they were out of the money (OTM), they would expire worthless. For example, look at Option Chain 4.1, which is the IWM (Russel 2000 ETF), trading at $193.13. A 191 call is $2.13 ITM, so it will have an intrinsic value of $2.13. However, a 194 call that is OTM would be worth zero as it would have no real value if it expired now. Any strikes above $194 would also have no real value, so they also have zero intrinsic value. Any strike below $193 would have an intrinsic value by the amount it is ITM. With intrinsic value, time doesn't matter, so equivalent options in different expirations will have the same intrinsic value.

Calls have intrinsic value if the stock price is above the strike price.

Puts have intrinsic value if the stock price is below the strike price.

If it's confusing, you can look at the option's Delta: if the Delta is around 50, then an option is at the money. When the Delta is over 50, the option is in the money and has intrinsic value. If it's below 50, it would be out of the money.

OPTION CHAIN 4.1 IWM

Source: TradeStation

Extrinsic Value

The catch is that options are not expiring right now and do have some extra value in them because they could be profitable in the future. This extra value due to time is called the *extrinsic value* and includes everything else that goes into an option's pricing. It's the money that you pay for the possibility of benefitting from price movements in the future, but it comes with a ticking timeclock.

Extrinsic value is typically referred to as time value, but I don't want to just call it "time value" because other factors like volatility and interest rates will also have an effect on an option's value. In the end though it does boil down to the more time an option has before it expires, the greater the extrinsic value will be, as there is more time for things to happen. Extrinsic value is directly related to the *expiration date* and will shrink or decay as time passes. It is the value all options sellers are after. At expiration when no time is left, extrinsic value will always be zero and an option is only worth its intrinsic value.

A 195 call trading for $3.88 with 24 DTE is $1.87 OTM and would have zero intrinsic value (see Option Chain 4.1). That $3.88 value is strictly extrinsic value. That same option with 6 DTE is only worth $1.44, or $2.44 less in extrinsic value over that time. This implies that if you had sold a 195 call with 24 DTE and held it till 6 DTE and IWM stayed the same, you would keep that difference of $2.44.

Remember that the extrinsic (time) value of an option will always be greatest for the 50 Delta option (the at the money option) and will decrease as it goes further in or out of the money.

SUMMING UP

Intrinsic value= In the money value

Before Expiration

Option value = intrinsic value + extrinsic value (time value)

At Expiration

Time value = zero

Option value = intrinsic value + 0 or the ITM amount

HOW OPTIONS ARE VALUED

Options are priced using pricing models like the Black-Scholes model that outputs a theoretical option value based on things like:

Stock price

Strike price

Time to expiration

Volatility

Interest rates

Expected dividends

I am not going to go into the actual pricing models, but instead the components themselves. The most important of these elements to the price of an option are changes in the price of the underlying, time till expiration, the strike price, and the implied or expected volatility. Interest rates and dividends, though contributing factors, are less important because they are more constant and don't generally move an option price much.

Stock Price

The price of the underlying stock is important for determining option pricing and has a huge influence on the price of options. This is simple; as a stock moves higher in price, calls will become more valuable and puts will lose value. If the stock moves lower, puts will become more valuable while calls lose value. Moves in stock prices will have the biggest impact on option prices, especially on an intraday level, as none of the other factors affecting option prices will usually move an option much during the day. Yes, volatility can spike during the day, changing option prices, but for the most part this will correspond with a stock's move in price, which will weigh on the option's value anyway.

Strike Price

The relation of the strike price of an option to the stock price has a direct effect on the price of that option. The deeper in the money an option is, the more it will be worth as it has more intrinsic value. The 195 put on IWM that is $1.87 ITM will be worth more than a 193 put that is OTM, which is worth more than a 192 put that is further

OTM. This is tied hand-in-hand to the underlying's price move and the moneyness of the option. As an option's strike moves from out of the money to in the money, an option will obviously gain in value.

Time to Expiration

I will deal with this in further detail when I talk about Theta in Chapter 6 along with all the Greeks. In general, the longer the time to expiration, the more valuable an option is. This is because an option with more time to expiration has a better chance of the stock moving to a location that is profitable for you. This should be common sense; would you rather have three days for a stock to move $20, or 60 days? Sixty days, of course. Every day an option will lose a little of its time value, until the final few days when it makes it way to expiration and has zero time value left.

Volatility

Out of all these factors that go into a pricing model, volatility is the only item that is not a definite input. Instead, volatility is implied by the pricing model and the option's price. While all the other inputs are known, volatility from now to expiration is unknown, so models work backward and use an estimated volatility to come up with option pricing. The volatility is in reality implied by the option's price and is called implied volatility.

Interest Rates

Option valuation models use the annualized risk-free one-year Treasury interest rates in their formulas. The Greek term for this is Rho. The effect of interest rates on option prices is relatively negligible, especially when dealing with very short-term options. In a nutshell: rising interest rates increase the price of calls and decrease the price of puts.

Dividends

Dividends affect option pricing, but you shouldn't lose sleep trying to figure out how they do so. Stocks generally drop in price by the amount of the dividend on the ex-dividend date (the first trading day where an upcoming dividend payment is not included in a stock's price). This will have an impact on the price of options, causing call options to become less expensive and put options to increase in value on ex-dividend. Because most dividends are regularly announced, option premiums already have the dividends factored into their price, and the effect of dividends on option premiums is negligible. Only when a company changes its dividend will it affect the price of an option, and even then it's not enough of a price change to worry about.

FINAL THOUGHT

These are the basics you need to know to understand how options get their value. Understanding volatility is a key to becoming a successful options trader, and I will cover it in detail in the next chapter. Then in Chapter 6, I will move on to the Greeks, where you will gain a better understanding of how time to expiration, amongst other factors, plays a key role in option trading.

CHAPTER 5

It's All About the Volatility

Understanding volatility is essential to options trading. It may be the most critical factor that lies behind much of the trading that occurs in option markets, and it helps you determine a trade's chance of working in your favor or not. You should never make an option trade without first knowing what the underlying's volatility is doing. This chapter may get a little math heavy, but it's stuff worth knowing.

WHAT IS VOLATILITY?

Volatility is a measurement that shows how much the price of a stock is expected to change over a given time period. There are two volatility measurements, and both are useful, especially when you use them together. *Historical volatility (HV)* reflects what the stock has done in the past; *implied volatility (IV)* is how the market thinks the stock will move in the future, a belief reflected by current option prices. A change in IV means that predictions about a stock's price action will change and this will be reflected by option prices. Volatility affects all options the same. When volatility increases, the price of both puts and call goes up; as it decreases, all option prices go down.

HISTORICAL VOLATILITY

Historical volatility looks at previous price actions for a stock, ETF, market index, etc. over a specified period and measures the average deviation from its price. Historical volatility typically uses a one-month look back period, which is 20 or 21 trading days. (A year contains 252 trading days.) Traders use historical volatility to compare future volatility estimates to past results, looking for opportunities when they diverge. Knowing what a stock has done in the past is a good starting point to help you get an idea of what it may do in the future, which is a great starting point for making smarter trades. Yet while knowing that a stock's average daily move in the past was, say, $2.00 is good information to have, there is no certainty it will continue to stay in that range moving forward.

IMPLIED VOLATILITY

While historical volatility is what has happen in the past, implied volatility is what is expected to happen moving forward and should be more important to your trading decisions. IV is an up-to-the-minute gauge of the mood of the markets, and it gets priced into an option's premium. It considers both past price performance (historical volatility) and any factors that might move the stock in the future. The result is the current volatility of the stock implied by its option's price. As an example, consider the stock of a pharmaceutical company that has a drug awaiting FDA approval. The stock will probably move up or down, potentially by a lot, when the drug either gets or doesn't get that approval. This big potential move will cause option premiums for that stock to get inflated as traders wait in anticipation. This in turn causes a spike up in IV when compared to its historical volatility. A few days after the announcement, the stock price settles down and IV typically reverts to its norm.

WHAT IT MEANS

IV is a constantly changing number. Though each strike and expiration has its own IV, when a stock's IV is quoted, it is based on the front-month ATM options, as they are usually the most liquid and highly traded options and so give the best indicator. It's not necessary to know how IV is actually calculated, as it's not an easy formula to understand. However it is important that you know how to use it.

IV is the market's current assessment of how an option's prices will move in the future, up to an option's expiration date, based on a stock or market's forecasted move over a year. It represents a one standard deviation range of potential movement either up or down from the underlying price.

Because implied volatility is an annualized expected move, it gets adjusted for each expiration cycle. Look at Option Chain 5.1 for Tesla options. The last two columns show the IV for the ATM options for each expiration and the expected move up or down during that time frame. The Feb 17 options have an IV of 79.06% with 41 days to expiration. This suggests that the underlying stock with a one standard deviations accuracy will move within a $24.63 range either up or down from today's price by the time that option expires.

In mathematical terms, the 79.06% IV implies traders expect the stock to move up to 79% from its current price in a year's time. That would be $113.68 × 0.79 = $90 (after rounding) from today price. That number is then used to figure out the expected move of +/– $24.63 over the next 41 days. I will explain this better later in the chapter. If the IV were lower, the expected stock movement would also be lower. The jump in IV from Jan 20 to Jan 27 expirations is because earnings reports are due that week, which will cause more volatility in the stock than usual.

Symbol		Description	Last	Net C...	Bid	Ask	Hist V...	Beta Weighting	Account	?
▽ TSLA	▾	Tesla Inc	113.68	3.34	113.55	113.68	67.15 %	SPY	All Accounts ▾	
Spread Single ▾	Filter NONE ▾	Strikes 10 ▾							Click to: Trade ▾	🔧

		CALLS								PUTS					
Pos	Open...	Volu...	Imp V...	Delta	Bid	Ask		Strike	Bid	Ask	Delta	Imp V...	Volu...	Open...	Pos
▸ 13 Jan 23	(6d)	Weekly										80.33%	(±10.01)
▸ 20 Jan 23	(13d)											74.30%	(±13.20)
▸ 27 Jan 23	(20d)	Weekly										85.57%	(±18.72)
▸ 03 Feb 23	(27d)	Weekly										83.19%	(±21.07)
▸ 10 Feb 23	(34d)	Weekly										80.42%	(±22.83)
▸ 17 Feb 23	(41d)											79.06%	(±24.63)
▸ 24 Feb 23	(48d)	Weekly										76.90%	(±25.92)
▸ 17 Mar 23	(69d)											75.29%	(±30.50)
▸ 21 Apr 23	(104d)											74.22%	(±37.14)

OPTION CHAIN 5.1 Expected Move and IV

Source: TradeStation

USING IV

Understanding the characteristics of volatility and how to use IV in trading situations will help improve your understanding of various option strategies and when to use them. IV will become a tool you will always want to look at. Volatility can be used to a trader's advantage in a several ways, which I will discuss throughout the book. The simplest of these as already mentioned is being able to see the expected range a stock should move in a given time period. Once you know a stock's expected range, then you have a starting point for great locations to place shorting strategies.

IV TENDS TO GET OVERSTATED

A piece of information you want to keep in your back pocket is that IV tends to get overstated. If IV indicates an expected move of plus or minus $13.50 in 30 days, there is a very good chance that the stock will move less than that expected range. If volatility is overestimated, options will be overpriced, and you can us this to your advantage. Over time, if you notice that a stock is moving less than the volatility suggests it should, you can benefit from this knowledge by placing short strategies that are at the expected range.

IMPLIED VOLATILITY VERSUS HISTORICAL VOLATILITY

Implied volatility by itself may tell you what expected volatility and a stock's expected range should be, but it doesn't present a full picture on its own. It's only when compared to historical volatility that you can start to gain some valuable insight. A critical aspect of volatility is that it tends to be mean regressing. In theory, a stock's IV will revert back to its one-year historical mean—maybe not overnight, but eventually. If you find that the current IV is much higher or lower than its historical level, there is a good change that in time it will go back to its normal level. You can this see in Figure 5.1 from MarketChameleon .com, which shows the 30-day IV for QQQ tending to return to its 252-day average historical volatility levels.

FIGURE 5.1 QQQ Implied Versus Historical Volatility
Source: MarketCameleon.com

When you know that IV reverts to its historical mean, you can find ways to take advantage of that fact. If IV is relatively too high, you can profit by selling strategies such as iron condors or strangles. If IV does return to normal levels while the stock doesn't move too much, those option positions will lose value. You could then buy them back cheaper at a profit. Likewise, when volatility is extremely low, you can look for trades that benefit from low volatility, like buying calls or puts outright or buying spreads.

MEASURING IMPLIED VOLATILITY

So how do you go about determining where the current IV stands in relationship to its historical volatility? For starters you can look at a chart that compares the two as in (Figure 5.1). Alternatively, it's easy to find metrics, such as IV rank and IV percentile, that give you much of the information you need in a snapshot. These are metrics that you should be using every time you trade an option.

IV Rank

IV rank (IVR) compares a stock's current IV to its range over a set time period, usually a year. This lets you know where the current IV stands in relation to its historical range. The higher the IV rank, the more volatile the stock is now versus its history. The historical range is the highest IV reading minus the lowest over the past year. To find the IVR, you'll compare the current IV minus its one-year low versus its one-year range.

The formula is:

$$\frac{\text{Current IV} - \text{1-year IV low}}{\text{1-year IV high} - \text{1-year IV low}}$$

For a current IV of 45% with a high and low IV for the past year of 50% and 20%, you would get:

$$\frac{45 - 20}{50 - 20} = \frac{25}{30} = 83\% \text{ for an IVR of 83\%}$$

This number is on the high side and tells us that the current IV is in the top 83% range of its normal volatility. An IVR that is below 30% would be considered low.

A high IVR can help a seller in two ways. The first is that high IV means inflated option premiums. This gets you bigger premiums, which in turn lowers your breakeven point on a trade, giving you a higher probability of success. Second, if IV does revert to normal levels, option prices will shrink, giving you a profit. Either case means a bigger cushion regarding a stock's directional move hurting you. As a seller, a decrease in volatility can result in a profit, even if the underlying security goes against you slightly.

IV Percentile

IVR can be misleading at times, so I also like to look at IV percentile (IV%). This indicates the percentage of days in the past that a stock's IV was lower than its current IV. Although IV rank does give you some good information, it may not show a complete picture. Say the example above was a stock that normally has an IV of 30, but had a two-week surge in volatility a month earlier to 80%. The current IV of 45 would put its IVR below average.

$$\frac{45 - 20}{80 - 20} = \frac{25}{60} = 41.67 \text{ IVR}$$

Yet in reality, this could be considered high if the stock's IV traded most of year in the 30% to 40% range and only had a few weeks of trading above 45%. If you know that the IV has been below its current level for say 220 days in past year, IV percentile would take that into account. That gives you a different perspective.

Here's the easy IV percentile formula:

$$\frac{\text{Number of trading days below current IV}}{\text{252 trading days}}$$

This formula gives you an IV% of 220/252 = 0.8732, or 87.32%. This means the stock's IV has been lower than it is now for 87% of the past year, so today's IV is relatively high compared to where it normally traded throughout the year. IVR wouldn't capture that, so it is a good idea to get in the habit of looking at both or visualizing IV on a chart.

IVR and IV% are important tools for options traders. I never make a trade without knowing them. I look at both metrics as gauges of a stock's current volatility level relative to its historical volatility and to confirm a high IV.

The good news is you don't have to do the math; any options software will have these values readily available. In TradeStation it looks like Figure 5.2 (using Tesla's info). The 77% is the current IV, not the IVR. The actual IVR (not shown) is 61%. You can still get a sense of its rank and see that it's higher than its median IV of 64%. Other software may just say IVR = 61%, but with TradeStation you have to look at the picture or do the math. The visual is enough. Knowing the actual number is not as important as knowing the value is on the high or low side of the average. The IV percentile of 87% you can read outright; it's pretty high. Combined, these metrics tell you that Tesla's IV is on the high side and if you think its IV will come back down to normal, you should look to trade strategies that benefit from that. On the other hand if the IV were relatively low, you should consider bypassing a trade or a using different strategy.

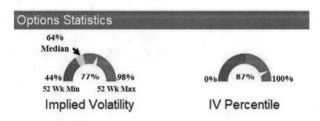

FIGURE 5.2 IV Rank and IV Percentile
Source: TradeStation

Looking at a Chart

I've recently started trading on the tastytrade platform, and I like that they make it easy to see a chart of a stock's IVR. They also let you easily see the IVR at the top of the page. They don't show IV percentile as readily, but you can find it on their watchlist screen. You can also get a sense of the IV% when you are looking at an IVR chart.

Looking at Rivian in Chart 5.1 tells a different story than looking at IVR alone. The bottom portion of the chart shows the IVR. At 41.2%, this could be considered to be on the low side, but when looking at the full chart of its IVR, you will notice a couple of very high IV peaks months ago. These two peaks have pushed the current IV to a comparative low level. But if you take these away, Rivian's current IV of 86% (not shown) is higher than it has been during the last nine months and is comparatively high to most of the year. Looking at this IVR chart, I tend to think IV is high and peaking, and I would be comfortable with strategies that were short volatility.

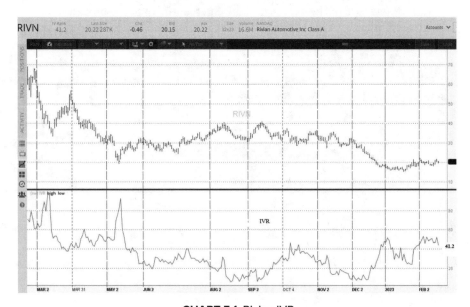

CHART 5.1 Rivian IVR
Source: tastytrade

WAYS TO USE IV

Options traders can use implied volatility several ways. Here are some of the most useful to help you be a high probability options trader.

IV, Mean Regression, and Contrarian Thinking

As I said, volatility is mean regressing. Now that you understand IVR and IV%, it should be easier to use and measure volatility. If you believe volatility levels are high or low and will revert back to their mean levels, you can make trades that reflect this. This thinking falls on the contrarian side of trading.

I will cover this more when I talk about the VIX in Chapter 7, but rising volatility is usually associated with falling markets, while low volatility means the market is steadily rising and expected to keep going up. As a contrarian and believer in mean regression, you could look for market tops and bottoms when volatility gets relatively very high or low. The theory is that as IV regresses to its mean, the market will change directions. Just be aware that volatility can stay high or low for a while. As I look at the RIVN chart with this idea in mind, if I believed that IV has peaked and will come down, I would also believe that the stock may be bottoming and due for a rally.

Stop Overpaying for Options

A grasp of volatility and understanding of whether an option is relatively expensive or cheap based on current IV levels will help prevent costly trading mistakes, such as overpaying for long options. The worse feeling is buying overinflated calls, then watching the market rally while volatility shrinks, sucking out the premium of your options. Trying to buy an option when its IVR is at 95% can be a costly proposition. Hopefully, this is something you will start paying attention to and realize that when IV is high, selling strategies are the best way to go.

Comparing Options

Comparing the prices of two options in different stocks doesn't help you determine if one is relatively cheaper than another. Here too, IVR or IV% can help you. If you are looking at the 50 Delta calls in both Costco and Apple, trading at $9.25 and $3.05, respectively, a novice trader would instantly say the Apple option is cheaper. But taking a closer look at volatility, you get:

Costco: IVR of 7.1, IV% of 14.2

Apple: IVR of 67.9, IV% of 65.4

This tells you that the $9.25 Costco call is much cheaper, relative to its normal value, while the Apple call is relatively high.

You can also use this concept when comparing two nearby options in a chain. Maybe one has an IV of 55.2 and the other an IV of 57.4. The higher IV option is comparatively overpriced. If you put on a trade that involves selling an option, consider the option with a higher IV, as it has a richer relative premium.

Perceived Directional Risk

Volatility can also indicate the direction in which traders perceive a stock or the market is heading. Calls and puts that are equally distant from the current price should technically have the same IV. But if you notice that the puts have a higher IV, then the market thinks there is more downside risk than upside, and vice versa for calls. Puts tend to have a higher IV than equidistant calls under normal circumstances, because fear of a crash increases put premiums more than greed increases call premiums. This is known as volatility skew. (I've already written about this; however, I moved it to Chapter 7, so you will have to wait to read it.)

Figuring Out Expected Move over a Set Period

When you see implied volatility of say 40%, that is an annualized number. It says that in a year's time, the market expects the stock will be 40% higher or lower than its current price, with one standard deviation (SD) of assurance, or 68% of the time.

But that information is not so helpful if you have an option that expires in 30 days. You need to work backward to figure that out. Though an option table will give you this information, you should understand how to figure it out. This involves understanding how standard deviation works.

To calculate volatility over some period of time other than one year (like a day), you first need to determine how many of those periods you expect to occur in a year, then calculate the square root (sq rt) of that number. For daily volatility, for instance, you would assume 252 periods in a year, because a year contains 252 trading days. It's easier (and nearly as accurate) to round that number up to 256, giving a tidy square root of 16 rather than 15.87 (the square root of 252). For a weekly time frame there would be 52 periods a year, and a monthly time frame has

12 periods a year. The square root of this period is the denominator. You would then divide the annual volatility by this amount.

To determine daily volatility using 40% as your IV:

$$\frac{\text{Volatility}}{\text{Sq rt of 256}} = \frac{40\%}{16} = 2.50\%, \text{ or } 0.025$$

This implies a daily one standard deviation price change up or down of 2.5%, meaning you would expect to see a price change of 2.5% or less approximately two trading days out of every three, or 68% of the time. In dollar terms, if the stock currently trades at $100, your expected range would be $100 × 0.025 = +/– $2.50, or expected prices between $97.50 and $102.50.

For a move of two standard deviations, double the previous result to 5% ($5.00) and except to see prices stay within that range 95% of the time, or 19 out of 20 days. So only 1 out of 20 trading days you should get a move outside this two SD +/–$5.00 range.

You don't multiply the daily volatility by 5 to get *weekly volatility*. Instead, divide volatility by the square root of 52, which is 7.2, to get:

$$\frac{\text{Volatility}}{\text{Sq rt of 52}} = \frac{40\%}{7.2} = 5.56\%$$

This implies that the standard deviation of a typical weekly move will be within +/–5.56%, while a two standard deviation move will stay within a +/–11.12% range.

You can now easily find the volatility of any different time frame, say, three days or five weeks. You just need to first figure out the number of trading days in the time period you are looking at. For five weeks you would use 25, as there are 25 trading days in five weeks (remove any holidays). Then figure out how many of those periods occur in a year. Don't let this confuse you: it's just 256 divided by the number of trading days in the time period you are looking at.

$$\frac{\text{Number of trading days in year}}{\text{Number of days in your time frame}} = \frac{256}{25} = 10.24$$

Then plug the 10.24 into the time frame volatility equation:

$$\text{Volatility of 5 weeks} = \frac{\text{Volatility}}{\text{Sq rt of 10.24}} = \frac{40\%}{3.2} = 12.5\%$$

With a $100 stock you could then expect a five-week one standard deviation move of up or down of $100 × 0.125, or $12.50.

Luckily, you will never have to figure any of this out, as it's a lot easier to look at an option table for expected range, but hopefully it helps you understand how expected range works.

STANDARD DEVIATION

While I am at it, I will explain standard deviation for those who don't really understand what it means, as it is vital to understanding option moves and probabilities of success.

In trading, standard deviation is a measure of how widely prices are dispersed from the average price. The standard deviation is closely related to IV and is based on an estimate of the future volatility, a time frame, and the current stock price:

- The higher the volatility, the bigger the potential moves and the higher the standard deviation.
- The farther in the future the date is, the more chance it has to move, yielding a bigger standard deviation.
- The larger the stock price, the bigger its moves will tend to be, so the standard deviation is bigger.

If a stock trades in a narrow range, its standard deviation will be lower than if prices moves rapidly. For example, compare two stocks trading at $100. One has a steady uptrend moving one or two dollars a day, while the other has recently gone from $300 to $50 to $100 in a few weeks, with 20 point daily moves being normal.. The first stock has a much lower volatility, so the standard deviation move from its current price will be smaller as well.

STANDARD DEVIATION AND PROBABILITY

Standard deviation can also help tell you the probability of a stock being at a specific price at a future date, or better said a within a specified distance from the current price. If you know that a $100 stock has a one standard deviation of $2, then you know that 68% of time it should move less than that.

WHAT YOU NEED TO KNOW ABOUT SD

±one standard deviation takes in approximately 68.27% (about 2/3) of all occurrences.

±two standard deviations takes in approximately 95.45% (about 19/20) of all occurrences.

±three standard deviations takes in approximately 99.73% (about 369/370) of all occurrences.

Figure 5.3 shows standard deviation on a bell curve. The center line is the current price. The 34.1% one standard deviation on either side accounts for 68.2% of all occurrences. When you look at an option table and see an IV of 26 and an expected move +/–$20.75, it means that 68.27% of the time, price moves will fall within that one standard deviation range. You should also expect that 95.4% of the time prices will stay within a two standard deviations move of $41.50. This insight is helpful in knowing the probabilities that different option Deltas will be in and out of the money by expiration.

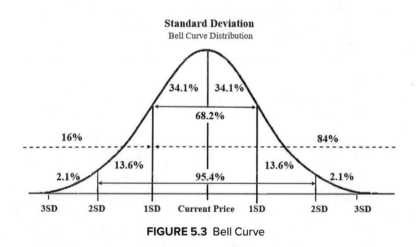

Standard Deviation
Bell Curve Distribution

FIGURE 5.3 Bell Curve

To help make standard deviation clearer, imagine you hit 100 golf balls with the same driver. Your average shot is 100 yards (you are not a great golfer). Your one standard deviation is plus or minus 30 yards from your average 100-yard shot. If your shots fell perfectly in a bell curve, you would expect to see 68.27% of the shots land between 70 and 130 yards. Two standard deviations is plus or minus 60 yards, so 95.45% of your shots would land between 40 and 160 yards. Three standard deviations is plus or minus 90 yards. Of all your shots:

34.1% would travel 70 to 100 yards: one SD of 30 yards below the average 100 yards.

34.1% would go 100 to 130 yards: one SD above the average.

13.6% would go 40 to 70 yards: two SD of 60 below the average.

13.6% would go 130 to 160 yards: two SD above the average.

2.1% would go between 10 to 40 yards: three SD of 90 below yards average.

2.1% would go 160 to 190 yards: three SD above the average.

You may also hit an outlier or two that go 230 yards, or you may hit one that travels 9 feet and another that bounces off a tree and ends up behind you—though rare, these outliers will happen. And of course 40 of your balls may end up in the woods, but that has nothing to with this. The point though is you're a pretty volatile golfer whose shots can go anywhere and you should consider golf lessons. A good consistent golfer would be able to hit those balls an average of 200 yards with a standard deviation of 10 yards, so his one standard deviation range would be 190 to 210. This lower-volatility golfer has more predictable shots that stay within a narrower range.

This can be translated to trading. If a stock trading at $100 had an IV of 30%, the 1-year standard deviation would be $30.

A one standard deviation range would be $70 to $130 with a 68.27% chance the stock will be in this range a year from now.

A two standard deviation range would be $40 to $160 with a 95.45% chance the stock will be in this range a year from now.

A three standard deviation range would be $10 to $190 with a 99.73% chance the stock will be in this range a year from now.

84 AND 16 PERCENT:
NUMBERS WORTH KNOWING

The above percentages relate to option trading because you can use them to figure out the probabilities that an option will expire in or out of the money. Going back to golf, what are the chances you will hit a ball at least 70 yards, or a one standard deviation shot? After rounding, the answer is 84% of the time. This is because half the time you should hit it 100 yards or more and 34% of the time you will hit between 70 and 100 yards.

Broken down, it's:

$$34.1\% \; + \; 34.1\% \; + \; 13.6\% \; + \; 2.3\% \; = 84\%$$
$$\text{(70–100)} \quad \text{(100–130)} \quad \text{(130–160)} \quad \text{(160+)}$$

This implies that only 16% of the time, your shot will not reach the one standard deviation distance of 70 yards. These 84 and 16 percents are represented by the dashed lines in Figure 5.3. This 16 is an important number in options, as the 16 Delta option is a one standard deviation level from current prices. You know now that the stock shouldn't go beyond that level in your chosen time frame 84% of the time. This now lets you know where you can place trades that have the highest probabilities of working.

If you only remember one thing from this chapter, make it this: The 16 Delta option is one standard deviation away from the current price and has an 84% chance of expiring out of the money.

I just want to reiterate, if a $100 stock has a one standard deviation expected range of $10 and you make a trade thinking the market will not go above $110, you should be right 84% of the time. If everything falls into a normal distribution, 50% of the time the market will drop and 34% it will stay within the $110 one standard deviation level if it does rally. This leaves 16 as the percentage of times you will be wrong, and is an important number to know when choosing strike prices, something I will talk about several times throughout the book.

OUTLIERS DO HAPPEN

On a different note, a two standard deviation move of 95% is what brokerage firms typically look at when figuring out a maximum loss level for margin requirements. Yet for those who think they can never be really wrong, the market may surprise you one day and move five standard deviations against you. At the very least, 5% of the time you should see a more than two standard deviation move. It does happen (recently Nvidia moved eight standard deviations in a day), and you can't really prepare yourself for it except by keeping your position size small enough to let you handle one of those outlier moves.

FINAL THOUGHTS

Always check volatility. It will play a big part in your trading, whether you know it or not. Putting volatility on your side increases your chances of making money. And don't ever forget, if you short a 16 Delta option you will be right 84% of time.

CHAPTER 6

A Dive into the Greeks

I will try my best to discuss how to understand Delta and Company and how to use them to increase your probabilities of making money while reducing risk. Hopefully not being too boring or technical in the process. Whole books have been written on this topic. Most can be mindboggling. Still, understanding the Greeks and how they affect your positions is a crucial part of successful trading.

THE GREEKS

The Greeks are tools that will give you insight into how you can expect an option's value to change as certain factors change. For example, **Delta**, the most common Greek, tells you how much an option's value changes versus a $1 move in a stock. **Theta** tells you how time will affect an option's price. **Vega** can tell you how a change in volatility will affect an option's price, and **Gamma** tells you how much Delta will move as the price of the underlying moves. There are a few other factors that affect the Greeks, such as Vanna, Color, Vomma, Speed, and Charm, but I won't get into them, as they don't directly affect my trading decisions. You may want to look into them on your own once you have a thorough understanding of the basic Greeks as part of your never-ending learning process.

As I explain trading strategies and risk later in the book, some of this will become easier to grasp, especially Gamma. This chapter will sometimes give brief explanations of things that may make more sense later.

> Gamma, Theta, and Vega have their greatest impact on at the money options.

HOW CAN THEY HELP

The Greeks help you know just how much money you may make (or lose) as price, time, volatility, and interest rates change. They will tell you the magnitude of how option prices can be affected by these different market factors. The Greeks are also an incredibly valuable tool to have when managing risk and protecting your portfolio from being too lopsided, so you shouldn't ignore them.

Questions Greeks Can Answer

A few questions knowing your Greeks can easily answer:

If the underlying stock moves 5 points, how much does that change the value of my position?

If the underlying stock moves 10 points, how much does that change the Delta of my position?

What happens to my position if IV goes from 30 to 40?

What is my overall exposure?

Do I have too much risk on?

Is my portfolio too long or short the market?

What are my chances of breaking even on a trade?

If the stock doesn't move, how much will my option change in week?

How many contracts should I trade?

DELTA

First, here are a few notes:

1. Delta is not a whole number. It is a percentage. If you see or hear "a Delta of 50," it's really 0.50. Most of the time, people ignore the decimal when talking about Delta. I will go back and forth between the two throughout the book.
2. Calls have positive Delta and puts have negative Delta. And just as the French fail to pronounce half their letters, the negative on puts is sometimes dropped as well.
3. The Delta for an option is pretty much 50 when it is at the money. Its absolute value shrinks as you go out of the money and increases as you go into the money. As puts go out of the money, their Delta gets smaller as well. Even though technically –20 is a larger number than –50, for our purposes it is smaller.
4. Delta ranges from 0 to +/–100, or 0 to +/–1.00 when using decimals.
5. When shorting an option, the Delta gets flipped. A short call with a 28 Delta has a negative 28 Delta and is a bearish position.
6. As Delta increases, so does the value of the option.

Delta 101: Predicating an Option's Move

Delta is fairly simple to understand, and it's one of the first thing you should look for on an option table. In addition to its primary use, Delta can give you an estimate of the likelihood that an option will be in the money at expiration. This is a way to estimate the probability of a trade working, a way to keep track of the directional risk of your portfolio, and a hedging meter. But for now let's get to that primary use: estimating an option's move versus the underlying asset.

Delta is the percent an option will theoretically move given a $1 move in the underlying asset.

This means that if an option has a 40 Delta, the option price should move 40 cents for every $1 the stock moves.

Looking at Option Chain 6.1, you'll see Apple is trading at $146.50. The closest at the money options are the 146 and 147 calls and puts. In the Delta column, you will see the 147 call has a Delta of 0.48 and the

146 put has a negative –0.48 Delta. What this means is that a $1 move in Apple from the current price will move these options by 0.48 cents. In the case of the put, a $1 move up in Apple will lower the price of the 146 put by 0.48 cents ($1.00 × –0.48), from around $3.65 to $3.17. If you had bought a 155 call with a Delta of 0.17, then you would see a 17-cent drop in its price if Apple dropped a dollar (–$1.00 × 0.17). This use of Delta is pretty straightforward.

Symbol		Description	Last	Net Chg	Bid	Ask	Volume	Hist Volati...	Beta Weighting	Account	
▽ AAPL		Apple Inc	146.50	1.12	146.45	146.49	71,598,3...	37.50 %	$SPX.X	All Accounts	
Spread Single		Filter NONE	Strikes 20							Click to: Trade	

		CALLS							PUTS			
Pos	Imp Volat...	Prob ITM	Delta	Bid	Ask	Strike	Bid	Ask	Delta	Prob ITM	Imp Volat...	Pos
▸	10 Jun 22 (3d)	Weekly									40.66%	(±4.73)
◂	17 Jun 22 (10d)										37.71%	(±7.53)
	47.29 %	77.74%	0.80	9.60	11.50	137	1.04	1.10	-0.18	19.80%	42.94 %	
	43.72 %	76.87%	0.79	9.35	9.70	138	1.16	1.26	-0.20	22.08%	41.91 %	
	39.80 %	76.05%	0.78	8.15	8.80	139	1.39	1.46	-0.23	25.03%	41.63 %	
	42.51 %	71.21%	0.74	7.60	8.30	140	1.61	1.69	-0.26	28.07%	41.12 %	
	42.16 %	67.94%	0.70	6.95	7.50	141	1.79	1.94	-0.29	31.11%	40.14 %	
	40.06 %	65.20%	0.68	6.20	6.55	142	2.13	2.23	-0.32	34.77%	39.98 %	
	39.07 %	61.68%	0.64	5.55	5.75	143	2.44	2.56	-0.36	38.46%	39.48 %	
	38.26 %	57.86%	0.60	4.85	5.10	144	2.79	2.88	-0.40	42.28%	38.76 %	
	38.08 %	53.71%	0.56	4.35	4.45	145	3.15	3.25	-0.44	46.27%	37.96 %	
	37.74 %	49.52%	0.52	3.75	3.95	146	3.55	3.75	-0.48	50.48%	37.62 %	
	36.97 %	45.26%	0.48	3.25	3.35	147	4.05	4.25	-0.52	54.72%	37.36 %	
	36.47 %	40.95%	0.43	2.74	2.90	148	4.55	4.70	-0.57	59.06%	36.41 %	
	35.83 %	36.63%	0.39	2.32	2.42	149	5.15	5.35	-0.61	63.17%	36.55 %	
	35.41 %	32.43%	0.35	1.94	2.03	150	5.70	6.00	-0.65	67.34%	35.99 %	
	34.82 %	22.95%	0.25	1.21	1.28	152.5	7.05	7.75	-0.77	78.30%	32.81 %	
	34.29 %	15.18%	0.17	0.72	0.75	155	9.25	10.15	-0.82	83.27%	36.71 %	
	33.88 %	9.40%	0.10	0.39	0.43	157.5	11.15	13.05	-0.85	86.30%	41.21 %	
	34.33 %	5.84%	0.07	0.23	0.25	160	13.75	15.00	-0.89	89.89%	42.66 %	
	34.91 %	3.56%	0.04	0.13	0.15	162.5	15.05	18.25	-0.92	93.17%	42.64 %	
	36.12 %	2.31%	0.03	0.08	0.10	165	17.70	19.65	-1.00	~0	NE	
▸	24 Jun 22 (17d)	Weekly									34.84%	(±8.97)

OPTION CHAIN 6.1 Looking at Delta

Source: TradeStation

Delta and Share Weighting

Another simple use of Delta is that Delta also tells you what percent of 100 shares of stock an option is worth. A 0.20 Delta call position means that you are effectively long 20 shares of a stock. If the Delta were –0.20, that's the same as being short 20 shares of stock. A high Delta like 85 or 90 means you have a much larger position trading very close in value to the stock itself.

If you have five 40 Delta calls, your total Delta is 200 and your position would be the equivalent of 200 shares of stock. At least it will be for now, because as the stock moves, so will the Delta. More on that change in Delta later, when I write about Gamma.

Since an option's Delta tells you how much the option will move as the stock moves $1, you can use that information to figure out how many options you would need to equal any number of shares by dividing that number of shares by the Delta. Following along with Table 6.1, to equal 100 shares, you could have five options with a 20 Delta or two options with a 50 Delta. In either case a $1 move in the stock price would result in a $100 change in the stock's value as well as $100 in the options' total value. The five 20 Delta calls would move 20 cents each, while the two 50 Delta ones would each move 50 cents.

TABLE 6.1 Delta Weighting

Number of stock or options	Move of stock or options	Value of move
100 shares	$1.00	100 shares × $1 = $100
5 calls with 20 Delta = 100 shares	$0.20	5 calls × $20 = $100
2 calls with 50 Delta = 100 shares	$0.50	2 calls × $50 = $100

Knowing this weighting means you can use it to see how much directional bias you have in a position. If you have a position that is long 300 Delta, then you are equivalently long 300 shares of the stock.

Market Direction

This one is also very simple. If your position has a positive Delta, you have a long outlook on the stock. If the net Delta is negative, you have a short bias. If you bought a put spread, such as buying the 145 put (–44 Delta) and selling the 140 put (–26 Delta), you would want the stock to drop to make money.

If you aren't sure just by looking at the position, the Delta will tell you how short you are. This position has a negative 18 Delta, which you can figure out by adding together the Deltas of each leg. Remember, the short 140 put would have a positive Delta of 26. So the position's net Delta is –44 + 26 = –18. This is the equivalent of being short 18 shares of stock.

Probability of Expiring in the Money

Assuming that price moves randomly, a stock should have a 50/50 chance of moving up or down from current prices. This 50% chance that it moves in the direction you want coincides with an at the money option with a Delta of 50. As you look at options that are further out of the money, the chances of options expiring in the money are diminished and so are their Deltas. Likewise as Delta increases, the odds of an option expiring in the money do so as well, as these options are already in the money. One of Delta's great features is that it closely mimics the probability that an option will expire in the money so it can be used to estimate your chances of success.

To reinforce something from the last chapter, a 16 Delta option is approximately a single standard deviation move from the current price. So there should be an 84% chance that the stock price does not reach this level during the option's lifespan. Likewise the 17 Delta 155 call in Apple tells you there is a 17% chance the stock will reach the $155 strike target. We can use this to figure out that the option has an 83% chance of not reaching that target, in which case it would expire out of the money and worthless. Looking at the shaded expected move range, you can see that the 17 Delta option falls just outside that range. Since most of the strategies I recommend involve shorting options, where you want the option you short to expire out of the money, knowing the odds of that happening makes things a bit easier.

Most software will allow you to see the probability of an option expiring in the money. In Option Chain 6.1 it is the Prob ITM column. When you compare Delta to Prob ITM, you can see they are very close to each other. There is also a probability of out of the money (Prob OTM) column you could use if you wanted to. To save space on my screen, I don't typically have either the Prob ITM or Prob OTM columns; instead, I rely on Delta to get a close-enough estimate.

Thinking in Terms of Delta

When you trade options, get into the habit of thinking about them in terms of Delta, and not so much price or strike. If you want to sell a put spread in Apple, you could think about it in terms of strike prices, as in a 144/139 put spread. You would be selling the 144 put and buying the 139 put. The 144 is the price you want Apple to stay above when shorting. Or you could think of it as a $5-wide 40 Delta put spread, which again is selling the 144 strike 40 Delta put and then buying the 23 Delta 139 put, which is $5 below. This thought process will be more intuitive as you go on, especially if you're trading strangles and iron condors where you want to sell (for instance) a 30 or 16 Delta strangle.

Thinking this way gets you to start considering the probabilities that options expire worthless and of the profit potential in trades. It will let you make the same probability trade over and over again, regardless of the underlying asset you choose. It will also be a necessity if you ever back-test a strategy. Even if you buy options outright, instead of buying a 155 call for $0.75, you have more information if you think of it as buying a 17 Delta option with a 17% chance of being in the money. Knowing that an option has a 17% shot of expiring in the money may cause you to think twice before throwing away $75 on a trade that has little chance of success.

Delta and Risk Trade-off

If you are selling an option, you can increase your potential returns by increasing your Delta. Selling an Apple 60 Delta call would get you about $500 in premium, compared to selling the 25 Delta call and collecting $125. There's a trade-off: you have a 40% chance of the 60 Delta call expiring worthless, as opposed to a 75% chance of the 25 Delta one doing so. Knowing these chances of success lets you compare two trades to see which fits your risk profile better. Do you want to be right more often with smaller wins or right less often but with bigger gains per win?

Delta Hedging

Delta lets you see a snapshot of how long or short your portfolio is as a whole. When you tally up the Delta on all your positions, you can easily see your net market exposure. And since not every stock has the same weight, you can Beta weight the Delta and compare each position to the market as a whole using the S&P 500 index as a gauge to get a better sense of how long or short you are in general. This lets you see and measure how much directional risk you have at any given time in either a single position or in all your positions at once. This allows you to use Delta as a way to hedge and protect your portfolio from directional risk, if needed.

When you start thinking in terms of Deltas, it becomes much easier to keep a balanced portfolio. A good rule of thumb is to keep the Beta-weighted Delta to +/– 0.2% to +/– 0.5% of total portfolio capital. These levels allow for some directional bias. To be Delta neutral, the number should be between – 0.2% and + 0.2%. If it starts getting too high in either direction, you can reduce risk by taking some trades off or putting on trades in the other direction. I will explain Delta hedging later in Chapter 19.

DON'T GET TOO COMFY

The Delta on options is not stationary. It changes as the underlying stock changes prices. If you are long a 50 Delta call and the stock rallies, that Delta will move up, and may be 60 or 70 in short time. If the stock drops, the Delta will shrink. Delta also moves as it nears expiration. What this means is that if you thought you were hedged with a Delta-neutral, balanced portfolio, a market move will throw a monkey wrench in your plan. You would no longer be hedged like before and may need to readjust.

THETA

With its multipurpose uses, Delta is the Swiss Army knife of the Greeks. Theta is the second most used Greek. It only has one purpose: to measure daily time decay.

Theta is the rate at which an option's
extrinsic value decays daily.

Time decay is an option buyer's worst enemy and plays a big part in why option buyers lose money. Every day, as an option gets closer to its expiration date, time decay eats into its value, regardless of other market factors. This is because, when you are long an option position, every day that passes means a smaller chance that the underlying asset's price will move to where you need it. Option sellers, on the other hand, love this decay. It is their reward for taking the risk of selling an option. It should make sense that, if a stock is trading at $100 and you buy a call with a 110 strike price, that option has more value to you with three months left to expiration than with five days. The more time you have, the better the chances of a stock moving to a favorable price. That extra cost is the option's time value. On a day-to-day basis, time decay is pretty small and you won't notice it much, especially when you are far from expiration. But when you are holding for a long period of time or have a few days before an option expires, you will see a noticeable drop in an option's value.

Theta measures how much value an option loses as one day passes. It is measured in dollars and cents and is a negative number, as it impacts an option price negatively. An option with a Theta of

−0.10 loses 10 cents of time value each day, or $10 per contract. This includes weekends and holidays. Theta is not concerned with market direction. What matters is whether you are long or short an option position. If you are long, Theta will be negative and will work against you. You can be right on the direction but still lose money because of time decay, if you don't get a big enough move or it takes too long for a move to happen. When you are short an option, it has a positive Theta. You would be happy with no directional move and to have the market sit still for a while as you collect time premium. If the market does move against you, the hope is that the gain in Theta outpaces the gain in the option's intrinsic value.

Some Theta Basics

The rate at which an option decays varies depending on market conditions, volatility, an option's moneyness, and time to expiration. Here are a few basics you need to know about Theta:

Theta increases as expiration nears.

Theta is highest for at the money options.

Short options have positive Theta.

Long options have negative Theta.

Theta increases as implied volatility increases.

Higher extrinsic value means higher Theta.

Theta and Moneyness

An option's time value is directly related to its moneyness and extrinsic value. An option's Theta is greatest when it is at the money (ATM). As an option moves either into or out of the money, its Theta shrinks along with its extrinsic value. When options get either very far into or out of the money, Theta plays an even smaller role, as the options are either close to worthless if they are far out of the money (OTM) or all intrinsic value when they are deep in the money (ITM).

You can see all this in Option Chain 6.2, where the Delta that is closest to 50 has the highest Theta and extrinsic value. Options that are ITM give up some of their time value (extrinsic value) in exchange for intrinsic value. A high Delta option that is deep ITM is mostly made up of its intrinsic value, with little extrinsic value. It doesn't have as much time value to lose as options nearer the money. Its rate of decay (Theta) is therefore less. In the other direction, as you get further OTM, options shrink in price, so they have less total value that can be eaten away every day. An option position worth $42 simply cannot lose as much per day as one worth $440, so its Theta has to be less.

In this example, the 48 Delta call ($4.40) has a Theta of 0.07. A long position would lose $7 a day in value, as opposed to the 9 Delta call ($0.42), which loses $2 a day.

Also notice that the 9 Delta and the 99 Delta calls are not that far apart in extrinsic values, so they will have similar Thetas and lose time value at about the same rate.

The closer to the ATM the strike price is,
the higher the time premium will be.

Symbol		Description			Last		Net Chg	
▽ JPM		JPMorgan Chase & Co			138.22		0.85	

Spread Single · Filter NONE · Strikes 19 ·

Pos	Vega	Gamma	Intrinsic	Extrinsic	Theta	Delta	Bid	Ask	Strike
17 Feb 23 (38d)									
	0.01	0.001	43.23	0.55	-0.02	0.99	43.65	43.90	95
	0.02	0.002	38.23	0.57	-0.02	0.99	38.70	38.95	100
	0.02	0.003	33.23	0.67	-0.03	0.98	33.80	34.00	105
	0.03	0.004	28.23	0.77	-0.03	0.97	28.90	29.15	110
	0.05	0.007	23.23	0.97	-0.04	0.94	24.10	24.30	115
	0.07	0.010	18.23	1.27	-0.05	0.91	19.40	19.60	120
	0.10	0.016	13.23	1.80	-0.06	0.85	14.95	15.10	125
	0.14	0.022	8.23	2.70	-0.07	0.76	10.85	11.00	130
	0.17	0.029	3.23	4.07	-0.07	0.64	7.25	7.35	135
	0.18	0.032	0.00	4.40	-0.07	0.48	4.35	4.45	140
	0.16	0.031	0.00	2.30	-0.06	0.32	2.28	2.32	145
	0.12	0.024	0.00	1.04	-0.04	0.18	1.03	1.05	150
	0.07	0.015	0.00	0.42	-0.02	0.09	0.41	0.43	155
	0.04	0.008	0.00	0.17	-0.01	0.04	0.16	0.18	160
	0.02	0.004	0.00	0.08	-0.01	0.02	0.07	0.08	165

OPTION CHAIN 6.2 Theta
Source: TradeStation

Time to Expiration and Rate of Decay

Besides moneyness, Theta is also very influenced by the amount of time left to expiration. Time decay doesn't occur at a constant linear rate. Instead it accelerates as an option gets closer to the expiration date. This means options with plenty of time to go have lower Thetas than those closer to expiration. Options start their Theta acceleration in their last 30 days; the pace then really increases in the last few days.

As Figure 6.1 shows, you can visualize Theta as if you were skiing. The loss in time decay is fairly mild from 90 to 60 days, like an easy green ski slope. From 60 to 30 days it picks up a little bit, like a moderate blue slope. At around 30 days to expiration, Theta acceleration kicks in like a steeper black slope. The last few days are even steeper and riskier, like a double black diamond. This is how the typical at the money options react. As options get in or out of the money, their increase in Theta isn't as prominent, as they have less extrinsic value to decay.

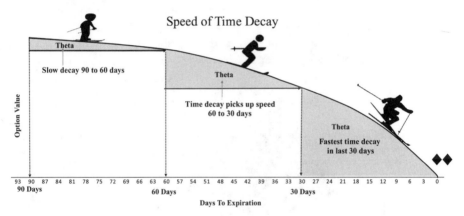

FIGURE 6.1 Theta Acceleration

To see the rate of decay better, look at Option Chain 6.3 of a few Microsoft options for three different months. You will see Theta increase through every time frame as you near expiration. Those increases increase in size as well. Looking at the 230 calls (the closest to ATM), with 65 days to go, it's trading at $12.25 and the Theta is –0.10. With 37 days to expiration (DTE), it's at $9.65 and the Theta is now at –0.14, a loss of $2.60 just due to time value. This same call with only two DTE has a –0.62 Theta and is trading at $3.00, losing another $6.65 in value over 35 days. That's a significantly larger amount lost compared to the previous time frame. With Theta now at –0.62, it will decay at an accelerated pace, eventually losing all its value if Microsoft stayed out of the money. By comparing these periods, especially the last two days, you can see just how fast the time decay accelerates as it nears expiration.

These steeper losses in time value can be dangerous to both buyers and sellers. As a buyer, you can get the call with two days to expiration much more cheaply than the 37 DTE call, but the trade-off is that quicker acceleration of Theta. If you are wrong in direction by even $1, with two days to expiration you will have nothing left. You wouldn't be that badly off with the longer time frame. Yes, you put up more money to do so, but in reality you are risking less on an option with more time to expiration if you exit before the acceleration begins.

> **The best way to minimize the effect of time value decay on long option trades is to trade options with more time to expiration.**

There is risk for sellers as well as an option nears expiration: a trade-off with Gamma risk. I will discuss that in the Gamma section, but since we are here, notice and remember how much Gamma increases as options get closer to expiration.

Symbol			Description			Last		Net Chg	
▽ MSFT			Microsoft Corp			229.15		2.03	
Spread Single	Filter NONE	Strikes 4							

			C A L L S						
Pos	**Vega**	**Gamma**	**Intrinsic**	**Extrinsic**	**Theta**	**Delta**	**Bid**	**Ask**	**Strike**
▲ 13 Jan 23 (2d)		Weekly							
	0.07	0.040	3.85	2.00	-0.58	0.68	5.80	5.90	225
	0.08	0.044	1.35	2.95	-0.63	0.57	4.25	4.35	227.5
	0.08	0.045	0.00	3.02	-0.62	0.46	2.99	3.05	230
	0.07	0.043	0.00	1.98	-0.57	0.35	1.96	2.00	232.5
▸ 20 Jan 23 (9d)									
▸ 27 Jan 23 (16d)		Weekly							
▸ 03 Feb 23 (23d)		Weekly							
▸ 10 Feb 23 (30d)		Weekly							
▲ 17 Feb 23 (37d)									
	0.27	0.014	8.85	6.80	-0.14	0.67	15.55	15.75	220
	0.28	0.016	3.85	8.60	-0.14	0.60	12.35	12.55	225
	0.29	0.016	0.00	9.65	-0.14	0.52	9.60	9.70	230
	0.29	0.017	0.00	7.25	-0.13	0.44	7.20	7.30	235
▸ 24 Feb 23 (44d)		Weekly							
▲ 17 Mar 23 (65d)									
	0.35	0.012	8.85	9.10	-0.10	0.66	17.50	18.40	220
	0.38	0.013	3.85	11.10	-0.10	0.60	14.80	15.10	225
	0.39	0.013	0.00	12.23	-0.10	0.54	12.15	12.30	230
	0.39	0.014	0.00	9.73	-0.10	0.47	9.65	9.80	235
▲ 21 Apr 23 (100d)									
	0.44	0.010	8.85	12.60	-0.09	0.65	20.85	22.05	220
	0.46	0.010	3.85	14.15	-0.08	0.60	17.80	18.20	225
	0.48	0.011	0.00	15.25	-0.08	0.55	15.15	15.35	230
	0.48	0.011	0.00	12.73	-0.08	0.49	12.65	12.80	235

OPTION CHAIN 6.3 Microsoft: Theta Acceleration and Gamma Too

Source: TradeStation

Using Theta to Your Advantage

Time decay can be used to your advantage. Simply selling options outright or through spreads and other trades can put Theta to work for you. A bonus of selling options is that when you take advantage of Theta, you can be slightly wrong in market direction and still make money. If you short a 235 call with 37 days to expiration for $7.25 with Microsoft at $229.15, you are technically bearish, hoping the market goes down. Yet even if the stock rallies a bit, to, say $234, and you hold to expiration, the option will expire worthless and you would see a profit as your Theta gain outpaces the loss from the rally. In this case, you would keep the $725 premium.

Perhaps you're thinking, "Cool, let me just load up on Theta and I will make a fortune." But Theta comes with risk. If you just short an ATM call or put, you will have maximum Theta, but even a moderate move in the wrong direction will overcome that Theta gain. A big move will really hurt. Being long Theta will always come with a directional risk (Gamma), so you should control how much Theta you have on. An easy way as a seller to lower Theta is to trade options that are not at the money, but well below it; this will buffer you from directional risk. How far out of the money you go will depend on your risk profile and the type of trader you are. I prefer to sell naked options that have a Delta of less than 20 and Deltas of 30 to 40 on spreads.

Like Delta, you want to keep the total Theta in your account to +/– 0.2% to +/– 0.5% of your total portfolio.

VEGA

Vega measures how changes in a stock's volatility affect option prices. Volatility affects the time value of an option because if volatility increases, stocks are more likely to make wider moves. This causes the extrinsic value on options to go up, as traders are willing to pay more for options that have a better chance of moving.

Vega measures the rate of change of an option's value relative to a 1% change in implied volatility.

Vega is a positive number that's measured in dollars and cents and that affects both puts and calls in the same way. When volatility rises, options prices go up; when it drops, prices go down. A Vega of 0.25 means that a 1% increase in volatility will drive options prices up 25 cents, and a decrease in volatility will drop an option's value by 25 cents. Vega is something an options trader should understand to estimate a move in option prices, especially when trying to take advantage of spikes in volatility. If you shorted an option that traded for $5.00 when IV was 50 and wanted to estimate what it would be worth if IV came down to 40, Vega can tell you that. Assuming nothing else changes, if the Vega was 0.20, then that 10-point IV drop would drop the option by $2.

Change in IV × Vega = Change in option's value

10 × 0.20 = $2.00

Some Vega Basics

Vega is greatest for options that are at the money.

The higher the stock price, the greater the Vega.

Similar Delta options will have a greater Vega for higher priced stocks.

Vega gets higher the further you go from expiration.

Increased volatility will increase the value of an option.

Vega only affects extrinsic value.

Option sellers are short Vega and want volatility to drop.

Vega has a bell-shaped curve around the at the money option. The at the money options have the highest Vega, and it gets lower as you move both further in and further out of the money. This means volatility has less of an effect as options move away from at the money. Go back and look at Option Chain 6.2 for JPM to see this. Because ATM options have the highest Vega, they are most sensitive to changes in volatility. Both ITM and OTM options have less extrinsic value, and since Vega only affects extrinsic value, they have less sensitivity to changes in IV. This is similar in concept to Theta. One thing to note is that the sell-off in Vega from ATM options is a bit faster for options that are closer to expiration.

Using Vega

Looking at Option Chain 6.3 for Microsoft, you can see that Vega is larger as you go out in time. One way to use Vega is to put on calendar spreads that take advantage of the discrepancy in the Vegas between two expiration cycles. If you put on a trade expecting a change in volatility, you will get more bang for your buck using longer term options. But you don't want to go out too far in time, because those options are less liquid. You also don't want too much Vega exposure, because a swing in volatility can hurt you as easily as it can help you.

RHO

Before I get into Gamma, which I think is really important, I will very quickly touch on Rho. Rho is an estimate of how a change in interest rates affects an option's price. Typically, a 1% increase in interest rates means that premiums on call options rise by the Rho amount and put option premiums decrease by that amount. Since interest rates do not move much on a day-to-day basis, Rho is not significant enough for the average trader to worry about, nor have I ever looked it at in 35 years of option trading. I am pressed for space, so let's continue to Gamma.

GAMMA

Gamma is the Greek that is least understood and tends to not get enough love from traders, as it isn't directly involved in making money. But it is the risk that you should fear the most. Delta, Theta, and Vega are first derivative Greeks and tell you how an option's price will change. Gamma is considered a second-derivative Greek. Gamma doesn't directly measure how an option will change, but instead how its Delta will change.

Gamma is stated in terms of Delta. It is the speed that an option's Delta moves. Traders use it to gauge an option's price movement. A large Gamma means Delta will increase faster as the market moves, which means an option will gain value more rapidly than with a smaller Gamma reading. And while it's great to have fast-moving options if you are on the right side of that move, it's not too good if you are wrong.

Gamma measures how much an option's Delta will change per 1 point move in the price of the underlying asset.

The most important thing about Gamma is understanding the risk it gives option sellers as time to expiration nears. There will always be a battle between Theta and Gamma that intensifies as you get closer to expiration. You can think of Theta as your reward and Gamma as your risk for selling.

Some Gamma Basics

Gamma is largest at the money or near the money.

Gamma for near the money options increases as you get closer to expiration.

Gamma is the risk you assume that a short option will move against you.

Gamma and Theta have opposite effects on an option.

Gamma risk increases near expiration.

Gamma is positive for long options and negative for short options.

Understanding Gamma

If a stock trading at $80 has its 80 strike –0.50 Delta put trading for $3.00 and the stock drops by $1 to $79, the option's value should increase by $0.50 and be worth $3.50. Now that option is no longer at the money because it moved to in the money by $1.00. Its Delta will no longer be –0.50. Now with the stock at $79, the put may have a Delta of –0.54. This means the Gamma on that option was 0.04. If the stock had rallied $1.00, then the Delta would have fallen to –0.46. If the Gamma were 0.20, then the option would have a 0.70 Delta after a 1-point drop. This seems like an excessive move for a $1.00 change in a stock's price, but this does happen close to expiration, as the option becomes very sensitive to price movement.

That was working backward. Instead you should see it as:

$$\text{Gamma} \times \text{move in the stock} = \text{change in Delta}$$

$$0.04 \times \$1.00 = 0.04$$

For an example, look at the 230 two DTE call with a 0.46 Delta on Option Chain 6.3. It has a Gamma of 0.045. This means that if MSFT rallied $1.00, the new Delta would be 0.46 + 0.045 or about 0.505. If it rallies by $5, then multiply the Gamma by 5 to get 0.225. The new Delta when thinking without the decimal would be 46 + 22.5, or 68.5, which is the Delta of the 225 call that is $5 deeper in the money.

Gamma and the risk it involves may be easier to understand as I look at Gamma's interaction with certain variables.

Gamma and Direction

Gamma itself is a positive number for calls as well as puts. What matters is if you are long or short the option position. When long an option, you want price to move in the direction of higher Delta, up for calls and down for puts. When long, Gamma is positive, which means Delta will change in the direction you want if the stock moves in the direction that works for you. For example, if you are long a 30 Delta OTM put, you'd want the market to drop, as this would increase the Delta by the Gamma amount and hopefully get the option ITM. When you're long Gamma, a big move in your direction is your friend.

When short an option or spread, Gamma is negative, so moves toward higher Deltas are bad for you, as you need an option to expire below a 50 Delta to be worthless. When short Gamma you don't necessarily need the market to move in any direction, but you definitely want it to stay out of the money.

Gamma and Moneyness

Gamma is highest when an option is near or at the money. As options move away from at the money in either direction, the Gamma is reduced and options lose their sensitivity. When options are near the money, Gamma stays in a narrow range, not changing much until you start to get a bit in or out of the money. Eventually they have virtually no Gamma. You can see this on the JPM Option Chain 6.2. Near the money, even a small change in underlying price can cause a significant change in Delta, whereas the options at the extremes need a fairly big move to move an option's Delta. When an option has a very low Delta, neither the option's premium nor its Delta are going to be very sensitive to changes in underlying price.

With JPM trading at $138.22, if it goes to $141, it doesn't really matter much to someone short a 165 call. It will still be far out of the money. With a Gamma of 0.004, you won't even see a move in Delta. The same holds true for Deltas that are deep in the money. Their Deltas won't move much either. But if you were short a 140 call, you would feel a move that changed the Delta from 0.48 to 0.57. This changes the option from being OTM to $1 ITM. If this was the day before expiration, there would be a good chance that a winner turned into a loser.

What all this tells you is that if you are short option strategies that started out of the money but have moved to at the money, then your

Gamma has most likely increased. You are now more Delta sensitive, and it takes smaller price moves to hurt you, compared to when the position was out of the money. This makes you more vulnerable to price moves.

Gamma and Time to Expiration

Moneyness is one piece of the Gamma puzzle. The bigger piece is how Gamma reacts to passing time. This is pretty easy to understand. As you saw in Option Chain 6.3, Theta Acceleration and Gamma Too, Gamma accelerates like Theta as you near expiration. For the 230 calls, Gamma goes from 0.011 to 0.045, quadrupling in just over three months. As I said, Gamma should be thought of as a risk to option sellers, so this increase in Gamma is how much risk increases if you hold options too close to expiration. When there is plenty of time left, risk is lower because you have plenty of time for the price to come back if it goes against you. With little time, a move against you may be final. Actually, this is not entirely true. With near the money options, Gamma will rise exponentially with time. However deep in or out of the money options with Deltas at extreme levels that have little sensitivity left in them have Gammas that approach zero as they near expiration.

HOW TO USE GAMMA

There are professionals who make a living scalping Gamma, but that really is the level after the next level of trading, which I won't get into in this book. Leave that to the market makers. Instead, you should use Gamma as a means of controlling your risk. *Gamma risk* can be thought of as the risk that an option that is profitable will become unprofitable. This risk increases as you get closer to expiration, where a $5 move in a stock can mean the difference between being in or out of money with not much time left to get back to where you need to be. A $5 move with two months to go is not going to change the speed of an option's move or its price all that much. In order to curtail this Gamma risk, most option strategies in this book exit trades with two to three weeks to go or when they've achieved a set profit. Otherwise you run the risk of giving it all back. This will become clearer as you get deeper into the book. You've just gotta survive this chapter.

Gamma and Theta

Gamma (risk) and Theta (reward) always work against each other. You can never have both in your favor. A positive Theta position has a negative Gamma, and vice versa. The size of the risk to reward tends to be correlated, so a large Gamma is accompanied by a large and opposite Theta, and a small Gamma is accompanied by a small Theta. This means that if you take on too much Theta in hopes of making alot of premium, you will be exposed to greater Gamma risk. When you are short an option, you benefit from Theta, but negative Gamma can hurt you in the interim. Your hope for assuming Gamma risk is that the reward from time decay outweighs the risk of price movement.

For option buyers, Theta is the risk and Gamma is the reward. You put on long directional trades looking for Gamma to help accelerate the option's value as the stock moves. In exchange for this, you are short Theta. If the stock doesn't see that move you need, time decay will eat away your money.

A trader's goal is to find the best balance between the two. The ideal is a trade frame that maximizes time decay (entering with 30 to 60 DTE) and minimizes risk (exiting at around two to three weeks to expiration). That is step one in becoming a high probability options trader.

Gamma and Volatility

Volatility and time affect Gamma similarly. Just as more time to expiration gives a move against you time to come back, so does a higher volatility. For ATM options, Gamma decreases as volatility goes up. Higher volatility stocks have less Gamma, as a $1.00 move means less to a volatile stock. The higher a stock's IV, the harder it is to move it away from ATM strike prices. This relationship is different for OTM and ITM options. These have a higher Gamma when volatility is greater. This is because with a larger volatility, ITM and OTM options have a greater chance of becoming an ATM option.

That was gamma in a nutshell—a rather large nutshell at that. I will talk about it more throughout the book and hope you will realize it's nothing more than a fear tactic to get you to exit trades before the risks get too big.

SOME MORE GREEK RELATIONSHIPS

I've already mentioned some relationships between Gamma and other Greeks. Here are a few relationships between the Greeks I haven't discussed yet that should tie everything together.

Delta and Time to Expiration and Volatility

Delta is not only affected by Gamma and a stock's price movement. It also moves as you get closer to expiration and with changes in volatility. At the money options will stay around 50 regardless of time or volatility. But for in the money and out of the money options, Delta values move away from 50 when you get closer to expiration or volatility decreases. With less time or lower volatility, options away from the money have a smaller chance of a big move that can put them back to at the money. This is the case for both in the money and out of the money options, as it easier for an option to move from in the money to out of the money and vice versa with more time and volatility.

At actual expiration, an option has two possibilities: It can have a zero or 100 Delta. You can see this starting to happen on Amazon's Option Chain 6.4. Look at the 89 and 98 options and the difference in Deltas just from 17 days to expiration to 3 days to expiration. The 89 call goes from a 73 to 87 Delta, while the puts go from a –26 Delta to –11. The 98 options show similar relationships. Here's why: The 73 Delta on the 17 DTE 89 call implies that there is 73% chance of it being ITM at expiration. But as expiation approaches and nothing else happens, that 89 call has a much greater chance of being ITM since there is less time for the stock to move from $89 to $93. The higher Delta reflects this. The same holds for an option that is OTM. At three DTE the 89 put has a much lower chance of being ITM. Here the Delta is saying that chance is 11%. With 17 DTE, the chance was 26%.

Symbol	Description	Last	Net Chg	Bid	Ask	Hist Volati...	Beta Weighting	Account	
▽ AMZN	Amazon.com Inc	93.64	0.14	93.64	93.70	47.09 %	SPY	All Accounts	
Spread Single	Filter Spr Width:5	Strikes 10						Click to: Trade	

		CALLS						PUTS						
Pos	Gamma	Vega	Theta	Delta	Bid	Ask	Strike	Bid	Ask	Delta	Theta	Vega	Gamma	Pos
03 Mar 23 (3d) Weekly												41.17%	(£3.06)	
	0.048	0.02	-0.14	0.87	5.00	5.15	89	0.21	0.23	-0.11	-0.11	0.02	0.046	
	0.061	0.02	-0.16	0.82	4.10	4.30	90	0.34	0.37	-0.16	-0.14	0.02	0.061	
	0.075	0.03	-0.18	0.76	3.30	3.45	91	0.54	0.56	-0.23	-0.17	0.03	0.077	
	0.090	0.03	-0.20	0.68	2.56	2.66	92	0.78	0.83	-0.31	-0.19	0.03	0.092	
	0.099	0.04	-0.21	0.59	1.93	2.02	93	1.12	1.18	-0.41	-0.20	0.04	0.103	
	0.104	0.04	-0.21	0.48	1.38	1.45	94	1.56	1.62	-0.52	-0.20	0.04	0.108	
	0.102	0.04	-0.20	0.38	0.95	0.99	95	2.11	2.22	-0.62	-0.19	0.04	0.104	
	0.092	0.03	-0.17	0.28	0.62	0.65	96	2.71	2.88	-0.73	-0.16	0.03	0.095	
	0.076	0.03	-0.14	0.20	0.39	0.40	97	3.50	3.65	-0.81	-0.13	0.03	0.077	
	0.059	0.02	-0.11	0.13	0.23	0.25	98	4.30	4.50	-0.89	-0.08	0.02	0.057	
10 Mar 23 (10d) Weekly												38.71%	(£4.94)	
17 Mar 23 (17d)												40.18%	(£6.63)	
	0.037	0.07	-0.09	0.73	6.35	6.50	89	1.37	1.43	-0.26	-0.08	0.07	0.039	
	0.040	0.07	-0.09	0.69	5.60	5.80	90	1.65	1.71	-0.30	-0.08	0.07	0.042	
	0.043	0.08	-0.09	0.65	4.95	5.10	91	1.99	2.03	-0.35	-0.08	0.08	0.045	
	0.045	0.08	-0.10	0.60	4.30	4.45	92	2.35	2.39	-0.39	-0.09	0.08	0.047	
	0.047	0.08	-0.10	0.56	3.75	3.85	93	2.76	2.81	-0.44	-0.09	0.08	0.049	
	0.048	0.08	-0.10	0.51	3.20	3.30	94	3.20	3.30	-0.49	-0.09	0.08	0.050	
	0.048	0.08	-0.09	0.46	2.74	2.79	95	3.70	3.80	-0.54	-0.09	0.08	0.051	
	0.048	0.08	-0.09	0.41	2.29	2.34	96	4.25	4.40	-0.59	-0.08	0.08	0.050	
	0.047	0.08	-0.09	0.37	1.90	1.95	97	4.80	5.00	-0.64	-0.08	0.08	0.049	
	0.045	0.07	-0.08	0.32	1.55	1.60	98	5.45	5.85	-0.69	-0.07	0.07	0.047	
Options Analysis Manage Search														

OPTION CHAIN 6.4 Amazon: Delta and Time

Source: TradeStation

Vega and Theta

If Vega goes up, Theta increases with it. This is because higher volatility adds to an option's extrinsic value, increasing its time value. This is amplified as you get closer to expiration. When IV goes up, you can look for trades that take advantage of higher option premiums.

Tying It All Together

Once you understand the different Greeks individually, you need to understand how they work together to affect your positions. Suppose you are short the 89 put. With a –26 Delta and 17 DTE in Option Chain 6.4, you will make money over the next few weeks if the stock stays above the 89 short strike price, as long as volatility does not go up too much. In this scenario you are:

Long Delta: Technically you are short negative Delta, but either way you want the market to rally.

Long Theta: When you are short options, you are making money on time decay.

Short Gamma: All short positions have negative Gamma and prefer little movement.

Short Vega: You don't want volatility to increase.

If implied volatility rises, your OTM short position may start to hurt because of its Vega exposure, which gives it a better chance of being ITM. With increases in volatility, this position will be more sensitive to price changes in the underlying as Gamma increases with an increase in volatility. This increase in Gamma will then make your position more Delta sensitive and riskier than it was under the initial IV level. All the while, Theta keeps chugging along as long the option is out of the money. Theta will lose its benefits if the option goes in the money gaining intrinsic value while losing extrinsic value. You want it to expire with no intrinsic value at all.

A cheat sheet can help you understand how the different Greeks affect your positions (Table 6.2).

TABLE 6.2 Greek Cheat Sheet

Your position is:		Calls	Puts	You Want:
Delta	Positive	Long	Short	Stock price to go up
	Negative	Short	Long	Price to go down
Theta	Positive	Short	Short	Time to go by and little price movement
	Negative	Long	Long	Time to stand still and big price movement
Vega	Positive	Long	Long	Implied volatility to rise
	Negative	Short	Short	Implied volatility to fall
Gamma	Positive	Long	Long	Big, fast moves in direction of larger Delta
	Negative	Short	Short	Not much to happen

To help get this chapter through your head better, here's a little quiz without the answers.

Delta

A call option has a Delta of 0.30.

If the stock drops by 60 cents, how much does the option move?

Does the call rise or fall?

Theta

An option is worth $2.40 with a Theta of 0.10.

If nothing else changes, how much would the option be worth in 3 days?

Vega

Implied volatility is 30% and an option is worth $3.00 and has a Vega of 0.20.

If implied volatility increases to 35%, what is the new value of the option?

Gamma

An option has a value of $2.50, a 0.30 Delta and a 0.05 Gamma.

If the stock moves up $1, what is the option's new Delta?

FINAL THOUGHTS

This could be a lot to take in, especially, if you are newish to options. In time it should kick in and be second nature. Until then keep in mind that as you approach expiration, options are more sensitive to their Greeks. At the very least remember you can reduce risk by exiting trades a couple of weeks before they expire.

CHAPTER 7

A Few Helpful Things to Know

Now that you hopefully have a better idea of how options are valued and what makes them move, I will throw in a few more things that will help you understand some nuances of options trading better. I've already spent some time discussing volatility, but this chapter takes a deeper dive into that topic, discussing the VIX, volatility skew, and how to use them to your advantage to become a better options trader. It also discusses how to calculate your probability of success on any given trade and a few other helpful things.

THE VIX

Stocks have their own volatilities that move and react differently than those of other stocks. Still, there are times when the volatility of all stocks and the market in general move in sync. If you watch CNBC or any other financial show, you will occasionally hear some traders or analysts refer to the VIX when describing market sentiment. If the VIX is low, they may say the market is overbought and due for drop. If the VIX is too high after a market drop, they will say a retracement in the VIX is due that may turn the market around. Understanding how to interpret the VIX is a great skill that will improve not just your options trading, but your ability to read the markets in general.

The Fear Index

The CBOE Volatility Index, or simply *the VIX*, is *an index that measures the stock market's current expectation for volatility*. The VIX is the benchmark for overall market volatility; it reflects how much investors think the S&P 500 will fluctuate in the next 30 days. This volatility can be seen as current market risk. Some traders refer to it as the Fear Index, as it measures the fear of market uncertainty. Low readings mean everything is great, but when the VIX goes up, traders get a little nervous and the fear of decline sets in.

How It's Measured

Before getting further into the VIX, here is how it's created and what it tells you. The VIX gives you the market's expectation for volatility over the next 30 days by looking at all the OTM option prices for the S&P 500 Index (SPX). It doesn't measure the options on the stocks in the S&P 500— just the options on the SPX index itself. It uses the weighted prices of the index's put and call options for the two expiration cycles that straddle 30 days to expiration. It weights these by how close each expiration is to 30 days. I will spare you a more detailed explanation of how VIX is calculated, as the average person would not understand it. Instead, it's more important to learn how to interpret it.

What the VIX Implies

In percentage terms, the VIX tells you how much the market believes the S&P will move in the next 12 months within a one standard deviation range. A VIX of 20 means that the S&P has a 66.7% chance (one standard deviation) of trading 20% higher or lower in the next 12 months. A low VIX (under 20) implies complacency; and a high VIX (over 30) implies uncertainty. These aren't set numbers, and you should look at long-term charts to see the current range, for the five years pre-Covid 12 and 25 was a more accurate range. The VIX gets high when traders start buying deeper out of the money puts for protection when they fear a big down move. This drives up the put's prices and IVs. When implied volatility starts getting extremely high, this is a sign of market panic. It doesn't actually mean the market will fall, but that traders are perceiving it may and are protecting themselves. When the VIX is high, you are more likely to see choppy trading and a whipsawing market with wider moves, making it scarier to trade. When the VIX is low, trading can be boring to some, as there is not much movement. The S&P may move 10 or 15 points in a day. But as the VIX increases, the S&P can get very erratic, moving up or down 15 points in a minute or by 100 points in a day. This makes the market harder to trade and traders get fearful of being whipsawed.

STAGES OF THE VIX

1. **Happy times:** The VIX is low and at normal levels—around 13% to 19%. The market is probably trending upward at mellow pace, with little fear of big moves. Long traders are happily reaping steady gains.
2. **Concern:** The VIX starts to increase to the low 20s, but it is still fairly low. People are starting to think about a potential downward move and start buying out of the money puts, just in case.
3. **Fear:** The VIX goes to 30% or higher and panic sets in, usually accompanied by a market drop. You can expect a volatile market.
4. **Relaxation:** The VIX heads back down to the low 20s. There is still concern in the market, but volatility is coming back down. The market can still be choppy, but traders are now selling closer to the money options for their rich premiums and buying out of the money options for protection.
5. **Return to normal:** As the VIX comes back down to normal levels, you may see a little remaining out of the money skew, as traders' muscle memory keeps them weary. Eventually they forget and the market goes back to happy times and rallies.

Using the VIX

You can look at the VIX as a contrarian indicator, in that the VIX tends to get higher as the market falls, and vice versa. Look at Chart 7.1, which compares the VIX with the S&P 500. You can see that whenever the market was rallying—from mid-June 2022 to mid-August 2022 (points A to B) and later from October to December of the same year (C to D), for instance—the VIX was trending down as traders were content with the rally. You'll also notice that as the market drops, the VIX rises, as from points B to C. You can't do much with that information alone.

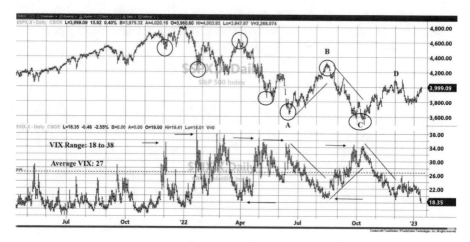

CHART 7.1 VIX vs SPX
Source: TradeStation

You should also notice that the VIX is range bound. While the market has been in a downtrend all year, the VIX has stayed in a range between 18 and 38, oscillating around 27 (the dashed line). Like magic, every time it neared or reached those extreme levels, the VIX reverted toward its mean or the opposite level, especially when it spiked near the top of the range. In the same way you can look at an option's IV rank, you can use the VIX as a mean reversion tool. Contrarian traders look at these extreme peaks as signs the market may be putting in a bottom, even if it's a temporary one. I always look at the VIX as a barometer for market sentiment as I look for market tops and bottoms.

Looking at this chart, a contrarian could be looking to short the market right now, as the VIX is at a nine-month low. Meanwhile if you look at the first half of the chart, you will notice that the VIX is a bit high in general right now. When the market rallied all year in 2021, it had a range of 14 to 25, where much of that time it was below 18. A different trader looking at the same info might think the VIX could drop further back down to the 14 level and that the market may finally break out of its yearlong downtrend, as it just failed to rally back to its mean. This is what makes trading hard. Different people can have sound but opposite market outlooks given the same information.

You can also use the VIX as a metric for general market volatility levels. Many traders will be more likely to short options when the VIX is high, as they believe this to be a great time to put on trades that benefit from the increased option premiums in high IV times.

I am willing to trade more aggressively when the VIX is high, as opposed to when it is low. When it is high I feel much more comfortable selling strategies such as iron condors on the SPY or strangles on stocks as opposed to when the VIX is low. This is because:

- My net premium received is higher, resulting in better breakeven prices.
- I can get the same bang for my dollars by using further out of the money options, again resulting in a better breakeven price.
- The chances that volatility will shrink are better. Without a huge market move either way, lower volatility would make my positions profitable just from the IV contraction.

EXTREME EXTREMES

The VIX doesn't always stay in a range. Though readings above 40 are rare, it can go there and stay above 40 for a while. In October 2008, during the financial crisis, and at the beginning of the Covid sell-off, it reached the low 80s, staying above 40 for two months as the market kept selling off.

Trading the VIX?

You can't actually trade the VIX, as it is an untradeable index. I don't recommend you do so, but if you really must, there are ways to trade it using options, ETFs, and futures that are based on the VIX. VIX options, VX futures and options, the VXX (IPath Series B S&P 500 VIX Short-Term Futures ETN), UVXY (ProShares Ultra VIX Short Term Futures ETF), and their options are all high-liquidity products that can help you accomplish this. There are other VIX-related products, but they have low liquidity, so I won't mention them. Trading VIX-related options is not so straightforward as they are not based on the VIX index itself, but on the futures contract. The different expirations in the futures contract may not react similarly to the current month, causing divergences in their prices. I would do a bit of research on them before jumping in.

VOLATILITY SKEW

Theoretically a put and a call that are equidistant from the current price should be priced the same, as there is the same chance of them expiring at the money. For example, if a stock is trading at $100, a 110 call and a 90 put are both $10 out of the money and have the same chance of being at the money, so they should be equally priced. But this is not usually the case, as implied volatility tends to be different for puts and calls.

You will also find a difference in volatilities at different expirations. This difference in IV among exercise prices, expirations, and puts and calls is known as volatility skew. It can help you better visualize the market and what traders expect to happen, providing you with trading opportunities. Like the VIX, you can also use skew to determine perceived directional risk.

Put-Call Skew

This is the skew that results when a put and call that are equidistant from the current price are priced differently. *Call skew* happens when the calls are more expensive than the puts. *Put skew* is the opposite. You can get a good sense of skew by looking at the puts and calls of the 16 Delta options (the one standard deviation option). If the option prices are different, there is skew to the more expensive side. Likewise, if one side is closer to the spot price, then it is perceived as having a higher chance of reaching that spot price, so there is skew to that side. You can also pick a spot X dollars plus and minus from the ATM strike price and look for skew in the puts or calls.

In Option Chain 7.1 of the SPY (trading at $398.50), you can see this skew in both option prices and their IVs. Start by looking at the 15 Delta option, as there is no 16 Delta option. The call is trading at $0.44 with an IV of 17.791%; the put is at $0.61 with an IV of 22.75%. The put definitely has more value, suggesting the options are skewed to the downside. This 391 put is $7.50 from the current price, while the 405 call is $6.50 away, also implying that traders are willing to bet that a further out of the money put has the same chance of being at the money as its same Delta call. You can also compare the prices of an equidistant out of the money put and call, say, $8.50 OTM. This would be the 390 put and 407 call. The put's price is about double that of the call, with a larger Delta, once again confirming the put skew.

Put skew is normal and is usually due to hedging. Most of the time, investors are long stocks and hedge by both buying out of the money puts as protection, which increases the puts' prices, while selling covered calls against their stocks, which causes price pressure on the calls. Traders generally use OTM options for these two purposes. This double pressure of buying OTM puts and selling OTM calls causes their implied volatilities to rise and fall, respectively.

Equities normally have a put skew, as risk is more likely on the downside, though this isn't always the case. Stocks sometimes have call skew when they are skyrocketing, as Tesla and many other tech stocks did after the Covid-related market drop. In these cases, people buy a lot of speculative out of the money calls. This drives up premiums, resulting in call skew. You also see it after a significant downward move, where the traders may see diminished downside risk and expect a move up instead.

Symbol		Description	Last	Net Chg	Bid	Ask	Hist Vol...	Beta Weighting		Account
▽ SPY		SPDR S&P 500 ETF	398.50	1.54	398.45	398.47	24.76 %	☐ SPY		All Accounts
Spread	Single	Filter NONE	Strikes 40							Click to: Trade

		CALLS				PUTS			
Pos	Imp Volatility	Delta	Bid	Ask	Strike	Bid	Ask	Delta	Imp Volatility
	20.25 %	0.96	11.39	12.07	387	0.29	0.31	-0.08	25.16 %
	20.67 %	0.94	10.46	11.13	388	0.35	0.36	-0.09	24.51 %
	20.77 %	0.92	9.54	10.20	389	0.41	0.43	-0.11	23.85 %
	20.63 %	0.90	8.63	9.28	390	0.50	0.51	-0.13	23.29 %
	20.43 %	0.87	7.75	8.37	391	0.60	0.62	-0.15	22.75 %
	20.21 %	0.84	6.89	7.49	392	0.73	0.76	-0.18	22.31 %
	20.82 %	0.80	6.22	6.64	393	0.90	0.92	-0.22	21.89 %
	20.27 %	0.76	5.46	5.75	394	1.10	1.12	-0.26	21.48 %
	20.38 %	0.71	4.75	5.03	395	1.34	1.37	-0.30	21.14 %
	19.35 %	0.66	4.07	4.11	396	1.64	1.66	-0.35	20.84 %
	19.13 %	0.60	3.42	3.45	397	1.99	2.01	-0.40	20.59 %
	18.87 %	0.54	2.82	2.85	398	2.39	2.42	-0.46	20.33 %
	18.64 %	0.48	2.29	2.31	399	2.86	2.88	-0.52	20.09 %
	18.46 %	0.41	1.82	1.85	400	3.39	3.42	-0.58	19.93 %
	18.24 %	0.35	1.42	1.44	401	3.99	4.03	-0.64	19.85 %
	18.12 %	0.29	1.09	1.11	402	4.66	4.71	-0.69	19.88 %
	17.97 %	0.24	0.81	0.84	403	5.14	5.68	-0.74	19.88 %
	17.89 %	0.19	0.60	0.62	404	5.92	6.50	-0.78	20.16 %
	17.79 %	0.15	0.43	0.45	405	6.75	7.37	-0.82	20.59 %
	17.78 %	0.11	0.30	0.33	406	7.62	8.26	-0.85	21.05 %
	17.85 %	0.08	0.21	0.24	407	8.54	9.20	-0.87	21.91 %
	17.96 %	0.06	0.15	0.17	408	9.48	10.16	-0.89	22.89 %

OPTION CHAIN 7.1 SPY Skew

Source: TradeStation

Horizontal Skew

Horizontal skew happens when options with different time frames have different volatilities. When the front month has a higher IV, it has positive skew. If the back month has higher than expected IV, then it has negative horizontal skew. Calendar and diagonal spreads are a way to take advantage of this horizontal skew by shorting the higher IV expiration's option while buying the lower valued option. Product announcements, earnings reports, or any market-moving event that affects a stock or market in a specific time period, like an Apple product launch, can cause horizontal skew.

Using Skew to Your Advantage

Knowing skew won't tell you where the market is going, but it does reveal which side of the market will have better premiums when you sell options. Getting the bigger premiums when shorting will always increase your probability of success on any given trade. When you trade a strangle or iron condor, for example, you could move the side with skew further away, as it will have higher premiums and may be priced similarly to a closer position on the other side. As an added bonus, the further out of the money protective options on the skew side will tend to hold their value better, with a slower premium decay that benefits those trades. Take any little advantage you can. Done repeatedly, they can make the difference between being a winning and losing trader.

PROBABILITY OF PROFIT

One of the nice things about trading options is that you can estimate your probability of success before making any trade. This lets you know if a trade has an excepted return that makes it worthwhile making, or you can compare it to any other possible trade. Knowing these probabilities lets you make more intelligent decisions while also helping you pick the best strategy for a trade idea. Probability should play an important role in your decision-making process, so it is worthwhile to get a grasp of some probability concepts.

Efficient Market Theory

Keep in mind that there are no gimmes in trading. The option market is pretty much efficiently priced, with options prices taking into account every possible outcome. At least, that's what I believe; others may believe they have an edge. In an efficient market, there should be no edge. Your risk/reward ratio should be a reflection of the probability of profit (POP) on a trade. This just means that trades that have a higher chance of succeeding should have lower potential profits than trades with lower chances of success. A trade that risks $900 to make $100 should have a probability of profit of 90%, while a trade that risks $100 to make $900 should have a POP of 10%. If you were to make both of these trades thousands of times, the result should be the same. In the long run, enough long shots should pay off to justify making them in the first place, much as if you sell 0.02 Delta options for $0.05 that have virtually no chance of being in the money, once in a while they will come around to hurt you, taking away all your previous profits.

What Is Probability of Profit (POP)?

Probability of profit is the chance that a trade makes at least a penny at expiration. I go back and forth sometimes calling it probability of success but will usually just say POP. Probability of profit is a measurement used to get a general idea of a trade's chance of success, if you made the same trade repeatedly. A POP of 60% means this trade should make at least a penny 60% of the time if held to expiration. POP then is not a complete metric, with the issue that most of your trades should not be held to expiration. Some trades may be exited early for losses that would have ended up being profitable, while some pocketed winners could have become losers at expiration. This will throw off the long-term expected outcome.

Another issue is that POP doesn't estimate a potential profit. A trade could have a 65% chance of making at least one cent, but how much it actually makes it an uncertainty. Still, knowing the probability of profit is a great place to start.

ANOTHER DISCLAIMER

I will start using the tastytrade platform a lot for examples from now on. Unfortunately, tastytrade option tables may not be as readable in print as the TradeStation ones. Still, the tastytrade platform has better features for options traders. For instance, one of the things I like about tastytrade is that it lets you see the POP easily for any trade. On TradeStation, you would need to estimate probability of profit using Deltas and a trade's breakeven point.

Estimating POP

Probability of profit is the probability that a trade will be at breakeven (BE) plus a penny at expiration. This is the same as the chance that a long option will be in the money by the amount you paid for that option. It's also the probability that a short will be out of the money by the amount of the premium received. I will show this in more detail when I discuss individual strategies, but for now here is a simple example on a long call using the IWM (iShares Russell 2000 ETF). In the IWM Option Chain 7.2, look at just the long 188 call. In the lower left corner, you'll see that the POP is 30%.

Hopefully you recall that an option's Delta can be used as an estimate of an option's chance of being in the money. The Delta for the 188 call is 46, implying a 46% chance of it being ITM at expiration. However, you won't break even if IWM goes to $188, as you need to recoup the $4.29 you paid for the call. Instead you need to find the Delta of the breakeven price of $188 + $4.29, or $192.29. You would then estimate what the Delta for a $192.29 strike option would be. The option chain shows that this would fall somewhere between the 32 and 29 Deltas.

OPTION CHAIN 7.2 IWM Figuring out POP

Source: tastytrade

To compensate for the price being between two strikes you would estimate that $192.29 is about one-third of the way from the 192 to 193 strikes, and a Delta one-third of the way from 32 to 29 is about 31. You could be more precise if you want with a calculator, but this estimate is close enough. This 31% is the probability that IWM will settle at $192.29 or above, where you would start to profit. The platform calculates a POP of 30%, so the Delta method gives a pretty good estimate.

If you were shorting this call, the probability of profit would equal the chance that the option wasn't in the money at expiration. The probability of profit of a short trade is 100 minus the POP of a long trade. In this case, a short would have a 70% probability of being out of the money, as the chances of the trade being in and out of the money must add up to 100%. When estimating the POP for a short trade, you first find the breakeven Delta as before, but this time subtract it from 100. That gives you 100 – 31, or a 69% probability of this trade not going above $192.29.

Puts

For puts, the breakeven is the option price minus the premium. If you were long the 188 put, then you need IWM to fall to $188 – $4.88 = $183.12 to break even. At this level, the estimated Delta is 38 and the probability of profit is 39% (not shown). Again, the estimate is fairly accurate.

More Probabilities

You may encounter other, also helpful probabilities. Some may have different titles on different platforms.

Probability of touch: the chance that an option will touch a strike price at some point in the option's life.

Probability of being in the money (ITM%): a more exact measure than Delta to figure out an option's chance of being in the money. If you tried to estimate POP for the 188 call like above using ITM% you would get very close to the actual POP of 30%.

Probability of being out the money (OTM%): 100 – ITM%. This is for sellers too lazy to subtract.

Probability of making 50% (P50): This tastytrade feature tells you the chance that at some point your trade will make 50% of the premium paid or if shorting 50% of the trade's max profit.

Using Probability of Profit

Looking at a trade's probability of profit by itself doesn't give you a full picture. You should compare the probability of profit with potential monetary rewards versus risk, as probability of profit is directly correlated to a trade's risk and reward. Trades that have a high POP, like selling a way out of the money option that's a winner 95% of the time, are not going to pay off much. You might make $50 by risking $950 to make that trade. Trades with a low probability of profit may make a potential $900 while risking $100, but the problem is they are only winners 10% of the time.

The goal is to figure out the optimal chance of success versus the risk you are taking that fits your trading style. There is no right or wrong POP. If you like lots of small winners, use a high probability of profit. If you prefer a few big winners, then a low POP is right for you. If you prefer huge winners all the time and have found a method for achieving this, please email me how. I tend to aim for probabilities of successes of 60% to 70% with a 65% risk/reward ratio.

Increasing the probability of making a profit can be achieved by lowering your potential profits or increasing your maximum loss on a trade. This could be done using different strikes, using spreads, or changing the wing width on spreads. Higher probability of profit also results in a higher margin or buying power reduction as trades get riskier.

Here are some examples based on the IWM option chain that show different potential trades with their POP, correlated profit and loss potential, and buying power reduction (BPR). Even though the first and last trades have a 70% probability of profit, the spread is the much safer trade. The short 188 call pays a lot more, but it has unlimited loss potential and ties up $3,736 in capital (Table 7.1). I would much rather trade a few of the lower risk spreads and have the extra money to make other trades. The spread also has a better return on margin.

TABLE 7.1 Comparing Trades

	Action	POP	Max Profit	Max Loss	BPR
Sell	188 Call	70%	$429	Unlimited	$3,736
Sell	182 Call	63%	$802	Unlimited	$3,736
Buy	182 Call	37%	Unlimited	$802	$802
Buy	195 Call	19%	Unlimited	$155	$155
Sell	191/195 Call Spread	70%	$134	$266	$266

Suggested Odds and POP

There is one more thing to consider: the actual odds of the trade predicted by its profit/loss potential. This only works for a trade with defined profits and losses. The formula is:

1.00 − profit ratio

Profit ratio = (max profit / (max loss + max profit))

In the 191/195 call spread, the max profit is $134. The total of the max loss ($266) plus the max profit is $400, or the width of the spread. The odds suggested by the reward to risk of this trade are a 1.00 − (134/400) = 0.665 chance of profitability. This should equate to 66.5% POP, but the tastytrade POP was 70%. When the probability of profit is better than the odds suggested by the profit ratio, you may have a slight edge.

Another thing you may want to do is add the probability of profit to the profit ratio. If this number is greater than 1, you have good odds on your hands.

Here the POP is 0.70 and the profit ratio of $134/$400 is 0.335. These numbers add up to 1.035, which gets two thumbs up from me. If you only had a max profit of $100 on this trade, then the profit ratio would be 100/400= 0.25. You would then want to see a POP of 0.75 to make the trade worthwhile. I will revisit this later when I talk about induvial trades, so don't worry if it's not too clear now.

USING YOUR CAPITAL WISELY

Learning how to best optimize your money will lead to becoming a better trader. Here are some things to consider in using your capital wisely.

Margin and Buying Power Reduction

Buying power reduction (BPR) is similar to margin requirement. It is the sum in your account that is used or placed on hold to make a trade. The difference between margin and buying power reduction is that when you short and collect a premium, the margin required for the trade is reduced by the premium to get the total buying power you've used. As an example, if the margin on shorting a call is $1,200 and you received $200 in premium on the trade, the BPR on your account is $1,000. Margin is based on a trade's size and risk, the strikes used, whether there is unlimited risk or defined risk, and a few other factors. Naked options in high-priced, volatile stock have the highest BPR, while spreads or buying outright options have the lowest. If you put on a trade that uses $500 in buying power, you cannot use that money again until you liquidate the trade.

Originally I wrote three pages on how to calculate margin, but they were so dry and tedious that I fell asleep rereading them, so I am sparing you the agony. It's more important to know how to use your buying power than how to calculate margin. Learning to use your buying power properly will let you make more trades, and it makes for a great way to compare trades.

Return on Margin

Margin or buying power reduction are useful performance measures. When you buy an option, pay $1,000 for it, and make $200, you know you made 20% on your trade. But you cannot do that when shorting options or spreads, as there is no set money outlay. Instead you can base your return on how much margin the trade costs or the buying power reduction of the trade. This lets you compare trades evenly. A $200 profit on a spread that used $600 in margin is a much more desirable trade than one that earns a $200 profit by selling a call outright that used $3,000 in margin. And last, tying up your buying power by staying in trades that have already captured most of their gains is a bad use of buying power. It's money that can be used better somewhere else.

FINAL THOUGHT

If you are still reading, you got through the dullish but important part of the book. I hope something in these last few chapter helps you understand and trade options a little better. The rest of the book is more about trading and less about fundamentals, so it will not be as tedious.

CHAPTER 8

Making a Watchlist

What you trade is as important as the actual trading strategies you use. This chapter will give you an idea of what types of stocks, markets, ETFs, etc. you should or should not be trading. I can write this chapter in one sentence, as it all comes down to this: You should without a doubt only trade options with high volumes, high open interest, and tight bid and ask spreads. But since I can be wordy, I will write a chapter instead.

THE CRITERIA

An option should meet certain basic criteria before you consider trading it. I first look at an option's liquidity. Without decent liquidity you should not even consider trading it, no matter how tempting it looks, or you may get stuck in a position for longer than you want. As part of liquidity, look for volume, open interest, and a tight bid/ask spread. Next I look at the IV and IV rank and percentile. I prefer a high IV if I am selling. This is not as important as liquidity in deciding what to trade, but more of how to trade. Finally, I like to know the correlation between stocks I trade. This helps me keep a balanced portfolio.

I use four different methods to choose what to trade:

1. A watch list of about 50 regulars that meet my criteria, these are the stocks, ETFs, and indices that I love to trade all the time.

2. Scanning for trades with a high relative IV and sufficient volume.
3. Looking for stocks with earnings reports coming out.
4. Keeping my ears open for ideas. I watch CNBC and tastylive .com while I trade, and every now and then I get a good trading idea from them as well as the occasional clunker.

Liquidity

This is number one on the list. Options with good liquidity have high trading volume and open interest, with many buyers and sellers, letting you trade in and out easily at a fairly competitive price. The big reason you want to have high liquidity is that without liquidity, you are at the mercy of the market makers. With liquidity, you can place a limit order at a price that's a little better than the market makers and another retail trader may take the other side. This will have a dramatic impact on your P&L.

You should only be trading liquid options
in liquid underlying stocks or ETFs.

I always look for the underlying asset to trade at least 2 million shares a day, before I would even consider looking to trade options in it. Anything less will not have much volume in the options, so you should skip it. High volume is not just for the stock or the total volume of all options traded in a stock. It also applies to each individual option for that stock. An at the money front month or expiring weekly option may have a volume of 2,000 shares a day, but an option with a 20 Delta, one month out may have traded 12 contracts in the last five days You should only look to trade stocks that have options with decent volume throughout while avoiding those that don't. Options that lack liquidity may not let you out at a good price and may trap you into a position.

As a general rule, the most liquid options are
those that are expiring soonest and that are
either at or slightly out of the money.

THE NO LIQUIDITY TRAP

I got stuck last year when I made a trade in Thor Industries (THO). I bought some call spreads on it as a bullish position.

Normally I prefer to sell options, but the IV was rather low, so buying was the best choice. I don't remember the exact numbers, but with the stock trading around $105, I bought some 105/115 call spreads with two months to expiration at maybe $3.75. The stock then ran up to over $140 in a few days, but the bid and ask on the spread was something like $8.40 by $10.60, when the fair value should have been in the mid-$9 range. There were no trades at all in the spread or either of its legs for days. I was now at the mercy of the market maker, as there was no liquidity to let me out. For days I tried getting out with limit orders near the halfway mark with no luck. My choices were to hold another five weeks till expiration or get out at the market maker's discretion. I choose poorly and held while trying to get filled. Eventually the stock dropped back down to under $100 and my spread was worth 75 cents. I was finally able to get out at 50 cents. All this because I traded a stock with poor volume whose best options trade 25 contracts a day, with a very wide bid and ask.

Volume and Open Interest

Open interest and volume give you similar information, but they are a bit different. Looking at both of them can help you select which options to trade. To get a good sense of liquidity, start by looking at the ATM option's volume and open interest. If there is little activity there, then you should not be trading that option, as it will be harder to exit if the option moves away from the at the money prices.

Volume

Volume is straightforward and easier to understand. It is the number of contracts that have been traded for that day. You will see it for a stock's total options, as well total put volume, total call volume, and for each individual option in a chain. I need to see at least 25,000 total options traded daily before considering a stock. Normally the options I trade have a total average daily volume of more than 100,000 shares.

Open Interest

Open interest, on the other hand, measures the total number of open contracts for any option. Open contracts are all long positions held by investors that have been opened but haven't yet been closed out, expired, or exercised. To make it easier to picture, on the first day an option is listed, the open interest is zero. If one person buys it (most likely from a market maker), there would be one open contract. If the trader sold that contract back to the market maker the next day, no open contracts would remain, as the position is closed out entirely. If instead the trader sold it to a second trader, the open interest would still be one, as the contract is still open and the second trader is long one contract. If instead of buying a call, someone sold a call to open a position, the open interest would still be one, because now the market maker would be long one contract.

Open interest is measured for each option and can be summarized by option type, expiration, or for all a stock's options. Open interest is updated nightly by the Options Clearing Corp (OCC), and it doesn't change during the trading day. When an option gets listed, it has no open interest. Open interest begins to rise during the option's life before declining closer to expiration as positions get closed out. When looking at an option chain, you will notice that open interest and volume are highest for at or near the money options and that the contracts with high open interest also have high volume.

Option Chains 8.1 shows the difference between Auto Nation (AN) with very little open interest and volume and wide bid and ask prices, and Apple, which is one of the most liquid stocks there is. Look how wide AN spreads are when you get away from the at the money options. You know with Apple you will always be able to get in and out easily without getting a bad fill, even far from at the money.

Symbol	Description	Last	Net Chg	Bid
▽ AN	AutoNation Inc	110.48	0.22	110.45
Spread Single	Filter NONE	Strikes 10		

		CALLS				
Pos	Open Int	Volume	Delta	Bid	Ask	Strike
17 Feb 23 (29d)						
	0	0	0.96	19.00	23.00	90
	25	19	0.89	15.80	17.40	95
	19	9	0.82	11.00	13.30	100
	278	7	0.70	7.80	9.20	105
	293	257	0.55	5.40	5.80	110
	87	3	0.38	2.25	3.40	115
	600	0	0.24	1.10	2.10	120
	55	0	0.16	0.75	1.30	125
	32	0	0.22	0.05	4.80	130
	5	0	0.07	0.05	0.75	135

Symbol	Description	Last	Net Chg	Bid
▽ AAPL	Apple Inc	135.40	0.20	135.40
Spread Single	Filter NONE	Strikes 10		

		CALLS				
Pos	Open Int	Volume	Delta	Bid	Ask	Strike
17 Feb 23 (29d)						
	1,000	40	0.93	21.15	21.50	115
	3,387	50	0.88	16.60	16.90	120
	13,051	246	0.79	12.45	12.75	125
	25,794	1,132	0.68	8.75	8.90	130
	43,331	3,673	0.54	5.70	5.80	135
	36,825	4,099	0.39	3.30	3.35	140
	30,906	3,391	0.25	1.69	1.70	145
	44,009	4,273	0.14	0.78	0.79	150
	40,720	1,752	0.07	0.34	0.35	155
	19,239	1,295	0.04	0.16	0.17	160

OPTION CHAINS 8.1 Low vs High Liquidity

Source: TradeStation

Volume and Open Interest and Market Sentiment

Besides using volume and open interest to find suitable options, you can also use them to confirm market sentiment. Open interest can show you where the money is going. For example, if a stock's price is rising, with increasing call volume and open interest, that may indicate that the move is strong. But if prices are rising while call volume and open interest are decreasing, this could suggest less market interest in the move indicating the rally is weak and may soon be ending. The same is true of puts on the downside. When prices are falling if you see open interest and volume on puts increasing, this could confirm the downward move.

Bid and Ask Spread

One thing you will discover is, the more liquid a market is, the tighter its bid and ask spread will be. This means less slippage as you enter your orders, especially with multi-leg strategies such as spreads, condors, or butterflies. A tight spread lets you get in and out of a trade without giving up too much. Options on a stock such as Apple can have spreads of a penny or two, with thousands of trades a day at every strike price. If you put on a trade, you can get out right away without losing much.

Meanwhile, trading a less active stock could mean you're out $100 in a heartbeat. The 130 Apple call has a 15-cent spread, while a similar Delta Auto Nation call has a $1.40 spread with only 7 contracts traded. If you bought and sold both of these at the market, you would only lose $15 on Apple but $140 on AN. Generally, you should first try to work a price trying to get a better fill. But when you are wrong and need to get out, you will have to place a market order and be forced to take the worse price.

With a wide bid/ask spread on an illiquid stock, your best bet is to try to get filled at the midpoint, though this may not always be the case. However, when an option is very active, you can usually get a better fill then the midpoint price.

Slippage

Slippage is the difference between what you expect to pay for an option and what you actually pay. Fair value is typically the midpoint between the bid and ask price. You should always at least aim for it. There will be times when you get a bad fill and may not even realize it. Perhaps you want to do a credit spread in a low-volume stock with a market of $1.00 bid, $1.80 ask, and $1.40 midpoint. If you put in a market order, you would get filled at $1.00. That slippage is obvious. If instead you had put in the order at $1.40, you may not get filled right away and only do so when then the stock's price had moved. At that point, the option's midpoint wouldn't be $1.40 anymore. It might be $1.20. Here you don't actually have price slippage—you got your price—but you may have slippage in the other metrics. The price you end up getting may imply that the Delta or volatility of your position is different than what you expected.

Every time you enter an order you need to assume some slippage from the fair price. There is not much you can do about it, except trade tighter options and make fewer trades in general, especially the stupid, not carefully thought out ones. Do not ignore slippage. It adds ups.

SLIPPAGE AND VOLATILITY

When you trade an option, you are not just trading price, but also the implied volatility that equates to that price. Imagine a stock with an IV of 32%. That 32% equals an option price of $1.50. You sell a call, but only get $1.30 for it, so you effectively sold an IV of maybe 31%. With every penny you give up to the market makers, you are selling a slightly lower IV. If your goal is to capture as much IV as possible and you give some up through price action, you are giving up some of that hoped-for advantage.

MAKING A LIST

Keep a watchlist of your favorite products. I would venture to say 90% of my trades are made using the same 40 to 60 stocks, indices, or ETFs. This list is based on options that meet my criteria, which include liquidity, IV, diversification, and price. It's not etched in stone and it changes from time to time, but in general I stick to it.

MarketChameleon.com is a great place to start when making your own list. I reformatted the list in Table 8.1 to fit, so a few columns are missing. This list shows the underlyings that have the most option volume on January 13, 2023. I am only showing 24 symbols here, but their full list covers every possible tradable thing that has options. Most of this list with the exception of the lower priced ones are on my favorites list. The options with the highest volume do change, so search for "stocks with highest average option daily volume" to see what is most active when you are reading this book.

TABLE 8.1 Highest Option Volume for January 13, 2023

Symbol	Name	Price	Total Volume	90-Day Avg Volume	Call Volume	Put Volume
SPY	SPDR S&P 500 ETF Trust	388.64	8,865,049	8,442,462	3,805,301	5,059,748
QQQ	Invesco QQQ Trust	275.15	2,582,138	2,787,985	1,117,243	1,464,895
TSLA	Tesla	127.17	2,518,843	2,481,189	1,232,500	1,286,343
AAPL	Apple	135.27	1,071,566	1,415,048	507,522	564,044
AMZN	Amazon.com	93.68	810,551	1,114,969	448,488	362,063
IWM	iShares Russell 2000 ETF	182.04	849,707	882,864	346,148	503,559
META	Meta Platforms	136.15	465,639	604,519	224,331	241,308
NVDA	Nvidia	167.65	498,176	534,487	197,126	301,050
AMD	Advanced Micro Devices	67.71	415,150	502,820	235,784	179,366
TQQQ	ProShares UltraPro QQQ	18.85	395,349	465,969	214,073	181,276
HYG	High Yield Corporate Bond ETF	76.02	536,334	418,429	238,203	298,131
BABA	Alibaba Group Holding	116.58	267,390	357,246	155,374	112,016
MSFT	Microsoft	231.93	347,864	349,346	158,920	188,944
GOOGL	Alphabet - Class A	93.05	335,869	327,434	210,931	124,938
FXI	China Large-Cap ETF	31.70	227,927	309,544	155,120	72,807
NFLX	Netflix	315.78	475,322	305,221	221,852	253,470
EEM	Emerging Markets ETF	41.10	223,676	298,285	124,395	99,281
AMC	AMC Entertainment	5.52	347,643	264,855	175,997	171,646
TLT	20+ Year Treasury Bond ETF	107.95	181,195	242,993	98,647	82,548
F	Ford Motor Company	12.18	220,351	237,241	129,237	91,114
BAC	Bank of America	33.23	367,144	215,736	189,034	178,110
NIO	NIO American Depositary Shares	10.77	144,239	213,955	87,495	56,744
XLE	Energy Select Sector SPDR	89.59	147,901	210,026	59,864	88,037
GOOG	Alphabet	93.91	190,424	206,975	113,814	76,610

Though I tend to trade a core of about 15 to 20 markets/stocks at any given time, I do have more on my watchlist. My current favorites provide me with good liquidity and decent diversity, so I am not over-exposed in any sector. They are:

Stocks: AAPL, META, AMZN, NFLX, MSFT, UAL, BA, WMT, XOM, JPM, DIS, KO, UBER, NKE, CAT, MRK, GM, HD, ROKU, COIN, NVDA, CRM, ABNB, LVS

ETFs: SPY, IWM, QQQ, TLT (Treasury Bonds), GLD (Gold), XLE (Energy), XLF (Financial), XLI (Industrials), EEM (Emerging Markets), EWZ (Brazil ETF) FXI (China Large Caps)

Indices: SPX

Futures: Crude Oil, E-Mini S&P, Gold, Euro Currency

SCANNERS

Aside from your list of regular stocks, you can use a scanner to find trades that have whatever criteria you want. I scan for stocks with high IV ranks and percentile (over 50%). In my scan I only look for stocks/ETFs with average daily volume of over 2 million shares and total option volume of 50,000 traded. If I find something I like, I then look at charts to make sure I want to trade it. I also scan to see which stocks have upcoming earnings announcements.

Your trading platform should have a scanner. If not, I recommend MarketChameleon.com. It's one of the best websites for options traders and a free subscription gives you quite a lot. I use it to see which stocks have earnings announcements coming out, how a stock's price previously reacted to earnings, and the stock's current expected move for the upcoming earnings. You can also scan for unusual options volume or sort by option volume or market cap. It will help you find the most active stocks, ETFs, and indices and has many more useful features an options trader could use.

DIVERSIFY

Make a diverse trading list to help keep your trades balanced. Having the same strategy with the same time frames on AAPL, TSLA, MSFT, and QQQ (NASDAQ) is really like having one large position. Instead be inclusive and keep stocks in multiple sectors in your radar of tradable assets. Look for a mix of technology, energy, banking, software, chipmakers, airlines, infrastructure, gold, social media, biotech, healthcare, consumer products, pharmaceutical, and so on represented in your trades.

LISTENING TO OTHERS

Never believe anything you see or hear, but it's always good to keep your ears open to get new ideas. Trading from home you will be in a bit of a vacuum, so I have CNBC and tastylive.com on in the background during the trading day. Between these I hear perhaps a hundred recommendations a week. The crew from tastylive talks about option trades, including strategies they are using, plus things that will make you a better options trader. They tend to focus on selling strategies with high volatility. I highly recommend that every trader spend some time watching and learning from their website. You will learn a lot about how to properly trade options and get help finding potential trades. I watch CNBC mostly for the news. They do have analysts giving their own opinions and directional stock recommendations, but you should take these with a grain of salt. Many times these are fund managers who have positions in the stocks and are "talking their book."

Despite being weary of what I hear, it's nice to get some fresh ideas. Even so, I never, ever trade without looking at my own charts and making my own opinions. For example, I never thought about trading CROX (Crocs, the shoe company) until I heard it mentioned on CNBC many times during the post-Covid stay at home run-up, where stocks rallied like mad. A little research showed that the stock and the chart looked great, but the options didn't have enough volume and liquidity for me to justify making an options trade. Instead, I bought the stock outright for a few months and had a nice return. I have also come up with many good options trades watching tastylive. com, like a recent ratio spread I have in EWZ.

EARNINGS

Finally, you can search for stocks that have earnings announcements coming up. Their inflated volatility can provide good trading opportunities. I used to make a lot of earnings-related trades, but

I've curtailed that recently, as the moves have become wild. Lately it seems stocks are dropping or rising 20% when their expected move is 8%. I still make a few, but have been trading around them more and more. Whenever I put on a trade I make sure to know when earnings announcements are due, as I don't want to get caught in a potential 20% surprise.

I start by using Earnings Whispers' "Most Anticipated Earning Releases" for the upcoming week, which I get from their Twitter page (Figure 8.1). This table shows you the best earnings-related stocks for the week. You can then narrow it down by day using the MarketChameleon.com platform and EarningsWhispers.com websites for a more detailed analysis for each stock. These sites let you see all the earnings for any particular day, the expected and previous earnings moves, IV, options volume, and market capitalization.

FIGURE 8.1 Most Anticipated Earning Releases

Market Chameleon has many valuable features, even for the free user. Use it to find unusual options activity and implied volatility rankings, or see charts comparing historical volatility to current IV for any stock, ETF, or index. It has a good scanner to help you find trades, and much more. I recommend you take a look. Tastytrade also has an easy-to-use earnings watchlist.

FINAL THOUGHTS

No matter what you trade, make sure it has plenty of liquidity, a narrow spread, and diversity between products. Always keep your eyes and ears open for trading ideas, but do your own analysis before jumping in.

CHAPTER 9

The Sweet Spot

Or the Great Theta-Gamma Battle

The perfect trading period optimizes potential rewards while limiting risks. Having the ideal trading period comes from learning how to have a good balance between Gamma (price movement risk) and Theta (time decay). Though it may not click in yet, you should get a total understanding before the end of the book.

WHAT ARE THE PERFECT TIME FRAMES?

A good balance of days to expiration (DTE) when you enter and when you exit trades will play a big part in making money, regardless of whether you are buying or selling options. Though you can make general rules, not every type of trade will have the same time frame parameters. I will address this as I review different strategies. In general, as a seller your goal will be to have the proper balance that gives your trades enough time to work while getting you out before Gamma risk can hurt you. The ideal trading period to achieve this is to:

Sell with about 45 days to expiration and
cover with 14 to 21 days to go.

GETTING IN

There are two schools of thought, especially when selling options. One is to use weekly options with short expirations, which give you the quickest time decay. The other is to give yourself more time—like 60 days. The longer time frame comes with bigger total premiums that offset slower decay. That gives you some breathing room and less risk from price movement just in case you are wrong or have outlier days.

Option buyers will find that the further in time you go, the less time decay will hurt you. Though a longer time frame means that you pay more for an option and have a higher breakeven price, that option will hold its value better than a short-term option.

THE SWEET SPOT

Many traders like short-term weekly options. Buyers like them because they are cheap and can be quite lucrative if the market moves quickly. Sellers like them for their rapid time decay. Overall, I believe you are better off with longer-term options. If you are buying an option and believe a strong directional move is coming in three days, then maybe it's worth the risk to buy a cheap option. But if you are wrong, you will lose the full purchase price in those three days. As an option seller you may be tempted to get all of an option's time decay in its last few days, but trust me, one bad day can destroy this strategy. In either case, a small hiccup could be costly. Giving yourself ample time in a trade provides you with a safety net.

Going out too far in time also has issues. Time decay starts to pick up speed around 30 days to expiration. A seller who goes too far out in time—perhaps to three months—and tries to capture time decay will find that it's a very slow process. It's like looking in the mirror to see your hair grow for more than half the life of the trade. At the same time you tie up buying power on a trade that's doing nothing. You could use those funds instead to make money elsewhere.

When you buy options as a directional trade, even if you are only looking for a stock to make a quick three-day move, you're better off using an option with 45 to 60 DTE. Though you will pay more and potentially make a smaller return, neither time decay nor price move-ment will hurt as much as it would in an option with only a few days to expiration. If you buy an option with three days to go, the odds are strong that you will lose money on the trade—unless you get a powerful move. If you are just slightly wrong in your estimate, you still lose your whole investment. If instead if you went out a month or two, the option would still hold a significant amount of its value after three days, as it will still have plenty of extrinsic value left.

The sweet spot for entry tends to be 30 to 60 days; 45 days is the average. Look to use the monthly expiration that falls within that range, unless the weekly one has good liquidity. If there are two viable choices, as a buyer I would use the further expiration. As a seller, I would use the closer one. This lets me take advantage of the speed of time decay either way. I will be mostly concentrating on short strategies in this book, so I will tend to look at it from that point of view. As a seller, the ultimate goal is to capture as much time decay as possible, while keeping your risk level low. This is the great Theta-Gamma battle, which can be mitigated by using these trading time frames. This 45-day entry time period has a good risk/reward balance: if you are correct, you will get rewarded fairly quickly, and if you are wrong, you shouldn't get too banged up. The closer you get to expiration, the less control you have over how much an option can hurt if it goes wrong.

On the exit side, you may be tempted to hold out for every last penny. But the closer you get to expiration, the greater the risk becomes that you'll give back profits and/or tie up potential capital if you have made most of the money a trade has to offer. (More on that later.) In order to reduce this risk, get out of a trade with between 21 and 14 days to expiration.

WEEKLY OPTIONS AND DAILY TOO

When I first started trading, this wasn't even a discussion, as there were no weekly options. Options expired on the third Friday of each month, so I only had to deal with 12 expirations a year. Weekly options didn't come about until 2005. Now any stock with decent volume has 52 annual expirations to have to think about, which gives traders both more trading opportunities and more chances to lose money. It's not just for stocks. Some ETFs and indices like the SPY and QQQ now have daily expirations.

Weekly options with little time to expiration have soared in popularity in recent years, as action junkies demand more ways to hedge and speculate. Option buyers love them for their cheaper prices and lottery ticket feel. Options sellers like them for their fast time decay, which results in a greater annual return on capital. Day traders love them the most for their high sensitivity. There are typically five sets of weekly options, but that may eventually change. The front two or three expirations tend to be very active and have extremely high liquidly.

After the first few sets of expirations, volume and open interest diminish and bid and ask spreads are larger, so try to avoid these and stick to the regular monthly ones if you can. On the most highly traded stocks, this drop-off in liquidity may be insignificant; in others it's more noticeable. Look at Option Chain 9.1 for Alibaba as an example. If you want to put on a trade 45 days out, you could choose between 41 DTE (weekly) and 55 DTE (monthly). I would much rather trade the 55 DTE simply because of the volume.

OPTION CHAIN 9.1 Alibaba
Source: tastytrade

WEEKLY VERSUS MONTHLY OPTIONS

I do use both weekly and monthly options for putting on trades, as they offer different things.

A Case for the Weekly

I will use weekly shorter-term option as one leg in a calendar or diagonal spread. On a rare occasion if I think a big move is coming, I buy an option with a week to go if the IV is low, but this is not a typical strategy of mine. I trade near-term options when I sell iron condors as an earnings play. I also like to trade options with two weeks to expiration for covered calls and puts.

Weekly options can be a gold mine for more aggressive traders who like to take advantage of the rapidly accelerating time decay in an option's final week of life. They provide 52 possible paydays a year. I don't oppose selling a SPY call spread with seven days to expiration as a pure directional play, as part of a diversified portfolio. I would never recommend making that your primary trading strategy—yet some traders do.

Reasons for Weekly Options

Faster time decay.

Great for day trading.

Bigger potential reward over the same time period compared to longer-term options.

You can easily adjust the strike price and Deltas every week.

Useful for trading earnings, as they have the largest IV collapse.

Handy for rolling calendar spreads and covered puts and calls.

To exit trades prior to expiration.

To trade or avoid earnings.

Monthly Options

I prefer entering the majority of my trades using monthly options. Longer-term monthly options give you larger premiums with less work, fewer trades, less slippage, and lower commissions. Trading with about 45 days to expiration allows for more stability in your P&L. When you trade with only a few days left to expiration, it's pretty much an all-or-nothing trade. There is nowhere to hide if you're wrong. If it goes against you, it's relatively easy to lose the maximum possible on the trade. Then you're stuck holding the option and hoping for a miracle. When you go further out in time and exit before the last two weeks of trading, your losing trades will retain some of their value. True, your winners won't be as big, but this means less volatility in your trading.

Longer-term options are also better suited for those who can't constantly monitor the market. They let you hold one contract for longer, instead of forcing you to put on new trades constantly. By making fewer transactions, you give up less to total slippage over the long run. And even though commissions are much cheaper than they used to be, they still add up.

Longer-term options, with their higher price tags, let you use further out of the money options to achieve the same results that a higher Delta shorter-term option may offer. This allows for safer trades, with lower Gamma risk, and lets you sustain bigger price movements against you. Longer-term options will help preserve your precious capital and let you grow rich slowly but steadily. This is a lesson that took me years to fully understand. Once I did, I started seeing more consistent results.

Reasons for Monthly Options

Bigger premiums for sellers

Less maintenance involved

More stable trading results

Lower overall commissions and slippage

Greater liquidity

Less Gamma risk

A LITTLE ABOUT EARNINGS

When deciding which expirations to trade, make sure you know when earnings announcements are due. You can get caught with your pants down if you accidentally run into a stock that surprises you with a 10% move against you because you failed to do your homework. By checking for when earnings are coming you can either avoid the trade entirely, use options that expire prior to the announcement, or choose to trade the earnings with a proper strategy. If you do get caught with your pants down, it's easy to fall on your face if you have to run for the exits.

In Option Chain 9.1, notice that BABA has an earnings announcement in four weeks. To put a trade on it while avoiding earnings, you would need to trade the 27 DTE cycle. If this is too short an expiration for your liking, avoid the trade and find something else.

FINAL THOUGHT

As I go through the next few chapters on trading strategies, I will go into more detail on why specific trades may have shorter or longer time frames and when to use them. But when in doubt, remember the 45 day entry and 21 to 14 day exit suggestion.

CHAPTER 10

Options Strategies

The Prelude

The next few chapters explain some of the best trading strategies you can use. These aren't the end-all of trading. There are many more ways to trade options. Keep doing your homework after reading this book to expand your trading capabilities. The methods I discuss make a great foundation and account for 90% of my trades. I start with basic option trades and discuss how to use or not use them, then move on to more advanced methods.

Actually, I start off with some strategies I don't recommend, like buying or selling calls outright. These are building blocks you need to understand in order to trade more effectively, as is most of what I have already written. Throughout the next bunch of chapters, I expand and (I hope) clarify all the technical stuff that may have been Greek to you earlier. This short chapter is about general trading principles that apply to whatever methods you use.

ALWAYS MAKE HIGH PROBABILITY TRADES

Before putting on a trade, justify it by answering these questions:

What is your outlook on the stock?

How much time do you want to give the trade?

What is the stock's volatility, and what do you expect the volatility to do?

What is the VIX telling you?

How much are you willing to risk?

What is the potential reward?

How much will the trade cost?

How much margin will it tie up?

What strategy is best for this situation?

Is the risk/reward ratio worthwhile?

Does it fit into your current portfolio of trades?

How directional do you want to be?

This is just a sample, but you should get the gist. Think out a trade prior to making it. Asking these questions helps weed out some of the worst low probability trades, leaving you with a better overall chance of success.

EVERYONE IS DIFFERENT

Not all market conditions are the same. What may work in a volatile market may not work in slow one. Not every trader has the same account size, goals, or risk parameters. Beginners should not try to trade the same as experienced traders. They should gain experience and make the inevitable mistakes before moving on to riskier strategies. The bottom line is there is no one-size-fits-all strategy or style. You need to figure out what works for you, and that takes experience.

SINGLE VERSUS MULTIPLE OPTION LEGS

The first few chapters here start out with the simplest types of trade: buying or selling individual calls or puts. These include covered calls and puts, two of my favorite ways to trade. Then I move on to trading strategies with multiple option legs: spreads, strangles, butterflies, and more. Except for selling covered calls and puts, most of my trades involve some sort of multi-leg strategy.

DEBIT VERSUS CREDIT

Credit and debit trades, especially with spreads, refer to whether you are collecting money or paying for the trade.

Debit trade: a long trade that costs money to put on.

Credit trade: a short trade that collects a premium.

These do not refer to being long or short a stock—only to whether you bought or sold in an option trade. For the most part, you should be making *credit trades* and collecting premiums. These trades have the highest probability of success. They have Theta working for you, and the plan is to have volatility on your side as well.

DEFINED VERSUS UNDEFINED RISK

Trades can be separated into defined or undefined risk categories. Any trade with a naked, unprotected option, such as a short call or strangle, has undefined risk. In a defined risk trade, you know the most you can lose up front. These are the safest trades and should be your primary kind of trades at first, even though they limit your maximum profit. As you progress, undefined risk trade are acceptable to make and should be included in a well-diversified portfolio of trades.

Defined Risk Trades:

Have smaller rewards

Are slower to react to changes in the underlying asset

Have smaller daily gains or losses

Have less exposure to Greeks

Give you more time to be right or wrong

Are cheaper to make

ENTERING ORDERS

Whenever possible, use a limited order to enter a trade. Avoid market orders unless you absolutely have to get out of a trade and are not getting filled. This is easier if you don't wait until an hour before expiration.

A market order invites slippage and a poor fill. The higher the liquidity, the better your chances of a good fill. This becomes more important when you start trading multi-leg strategies.

As you trade different stocks, you will get to know where in the bid-ask spread you can get filled. Do not chase a trade that moves away from you. Pick the price you want, place the order, and see what happens for a minute or two. If you are not getting filled after a short period, move your order a little and repeat the process until you are filled. Always strive for the midpoint price or better first. Liquid options should let you get that price or close to it.

In a very liquid stock or ETF, try placing an order at around 75% of the spread distance. If the spread is $2.20 bid and $2.50 ask and you want to sell, try placing an order at $2.45 or $2.40. If it isn't filled, move to the midpoint of $2.35, assuming the stock hasn't moved. If it still isn't filled, go down a little—but I would never go too close to the bid. It's just not worth trading with a bad fill, as you will probably also have issues getting out.

LOOKING AT VOLATILITY

Know what the IV and IVR are doing and what direction volatility is trending. There are two reasons for this, as I've mentioned. First, when you sell options, your goal is to capture premium. With higher IV comes bigger premiums and rewards. The same option could be worth $3.00 at a 20% IV and $4.00 at a 25% IV. The higher premium gives you better breakeven levels and greater potential to make money, no matter how IV reacts afterward.

Second, if IV is high and reverts back to its mean, you increase your ability to make money. Always check where IV is within its normal range. Different IV levels favor different strategies. At an IVR of 6%, I would be leery of shorting options. If IVR is high, selling strategies make the most sense.

SLIPPAGE

With multi-leg strategies, such as a four-sided iron condor, you need to be extra careful of slippage as it will be magnified. Even a simple vertical spread involves four options: two legs when you enter and two when you get out. If you lose even 10 cents on each leg, that's $40 total you give away, which could be half your profit. Spreads aren't always as liquid as single trades. It may be a little difficult to get in and out at the midpoint price, unless all the legs have liquidity.

PAYOFF CHARTS

To better understand the mechanics behind the trades, I use payoff charts that assume trades are held to expiration. In practice, however, this is not how you should trade. I discuss proper holding times, targets, and how to manage trades as I go along. If your trading platform has analysis charts, especially ones that let you input hypothetical exit prices and alter the days to expiration, learning how to use them will be helpful.

MULTI-LEG TRADES

The vast majority of the trades you make should be multi-legged trades if you hope to make money consistently. These are trades that have both bullish and bearish components in them at the same time. They can include putting on a protective leg with the same type of option as in vertical spreads, or can combine puts and calls, as in an iron condor or strangle. Using multi-legged trades lets you start making high probability trades, limiting your risks, controlling your Delta exposure, and in general have better control of the Greeks. For simplicity now, I will refer to them as spreads. I will discuss:

Vertical spreads	Butterflies
Straddles	Iron condors
Strangles	Ratio spreads
Calendar and diagonal spreads	

MISSING CHAPTER

As I will discuss in the last chapter of the book, I ended up writing quite a long book and was asked to condense it. In an effort to shorten the book, the chapter on calendar and diagonal spreads was moved to my website, MarcelLink.com.

Why Trade Them

The main reason for multi-leg trades is to lower the risk in both the trade and your portfolio. Spread trades also lower your capital requirements. That lets you make more trades, allowing for more diversity and spreading out risk while reducing your portfolio's volatility. Spreads are cheaper to put on than buying or selling an individual option, and they let you better control risk. I would rather trade an option spread on a $400 stock where I know the most I can lose is $300 and still have a reasonable chance of making money. You can't do this with single options as the margin requirement could be too high.

Versatility is another reason to make multi-leg trades. If there is a scenario you can think of, you can find a trade to take advantage of it. You can use multi-leg trades if you think the market will move big or stay still, to take advantage of time decay, to capture moves in volatility, or to spread your risk over time.

Smaller, Steadier Gains

Trading credit spreads usually means profits tend to be small and defined. If you are the type of trader who is looking for massive gains, selling defined profit trades may not be for you. However, these trades have a higher probability of working in exchange for smaller returns. The limited rewards achieved from selling spreads can add up significantly over time. Would you rather be right 80% of the time and make a little each time or lose 80% of the time but make a lot per winner? The results may be the same, but the swings in your account will be smoother with the small, steady gains.

Legging in or Out

All trades are meant to be entered and exited as one order, so it's how I discuss them. If you enter a call spread, don't take off one side later, as this will expose you to the risk that you used the spread to avoid in the first place. I only consider legging out of a trade if the liquidity is so bad that I can't get out of two or four options at once at a decent price. If I do exit one side first I will exit the other side as soon as I get filled.

You can create spreads over time. If you are long a call, it can become a call spread later by shorting another call, and you can then combine that with a put spread to make an iron condor. You can also adjust part of a spread trade by moving one side of it and keeping the other side as it is. This is common in strangles and iron condors, as one side gets so far out of the money that it becomes barely worth anything.

TRADING EARNINGS

Be aware of when a company reports quarterly earnings, as its stock can move drastically in either direction after an earnings report release. I've lately seen regular moves of 15% to 20% when only 5% was forecasted. A stock that may move $2 on a normal day can move $10 either way after an earnings release. A stock's IV jumps dramatically in the week or two leading to the company's earnings announcement, especially in the soonest expiring option. Options in that stock will get very expensive leading up to the earnings report. After the earnings report, you can expect to see an implosion in volatility. IV can go from 90% to 40% overnight, potentially causing option prices to drop even if there is a big move in the stock.

This leads to trading opportunities with proper shorting strategies, such as iron condors, straddles, and strangles. These are all nondirectional strategies that don't care where the stock goes, as long as it stays within the expected range predicted by the option prices.

If you had a directional bias, you could trade a vertical credit spread or a diagonal spread. I prefer the diagonal spread if I have a bias. Overall the method I use the most is selling iron condors just outside the expected range. I use the nearest expiring contract, selling it the day before or of the earnings announcement and buying it back in the morning, looking to take advantage of the drop in volatility. I will go over some earning trades as I talk about different strategies.

The expected range can be found in several ways. You can look at the expected range on your options chain, on websites such as marketchameleon.com, or by adding the prices of the put and call that are closest to at the money. But be careful as a stock can blow past its expected range very easily, which is why I stopped using unlimited risk trades for earnings trades.

FINAL THOUGHT

There are so many ways to trade options that if I discussed them all, I would end up writing a book that would rival *War and Peace* in length, so I had to stop somewhere. Chapters 11 through 18 (plus the chapter on calender and diagonal spreads on my website) are the methods and strategies I believe to be the most important that every trader should know. These will help you build a solid trading foundation that you can later expand on.

CHAPTER 11

Don't Buy Options

F inally, what you have been waiting for: the riskless strategies that will help you make a fortune. They don't really exist, but after the next few chapters, you will have a good sense of how to find high probability options trades to take your trading to the next level.

BUYING OPTIONS

The strategies I want to emphasize are not the buying or selling of single-legged options. Still, single-legged options are easier to understand and are the way most traders start in option trading. Notice I said traders, not investors. Investors usually start out by selling covered calls. Traders are apt to start out by buying options because they provide limited risk, have alluringly large profit potentials, and are a lot easier to understand than an iron condor. They may also be limited to just buying options if their brokerage account is set at level 1, which only allows the buying of options or selling covered calls or puts.

Buying calls and puts can be attractive to new traders as well as those with small accounts, as they think they don't have much choice and/or want to make a fortune in one shot. They also see it as the easiest form of trading options. Realistically, though, buying options is the hardest way to make money, as you need to pick the right time frames, right strike price, and right direction And you are fighting against time and volatility. There is little margin of error when buying options, and getting all these things right is not an easy task.

Hedge funds, commercial hedgers, and institutional traders buy options by the boatload, but they rarely buy options for speculation. Instead they may be buying options for risk protection or Delta hedging, not as an outright main strategy. These are pros and they know the odds, so take a cue from them and for the most part avoid buying puts and calls outright.

QUICK REFRESHER

Buying a *call* means you want prices to rally.

Buying a *put* means you want prices to fall.

LEVERAGE AND LIMITED RISK

The big allure of buying a put or call outright is that, with a little amount of up-front money, you have potentially unlimited profits with a limited defined risk. Suppose you had a $50,000 trading account and wanted to buy 100 shares of MSFT trading at $241. You would need to put up $24,100, assuming you are not using margin. That's 48% of your capital. Assume you follow some reasonable risk management rule of never losing more than 3% of your total capital on any trade ($1,500 in this case). This means you would need a stop at $226 ($24,100 − $1,500 = $22,600). Using a $15 stop on a stock that can move $15 in two days is too close for my comfort—that has a good chance of getting hit, so I wouldn't do it. Instead you could buy a call for $5.00, spending $500 and knowing that is your whole risk. If you get a good move up in the time frame you hope for, you can easily double or triple that $500. If you are wrong, though, you lose the whole amount—but some traders love that leverage.

CALLS

Buying a call works as follows. After looking at the DIA (Dow Jones Industrial Average ETF; Chart 11.1), you decide it could rally from the current price of $333.67 to over $345 in the next two weeks. To try to profit from this, you can choose to buy one of many different calls on Option Chain 11.1. Let's say you choose the 18 days to expiration (DTE) Feb 23 with a 33 Delta 340 calls. You pay about $2.46 ($246 per option contract), making your breakeven $342.46 if you hold to expiration, which you shouldn't.

Breakeven of buying a call = the strike price + the option price

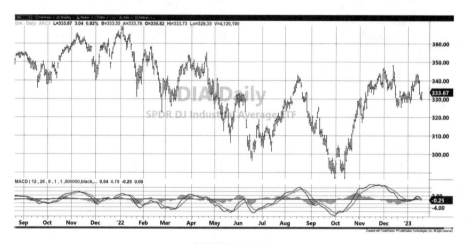

CHART 11.1 DIA

Source: TradeStation

OPTION CHAIN 11.1 DIA

Source: TradeStation

Before making a trade, get in the habit of checking its volatility. Chart 11.2, "IV Versus Historical Volatility" from MarketChameleon. com, shows a current implied volatility (IV) of around 16%. That's fairly low, compared to the historical volatility of about 21%. You can also see it is toward the bottom of the range it has been in for the last year, so it has a shot of going back up. I've added the implied volatility rank of 10.20% to the chart, which also tells you that the current level is very low.

To make educated trades, you should get used to noticing or figuring out the following things:

DIA's expected range is between 323 and 344.

The 21 Delta of the 344 call implies a 21% chance that it will reach that price by expiration.

The probability of profit is approximately the Delta of the breakeven price of $342.46, or about halfway between 24% and 26%.

The maximum loss is the $246 premium paid. The profit potential is unlimited.

Implied volatility rank is 10.2% and the IV is 16.84%, both fairly low.

CHART 11.2 IV Versus Historical Volatility

Source: Market Chameleon

Payoff Diagram 11.1 is a snapshot of how you would fare at different prices. Though the chance of success is only 25%, the payoff if your target price of $345 is right would be $2.54, which is the target price of $345 minus your breakeven price. This is a decent 100% return on investment. If the stock really took off, you could get a substantial windfall. Yet this isn't a trade I like to make. It fights time decay the whole time, especially with only 18 days to expiration. You also need a 3 point move just to break even.

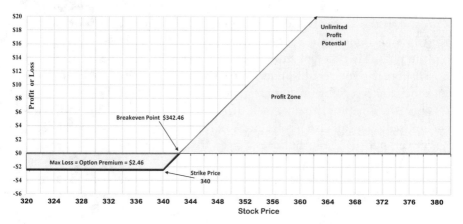

PAYOFF DIAGRAM 11.1 Long Call

PUTS

You can look at the same DIA chart and, if you think the market is going down, you can a buy a put instead of a call. Maybe you buy a 330 put for $3.43, hoping that the market drops below $326.57, as the *break-even point on a put is the strike price minus the premium paid.* Everything pertaining to calls applies to puts, except that with puts, you want the market to sell off. Your max risk is still limited to the initial debit paid, and your profit is unlimited as the market drops.

PROTECTIVE PUTS

Though calls and puts are both used as speculative instruments, one difference between them is that puts are often purchased for protective purposes. Many traders and fund managers are typically long stocks, not short them. This leaves them open to downside risk, so they will buy puts as an insurance policy to protect their portfolios or individual stocks against down moves, especially big ones.

As an example, maybe you own Apple at xxx. (The price doesn't really matter. I believe what price you paid for a stock is irrelevant. What is important is today's prices and how much you want to protect from there.) You like the stock and its dividends so you don't want to sell it, but you are scared of a market drop. Just in case it drops from today's price of $141, you could buy a put for protection. A 50 DTE 130 put would cost about $2.35. This will protect against a big drop in the stock. If it does drop to $120, you still keep your stock while also offsetting a large part of the loss with money earned on the put. This peace of mind will cost you $235. It's like having car insurance—you would prefer to never have to use it. You'd like the stock to keep going up, but are glad you have the insurance in case of a crash. If you only get a small drop in Apple, the insurance will go unused. You can also pay less for a deeper out of the money put if you prefer, but then your buffer is bigger, like having a bigger insurance deductible.

You might buy protective puts for two years and never need them, and then something major happens and you're glad you have them. I do not buy protective puts on individual stocks, but I balance my portfolio by buying way out of the money puts on the SPY or QQQ as protection against the "big one" when the VIX gets very low.

REASONS AGAINST BUYING OPTIONS

Overall I am not a fan of buying options. I have found it too hard to do so successfully. I have had some great individual trades that make up for 50 losers, but now I find it more rewarding to sell options instead. I still buy a few in low-volatility environments, but mostly I prefer the smaller, higher probability trades you can get by selling.

An issue with buying options is that people are hoping to make big gains with a small amount of money. They either buy out of the money options with little chance of working, or they don't go out far enough in time to give the trade time to work. If they buy at the money options, then they are paying up for extrinsic value. They may also ignore implied volatility rank and buy overvalued options. All of these factors can lead to the worst part of buying options: your directional call can be right but you can still lose money on a trade.

Options' cheap prices are also a reason that people lose money. Some people buy a call for $200 and think, "It's only $200 that I can lose. That's a risk I can handle, and it's not a big deal if I am wrong." Instead look at it as a 100% loss on a trade, which is quite expensive.

There are several factors working against you when buying options.

Theta

Time decay is the big killer. It eats away at your option every day, and there is nothing you can do about it. From the moment you buy an option you are fighting time decay. Not only do you lose time premium every day when you are long an option, but you start losing it at a greater pace as an out of the money option heads toward at the money. Most people tend to buy slightly out of the money options when speculating, and these have a slower time decay. If you look at the DIA option table again, you will see that the 33 Delta call has a Theta of 0.13, but goes up to 0.16 when it reaches 50 Delta. This means you start losing an extra $3.00 a day to time decay if the stock rallies, making it harder to make money as the stock moves in your favor.

Volatility

First, if volatility is high, you will be overpaying for options when you buy them. There is another factor that only affects calls. When buying calls, volatility may also work against you if you get the rally you want. Volatility tends to go down as markets rally—not always, but mostly. This means that call options lose some of their extrinsic value due to decreasing volatility as stocks begin to trend upward. Sometimes this decrease overshadows the rise in the stock price that should be making the call worth more. This will be exaggerated after a big run down that had caused IV to explode. When you buy out of the money calls, you need to be prepared for occasions when an underlying price increases but the value of those options actually decreases.

Directional Risk

To make money buying options, you must be able to pick market direction, as well as how much you think it will move in a specific amount of time. Most traders are just not good enough to pick the direction, magnitude of a move, and the time frame that it will happen in. If you fall just short in any one of these, you are probably going to lose.

Poor Strike and Expiration Selection

When your targets are unreachable, the odds are against you. You can miss a move altogether if you don't have enough time to expiration or go too far out of the money on a strike. It's easy to understand why people make these poor choices: these options cost less than the proper ones. To improve your chances, you would be better off paying more and buying in the money options with more time.

BUYING PUTS OR CALLS WISELY

Despite the lower chances of success, there are some tips you can use when buying options that will improve your overall odds of making money.

1. Use When You Expect a Big Move

Buying options works best when you get a big move, either in a strong trending market or if you are predicting a reversal. These are two scenarios where the market can move substantially making buying options profitable. Stay away from range bound markets, as selling options works better when markets are flat. I go back to Chart 11.1 (DIA) for this example. Maybe your analysis leads you to think the market tried to rally, failed, and will now continue its yearlong downward trend, with $280 as your eventual market target. You feel it will have at least a 20 point drop to $315 or below in the next month or so. If you nail this prediction, buying the right puts will be very profitable.

2. Know the Predicted Move

Start by looking at a chart for possible support or resistance levels, to give you an idea of where a stock might reasonably move to. Then check the expected range and/or the 16 Delta option in the time frame you choose to see where the predicted one standard deviation move is. This acts as confirmation that your target is reasonable. There is little point in buying an option so far out of the money that it has no chance of ever reaching its target, unless you are buying a put for protection.

3. Buy Further Out in Time Options

There is nothing more frustrating than being right on direction but having your option expire worthless, only to watch the stock make a big move two days later. Having sufficient time serves two purposes.

First and simplest, the stock has more chances to make a move in your favor when it has three months to do so, as opposed to one week. Buying time (which is exactly what you are doing, as you pay more for extra time) lets you ride out swings that may go against you. A $5 drop with three days left to go may leave your option out of the money, turning a $4.00 call into a 20-cent call virtually overnight. The same $5 move in the wrong direction with three months until expiration may move the option from $9 to $8.50, a much more reasonable change in both absolute dollars and percentage.

The other reason you want that extra time is that it eases the effect of Theta. Theta increases and starts to accelerate in the last 30 days of an option's life. This is where you see the fastest time decay, especially in the last few days, unless your option is already way in the money. In that case, Theta is usually relatively small and the option is pretty much all intrinsic value.

Table 11.1 shows information for the 335 put, which is the closest to 50 Delta, at different days to expiration, including their Thetas. DIA is a very low-volatility ETF; these numbers would be much more exaggerated if the volatility were higher. With DIA's current price at $333.67, all these options have an intrinsic value of $1.33. This is the amount by which an option is at the money and what the option would be worth if it expired at today's price. The extrinsic value is what you stand to lose if the option expired right now.

TABLE 11.1 Time Decay and DTE

DTE	Value of Put	Theta	Delta	Extrinsic	Intrinsic
4	3.20	−0.22	0.57	1.87	1.33
11	4.75	−0.15	0.53	3.42	1.33
18	5.40	−0.12	0.51	4.07	1.33
25	6.35	−0.10	0.51	5.02	1.33
32	6.85	−0.09	0.51	5.52	1.33
53	8.70	−0.07	0.50	7.37	1.33
88	10.95	−0.05	0.49	9.62	1.33

As you go further out in time, you lose less (with a lower Theta) per day in time value: 22 cents a day at 4 days to expiration as opposed to 5 cents at 88 days to expiration. More important is how much better the put holds up in value per period, assuming DIA doesn't move.

88 DTE to 53 DTE = 35 days passage with a loss in value of $2.25

53 DTE to 18 DTE = 35 days and loss of $3.30

32 DTE to Expiration = 32 days and loss of $5.52 (the extrinsic value)

18 DTE to 4 DTE = 14 days and loss of $2.20

4 DTE to Expiration = 4 days and loss of $1.87

The first three periods have about the same holding time, but you can easily see how you would fare better going further out in time. The move from 88 to 53 days is almost equal to the loss in value of a 14-day time passage from 18 to 4 days.

Though the 32 DTE put may seem like a better choice due to its cheaper price, the 88-day option for an extra $400 is a much smarter option to buy, especially if you plan on exiting after 30 days. If you do get the move you want, you won't make as much in percentage terms as you would if you bought cheaper options with shorter expiration times. But in the long run you will be better off thinking of trading in terms of losing less rather than about making more. If DIA just rallies 2 points, the 32 DTE option will expire worthless, losing all of its $6.85. The 88 DTE put may lose only $2.50 in those 32 days, and will still be worth about $8.50. You should be able to work these figures on your own. Despite the cheaper outlay and bigger potential returns, in the long run conserving capital will get you further than the few big moves you may catch using shorter-term options.

ANOTHER DISCLAIMER

You will most commonly hear and see implied volatility rank (IVR), but I like to look at implied volatility percentile (IV%) as well. Many times IV% gets ignored, but it is equally important. For simplicity's sake, if I say IVR, assume that you should look at IV%, too.

---

4. Look for Low-Volatility Rank and Percentile

I am not referring to a stock's actual volatility but to its IV rank and IV percentile. A stock such as Tesla can have normally high implied volatility. Even if it drops to below normal levels, its volatility will still be high, but it would now have a low implied volatility rank. The general rule in options is, be a seller when IVR is relatively high (over 50) and a buyer when it is low, I like to see it under 30 before I would think about buying strategies.

The reasoning behind this is that options will lose extrinsic value as implied volatility goes down, and vice versa. So if you were to buy a call for $4.00 with an IVR of 85%, the option could lose money even if the market moved up a bit but implied volatility came down. On the other hand, if you bought a call when IVR was low, a quick rise in implied volatility would really help your option out.

Currently DIA has an IV of 16.84% and an IVR of 10.2%. Both are very low. Chart 11.2, "IV Versus Historical Volatility," shows that in the last year, volatility has ranged from about 15% to 25%. This is one of the scenarios in which I would consider buying options. Here is why. With Vega at 0.39 and the help of an options calculator (there are countless free ones online), Table 11.2 shows what happens to the price of options and their Greeks when I change just the IV.

I used the low, average, and high end of the IV range. A drop in implied volatility by less than 2% to the low end of the range drops the option price by 71 cents, to $6.15. If volatility rallies to its average level of 21%, the put jumps to $8.45, and at 25% it is worth $10.05. You can also multiply the Vega by the change in IV to figure out how much an option's price will change.

TABLE 11.2 Implied Volatility and Price

Option Calculator						
IVR	IV	Price	Delta	Theta	Gamma	Vega
Low End	15%	$6.15	−51	−0.08	0.029	0.39
Current	16.84%	$6.86	−51	−0.09	0.024	0.39
Average	21%	$8.45	−49	−0.11	0.019	0.39
High End	25%	$10.05	−49	−0.14	0.016	0.39

You can clearly see that a rise in implied volatility would cause the option to gain value with no other factors involved. Getting into a position like this means you are buying a cheap option. I would much rather pay $6.85 for an option that could cost $10 at other times than the other way around. If implied volatility is low and settles back to normal level, that's one less thing that can hurt you. Now you only have to worry about time decay and direction.

5. Buy Deeper Delta

Natural instinct may lead you to buy cheap out of the money options with a 20 or 30 Delta or even an at the money option, but your chances of success are much better when you buy deep in the money options. This is because in the money options have a lower percentage of extrinsic value. You would not be fighting time decay to the same degree as you would with at the money or out of the money options. I like this approach because it almost acts like trading a stock at a fraction of its price. You still get quite a bit of leverage, just not as much as if you bought a cheaper option.

Let's go back to the original example where you liked DIA long. Instead of buying the 33 Delta 340 call for $2.46, you buy an 80 Delta 323 call for $13.00. Now your option would be trading very similarly to the DIA ETF. The 80 Delta means you are long the equivalent of 80 shares, which would cost you $26,694 if you bought them outright. Instead you can have almost the same position for only $1,300.

The difference between the two strikes is that you no longer need the same $9 rally in DIA just to get to breakeven. The new breakeven is now only $336. A rally to a level such as $338 would have the 33 Delta call moving toward being worthless, while the 80 Delta option would still make a profit. In both of these options, the extrinsic values are fairly similar—$2.35 versus $2.46—but the 33 Delta call is all extrinsic value. Extrinsic value accounts for just 18% of the 80 Delta call's value, so time decay affects a much smaller percentage of its price. If you were to compare a 50 Delta call to a 90 Delta call there would be more than a $4.00 difference in extrinsic value, giving you much more of an edge.

The downside to buying deep in the money options is that if you are dead wrong, you have a lot more cash on the table to lose. You will also find less liquidity at higher Deltas, so getting out at a midpoint price may become difficult especially as you get close to expiration.

Despite giving up a big percentage of gains if a big move comes, high-Delta options give you a much greater probability of success and more frequent profitability. The higher Delta also means the option will perform better in a rally.

6. Go Out Farther in Time, Then Get Out

If I do buy a put or call looking for a big move, I try not to overstay my welcome, right or wrong. When buying options, I look to enter a trade with about 60 days to expiration and get out after two or three weeks, before time decay kicks in hard. If I still like the trade, I reevaluate my strike and roll over to a further month. Doing this lets you keep more of your money if you are wrong, and as long as it's a liquid market, it's easy to get in and out. Of course this is not a strategy for a small account, as buying pricey options ties up a big chunk of capital.

7. Day Trading

I would consider buying options for day trading or very short term trading. This is similar to other strategies I've discussed, but you don't have to go so deep in the money, because as long as you don't hold overnight, you aren't really losing Theta. The problem comes when you are wrong and decide to hold for one more day to see what happens. Then you hold for another day, and so forth. Eventually your option has dwindled down to nothing and you keep holding it until expiration, looking for a miracle. If you have the self-discipline to exit a trade when you say you will, then buying very short term options could work. Even though I am not recommending day trading options, if you must, my one recommendation is to never day trade options that expire that same day. Go out at least one week to give yourself a little room for error.

8. Pure Speculation

Despite all I've said, it's OK every now and then to take a shot as a small part of your overall trading portfolio. I am more likely to buy cheap puts (20 to 30 Delta) when I think a market is topping, which has the added bonus of buying low implied volatility that could jump. The market also has a nasty habit of falling faster than it goes up. This faster directional boost can also quickly increase the volatility, doubly helping you.

FINAL THOUGHTS

In general, buying options is for amateurs. The pros prefer selling them. If you do buy options, your odds will improve by buying ones that have a low implied volatility rank and percentile. You can also help yourself in reducing Theta exposure by going further out in time and exiting before 30 days.

CHAPTER 12

Sell Them Instead

I f you have only bought options in the past, can you imagine how much money you might have made if you had sold all those options you bought, that expired worthless? Selling options may go against your natural instincts, but as an option seller, you gain a slight edge. You can become the casino. Shorting naked options outright is not all rosy. It does come with unlimited risk that can blow out an account if you are foolish. When done correctly and/or incorporated into a trade such as a spread or iron condor, however, it can be quite rewarding. This chapter explores the ins and outs of shorting options. You'll use this information later, as most of the trades in this book are short in nature though coupled with long options for protection.

INSURANCE COMPANIES

Selling options is like being an insurance underwriter that takes in a lot of small premiums and occasionally has to pay out a big loss. As with an insurer, the premium you collect when shorting options represents the maximum possible profit. Increasing that premium by shorting higher Deltas means a higher risk of losing money. There needs to be a balance between picking the strikes with the best potential profit and the chance of the option expiring worthless.

Insurers protect themselves against occasional losses by writing millions of policies that are worth more than their estimated eventual potential losses. As a trader you should also spread out your risk using multiple diversified trades, rather than having one big bet. Insurers also cap their losses by limiting their payouts. You can do this as well by putting on a protective leg and having a spread.

SELLING OPTIONS, THE BASICS

Directionally, shorting a call is similar to buying a put, in that you want the market to go down. In the same way, shorting a put is similar to buying a call: you want the market to rally. The difference is that you do not require as much as a move in a stock to make a profit when you are short. Heck, a stock can even go slightly against you and you can still make money. Now time decay is your buddy, as every day it shrinks the value of short options.

Directional Outlook

When you short a call, you want the market to stay below the strike price you chose and hope the option expires worthless. It doesn't matter if the stock's price moves lower, sideways, or rallies a little. It just needs to stay below the strike price you picked. What you don't want is a big rally. Selling a *put* means you want the market to stay above your strike price, so a higher, sideways, or slight downward move will work.

Implied Volatility

Selling options works best in relatively high and/or down-trending implied volatility. This is the opposite of buying options as in the last chapter. High IV gives you richer premiums. If it reverts lower, you profit as your options shrink in value.

Risk Profile

Selling options comes with a high probability of success, but also brings limited rewards and unlimited risk.

Breakeven Point

Here are a few things to know about the breakeven point: Call breakeven is the strike price plus premium received. Put BE is the strike price minus the premium received. If you short a 90 call for $3.00, your breakeven point is $93. You want the stock's price to stay below that. If you short a 90 put for $3.00, your breakeven point is $87. Everything above $87 is profit.

Probability of Profit for Short Options

POP = 100 – Delta of BE price.

Optimal Trade Length

When you short options, you should look to short the monthly contract that falls somewhere between 30 and 60 days and hold until two to three weeks before expiration. If you need more concrete dates, use 45 days to enter and 21 days to exit.

SELLING OPTIONS IN ACTION

Start by making your trade assumptions:

Directional outlook: Looking at Chart 12.1 of Amazon trading at $99.20, you may make the assumption that it will rally no higher than the resistance trendline in the next 30 days. This price target to the trendline should be no higher than $110 by then.

Strategy selection: You can try to capitalize on this by either buying a call or selling a put.

Volatility outlook: After making a directional evaluation, check where IV ranks. The current IV is 43%. At 41.9%, the implied volatility rank (IVR) is a little misleading, due to the huge IV spike in late October. Though I would prefer to see it higher, I do like that it's trending down from a recent three-month high, so I am OK putting on a short position here. I've become a big fan of being able to see IVR on tastytrade's charts.

Time frame: I use the 49 DTE options looking to exit within a month.

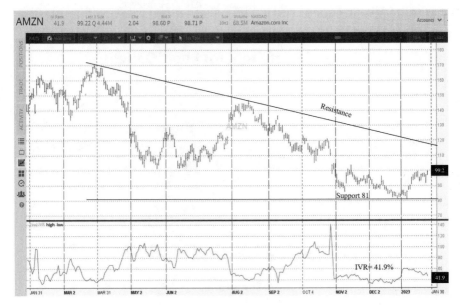

CHART 12.1 AMZN Chart

Source: tastytrade

Buying a Call

I will explain shorting a put by contrasting it to buying a call. When you buy a call, you can choose between many options. Let's look at the 65 Delta in Option Chain 12.1 in detail. You could try to figure out the same details for a 40 Delta call, so you can compare the two.

The 65 Delta 95 strike call costs $8.90 ($890) with a Theta of –0.07. You lose $7 a day in time decay, and your breakeven (BE) at expiration is $103.90 (95 strike + 8.90 premium). If Amazon rises to $110, you net $6.10. The 95 call is worth $15 if the stock expires at $110, so you subtract the $8.90 you paid for the option to get the profit. (The profit could be unlimited if the stock keeps rallying.)

A Few Things You May Want to Know

The current price is $98.70. The 110 call has a Delta of 28, so there's a 28% chance that the stock will reach that price. The probability of profit using the Delta of the BE price would be about 42%.

The risk profile is:

Target profit = $610

Max profit = Unlimited

Max loss = $890

AND YET ANOTHER DISCLAIMER

For risk profile, I am assuming everything is held to expiration to make it easier. In reality, if your exit target is around 21 days to expiration, you could make more as your call would still have plenty of extrinsic value left at 21 days to expiration. If you held to expiration it would have zero extrinsic value. I will explain how to figure what an option may be worth in the future later.

Symbol	Description	Last	Net Chg	Bid	Ask	Hist Volat...	Beta Weighting	Account	?
▽ AMZN	Amazon.com Inc	98.70	1.52	98.60	98.71	46.07 %	SPY	All Accounts	
Spread Single	Filter NONE	Strikes 30						Click to: Trade	

		CALLS							PUTS			
Pos	Imp Volatil...	Theta	Delta	Bid	Ask	Strike	Bid	Ask	Delta	Theta	Imp Volatil...	Pos
17 Mar 23 (49d)											42.83%	(±12.52)
	48.15 %	-0.05	0.86	17.05	17.25	84	1.41	1.46	-0.15	-0.04	48.39 %	
	47.56 %	-0.05	0.84	16.20	16.40	85	1.56	1.61	-0.16	-0.04	47.85 %	
	47.37 %	-0.05	0.83	15.40	15.60	86	1.73	1.78	-0.17	-0.04	47.39 %	
	47.00 %	-0.06	0.81	14.60	14.80	87	1.92	1.97	-0.19	-0.04	46.98 %	
	46.48 %	-0.06	0.79	13.80	14.00	88	2.12	2.18	-0.21	-0.05	46.56 %	
	45.81 %	-0.06	0.78	13.00	13.20	89	2.34	2.40	-0.22	-0.05	46.12 %	
	45.67 %	-0.06	0.76	12.25	12.50	90	2.58	2.65	-0.24	-0.05	45.75 %	
	45.14 %	-0.06	0.74	11.55	11.70	91	2.82	2.91	-0.26	-0.05	45.26 %	
	44.66 %	-0.06	0.72	10.80	11.00	92	3.10	3.20	-0.28	-0.05	44.90 %	
	44.42 %	-0.06	0.70	10.15	10.30	93	3.40	3.50	-0.30	-0.05	44.50 %	
	44.01 %	-0.07	0.67	9.45	9.65	94	3.75	3.85	-0.33	-0.05	44.31 %	
	43.63 %	-0.07	0.65	8.80	9.00	95	4.10	4.20	-0.35	-0.06	43.95 %	
	43.26 %	-0.07	0.63	8.20	8.35	96	4.45	4.60	-0.37	-0.06	43.61 %	
	42.90 %	-0.07	0.60	7.60	7.75	97	4.85	5.00	-0.40	-0.06	43.27 %	
	42.55 %	-0.07	0.58	7.05	7.15	98	5.30	5.40	-0.42	-0.06	42.94 %	
	42.21 %	-0.07	0.55	6.50	6.60	99	5.75	5.85	-0.45	-0.06	42.61 %	
	41.86 %	-0.07	0.53	5.95	6.10	100	6.25	6.35	-0.47	-0.06	42.46 %	
	40.45 %	-0.06	0.40	3.75	3.90	105	8.95	9.20	-0.60	-0.05	40.92 %	
	39.41 %	-0.05	0.28	2.26	2.30	110	12.55	12.70	-0.72	-0.04	40.59 %	
	39.17 %	-0.04	0.18	1.31	1.35	115	16.60	16.85	-0.81	-0.03	40.79 %	

OPTIONS CHAIN 12.1 Amazon
Source: TradeStation

Selling a Put

If instead you had sold a put, still thinking it would rally to $110, you can think differently. Depending on your risk appetite, you may decide to sell the –16 Delta 85 put, which is just outside the expected range based on current IV, for $1.58 ($158). Selling this option now earns you $4 a day on its Theta.

The breakeven is $83.42, or the strike price minus the premium collected. The probability of success is about 85%: 100 – 15% (the Delta between the 83 and 84 puts). The risk profile is:

Max profit = $158

Max loss = Unlimited

Table 12.1 is a summary of selling versus buying these options, with the 40 Delta call and –47 Delta put thrown in for comparison.

TABLE 12.1 Selling Versus Buying Options

	Buying Call	Buying Call	Selling Put	Selling Put
Delta	65	40	–16	–47
Strike	95	105	85	100
Price	$890	$385	–$158	–$630
Time Decay	–$210	–$180	$120	$180
Breakeven Price	$103.90	$108.85	$83.42	$93.70
Probability of Profit	42%	30%	85%	68%
Profit at $110	$610	$115	$158	$630
Margin Requirement	$890	$385	$850	$3,000
Return on Margin	69%	30%	19%	21%

Time decay is based on loss or profit after 30 days in the trade. If after 30 days the stock doesn't move much, the puts make a profit instead of giving you a loss. The max profit on the short trade is $158, regardless of how high above $85 Amazon goes. The long call can give you almost unlimited profits if the stock has an amazing rally, but you really need to get above $103.90 to have a profit.

Payoff Diagram 12.1 shows the potential payoff profile for the 85 put. Here you can easily picture the capped gain and unlimited loss if the stock plummets. Actually the loss isn't unlimited, as a stock can only go zero. Let's just call it a reeeeally large potential loss.

The best part of selling the 85 put is the much lower breakeven point. Instead of needing Amazon to actually rally to make money, you only need the stock to stay at or above $83.42, a much easier task.

With its much higher 85% POP, you double your chances of making money compared to the buying the 95 call. Yes, you make less by selling the more conservative –16 Delta put, but your chances of success are so much greater than with all the other choices. Even compared to the –47 Delta put you have so much more leeway to be wrong and still make nearly the same return on margin. This is the choice I prefer.

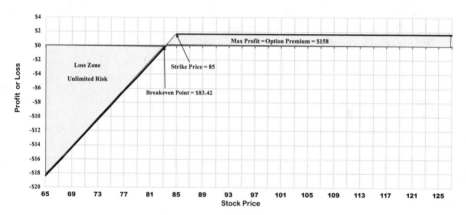

PAYOFF DIAGRAM 12.1 Short Put Payoff

WHY SELL OPTIONS?

It's easy to make a case why everyone should be selling options. Here are a handful of reasons why you should incorporate selling into your options trading strategy.

Higher Chances of Success

Though they come with higher worst-case scenario risk, selling options has a higher probability of success than buying options. With the right strikes you can be right as much as 75% to 90% of the time.

Time Decay

Selling options puts the odds in your favor. Option buyers fight an uphill battle where they need big directional moves to outpace time decay. The reverse holds true when selling. Let time decay work for you by being a seller.

You Don't Need to Be a Market Guru

A great part of selling options is that you don't have to be as smart or need as many factors working for you as when you buy. An option seller doesn't need to be as good a market forecaster as a buyer does. When you sell options, the market can move in your favor, remain stationary, or even move moderately against your position, and an option can still expire worthless—making you money.

Selling options lets you keep things simpler. You only need to determine a price level to which you believe the market *will not* reach and then let time decay do its thing. That's much easier than trying to guess where the market *will* go.

WOULD YOU RATHER?

It's December in New York City and 33 degrees outside. Would you rather?

1. Make a bet that pays you $100 if the temperature doesn't reach 90 degrees in the next two weeks and you lose $500 if it does?
2. Or would you prefer betting $10 to win $200 by predicting that temperatures will warm up and be above 50° in two weeks, with the chance to make $500 if it hits 90 degrees?

Your odds are much better with the first choice. Not many weather forecasters could screw that one up.

You've Got Leeway

Another benefit of selling options is that because you don't have to be as right, small fluctuations in prices are less damaging. If you use low enough Deltas, you can withstand pullbacks without affecting your position all that much.

More Tradeable Market Conditions

When you buy options, you need to catch a trend or a reversal and hope for a big move. Stagnant markets are a recipe for disaster. Option selling strategies work in any market, including range-bound or slow-moving ones.

GENERAL ADVICE FOR ANY OPTION-SELLING STRATEGY

Here is some sound advice to consider before engaging in option selling.

Give Yourself Time

Sellers have time decay working for them, and time decay works its fastest in the last couple of weeks before expiration—especially the last week of trading. Though this may seem enticing, do not forget that the closer you get to expiration, the more a market move can hurt you (Gamma risk). You are safer selling options further out: perhaps 30 to 60 days to expiration. These options provide a bigger premium, so they allow for more flexibility in price movement before hitting their losing level. Bigger premiums also mean you can use a smaller Delta to achieve the same monetary value as a shorter-expiration option. This provides yet more insurance against being wrong. Once again, that sweet spot for selling is about 45 days out and covering with about three weeks to go.

Placing Trades

When you pick spots to place trades, use technical analysis first. Look for trendlines, support and resistance, momentum oscillators, etc. for areas that you think the market will not reach. Combine this with picking a strike price outside the expected range to minimize risk. This is usually the 16 to 20 Delta strike option. Try to avoid selling an option that is within easy reach of a stock's movement or within support or resistance levels to which a stock can easily retrace. Using the Amazon chart and option chain, I would feel safest with a put under the support line of $81. I don't think I need to go below the $85 16 Delta put, but a $95 put would be too tight for my liking.

Keep Your Stress Level Low

Pick strikes that let you sleep at night. Look for Deltas of 30 and under. The smaller the Delta, the better your chance of success. If you want to make a more directional trade, you can increase your Delta to at or in the money strikes. If you shorted the $100 47 Delta instead of the 16 Delta put you stand to make four times the money. In the process, though, you lower your POP to about 68% and a 2 point move against you can have you biting your nails. I increase my Deltas when I have a strong directional bias, but I usually don't hold for very long.

Look for High IVR

Anytime you short options, you want a high IV environment to do it in. I don't think I need to expand on this again.

Don't Squeeze a Trade Dry

When you've made a good trade and an option has lost most of its value and is only worth a few cents, get out of it. How much more can you make? Not much. There is no point in tying up margin to make another $20 in two weeks when you've already made $200 in the first two weeks of a trade. Your trade is all risk (Gamma) now, with barely any reward. Why take the risk of losing it all? Get out and find another trade. This also applies to holding almost any trade to expiration. Set a target price and predetermined days to expiration, then get out when you hit either one. The longer you hold a trade, the bigger your risk of losing money.

OUCH!

Do not get into the habit of selling lots of way-OTM puts for a nickel, thinking they will never get filled. It doesn't happen often, but in my many years of trading I have seen some wild moves I never would have thought possible. Should you ever experience a crash—and they will happen every few years or so—*ouch* is not the four-letter word you will shout when your $5 potential gain has to be covered at a $5,000 loss. If you're going to wipe out, at least get paid more for it by selling higher-priced options.

DRAWBACKS OF SELLING OPTIONS

And of course selling options comes with a few hitches and risks.

Low Reward for High Risk

Selling options does have its drawbacks, including limited profit potential and unlimited risk exposure if you are wrong. Even when you try to take it into account, the worst-case scenario can be worse than you expect. If you'd sold a put, straddle, or strangle on Facebook (META) when it dropped from $323 to $235 on a bad earnings report on

February 3, 2022, you would have felt $7,000 to $9,000 worth of pain, depending on the strikes you used. If you had an account of $25,000, you would have lost a big chunk of it on one trade. Luckily, I only had an iron condor on that and lost a mere $780 thanks to its limited risk.

This is not a one-off. I've seen it happen in the past year in a few stocks after earnings reports, and not always to the downside. This is why I have cut back somewhat on my earning trades until the markets mellow out. The combination of low reward and high risk means that one really bad trade can wipe out the gains of 10 winners. However this high risk is no different than buying or shorting stocks outright. Your best defense is to keep your positions small, avoid abusing leverage, and stay diversified.

Cost

The second big drawback of selling options is that it ties up much more capital than buying does. Looking at Table 12.1 again, you can see the margin requirements for a few trades. The ATM short put has a $3,000 requirement, but the long calls require just the price of the option. The margin requirement is greater for higher-priced stocks and during increases in volatility. Higher margins also mean smaller returns on margin.

Volatility

Though high volatility has many advantages for an option seller, it should not be thought of as the Holy Grail to option selling. Just because you sell high implied volatility doesn't mean it can't go higher. An unexpected rise in volatility can hurt you regardless of what the market does. The ultimate goal is to sell high volatility that is falling, not just high volatility.

FINAL THOUGHTS

Shorting strategies opens up a whole new world of option trading that buying options cannot provide. You will need to get comfortable shorting options if you want to become a top-level trader, though I don't recommend shorting options outright unless you have plenty of capital. Even so, you need to understand the basics of shorting, as every strategy I mention from now on will have a short option it in, and the same principles will apply.

CHAPTER 13

Covered Calls and Puts

Option's Gig Economy

Many stock investors get their introduction to options by writing *covered calls* as a way to enhance profits on stocks they own. Fewer people write covered puts as a way to get into stocks. Even fewer do a wheel, and fewer still try a covered strangle. If you own or trade stocks, these are great strategies you can employ. I never make speculative option trades in my stock portfolio, but I do use all these methods on a regular basis to maximize my returns, especially writing covered calls.

COVERED CALLS

Writing covered calls is a simple but effective way to create a steady flow of income. It's a strategy that involves writing a call on a stock you already own, assuming you own at least 100 shares of it. If you own stock, this is a strategy you should not ignore, because it is a great way to increase your returns. The risk lies in the possibility of being assigned on the short call if the stock does rally above the strike price. If you do get assigned, you will be forced to sell your stock at the option's strike price. You would then lose your stock, missing out on a potential nice up move.

You don't have to already own the stock to write covered calls. You can make a trade where you purchase a stock and sell a call against it at the same time. This is known as a *buy-write*. Here you have no attachment to the stock and are trying to make a few percent on a trade, and you may be glad to get exercised.

BOOSTING YOUR RETURNS

Covered calls can boost your overall performance on a stock. Assume you bought 100 shares of Exxon years ago at $60 and it's currently trading at about $100. That's a not-too-shabby 67% return. But why settle for that? Instead of just owning the stock, you can sell calls along the way and gain even more.

With Exxon trading at $100, if you were to sell a 115 call trading at 55 cents, you would collect $55 in premium up front for it. This part works just like selling a naked call. In this case, though, your loss is limited because you own the stock. If Exxon rallied to $125 and you didn't own the stock, you would lose about $1,000 on a naked call. But since you own the stock, everything you lose with a call above the $115 strike is being matched by gains in the stock, so no monetary risk is involved. The only risk is potential lost profits that you could have made if you had not sold the call.

If the stock was at or above $115 at expiration, you would be required to sell your shares to some random person at $115, regardless of how high the stock's price gets. If you sell the 115 call, normally you would hope that the stock doesn't reach $115 and the call doesn't get exercised. Instead, you want it to rally close to $115 so that the stock appreciates, the call expires worthless, and you keep the premium. There are times when you might want to get exercised and finally get out of your stock, but for the most part covered call writers like keeping their stock.

As far as your broker is concerned, there is no risk and the trade doesn't eat up buying power as long as you own those shares. Instead, your buying power goes up and you can use the collected premium for something else. Because of the low risk, covered calls can be done in retirement accounts, which have tighter restrictions on options than regular trading accounts.

COVERED CALL EXAMPLE

This example will use the following parameters:

Exxon's current price is $98.43.

10 Delta 115 call with 37 days to expiration trading at $0.55.

19 Delta 110 call with 37 days to expiration trading at $1.12.

The expected range to the upside is $108.

First, look at the expected range on an options chain. I'm not showing the option chain for this example, but with 37 DTE it's $88.50 to $108. Then using Chart 13.1, confirm that this is a reasonable area. Looking at the chart I think the stock could rally to about that $108 top of the range area, but probably not more than that, so I would be OK with the 110 or 115 calls as targets. I prefer the 115 call for the lower Delta and a little extra buffer. If you sell the 115 call, as long as the stock stays below $115 at expiration, you keep the $55. But if the stock settles at or above $115, you will have sold the stock at $115. In a case where the stock rallies to $150, you will miss out on that $3,500 move, only to have made what feels like a crappy 55 bucks. This is one of the risks of covered calls, a trade-off between a little extra income and losing bigger potential profits should the stock move beyond the strike price you sold. If you sold a similar priced call 10 times a year, that's an extra $550 gain in your pocket, or 5% to 6%. I like to think of it as a steady stock dividend.

CHART 13.1 XOM Covered Call

Source: TradeStation

EXITING EARLY

As with any trade, you don't need to wait until expiration to get out. You can exit the call at any time. If the stocks drops or time decay eats away at it and the option becomes worth just a few cents, take the profit. At this point you are better off looking for a richer, further out option to sell, adjusting the strike price if necessary. You may also exit on a rally, if the stock is getting too close to your strike price and you are afraid you will lose a stock that you want to keep owning. This happens on occasion, and it's part of the game. It's OK to take a loss on the option now and then readjust or sit on the sidelines if the stock gets very strong. You will still make much more on the actual stock in a rally. If this stock rallied to $115 in a few days, you would lose about $500 on the option while gaining around $1,700 on the stock.

TIMES YOU MAY WANT TO GET EXERCISED

Getting exercised is not that bad. With Exxon trading at $98.43, you might think it will run out of steam and trade flat for a while. If you want to get out anyway, you could sell an at the money 97.50 call, currently trading at $5.30, and hope it gets filled, locking in some extra cash. Or if you had a $100 target on the stock, you could sell a $100 call for $4.05. This acts as a sort of limit order for your shares that earns an extra $405 along the way.

DISADVANTAGES OF COVERED CALLS

Covered calls also have disadvantages that you should be aware of.

Being Exercised

As I mentioned, the one big downside of writing covered calls on stocks you own and like is that you cap the upside gain and can potentially lose your stock. Inevitably, if you sell covered calls you will sometimes get called or have to close the call at a loss.

Not Meant for Protection

Selling calls doesn't protect you from downside risk. The small premium you receive on a covered call is not protection against a down move. I hear someone on CNBC all the time defending losing stock picks by saying they are selling calls against them so the losses are not that bad. They are just saving face. If a stock drops $20, the extra 50 cents you get selling a call isn't much help to offset the decline.

Tax Implications

If you get called on shares of a stock that's been profitable, you'll owe taxes on those profits. If that's a concern, you need to sell the option at a loss.

A ROLLER COASTER OF EMOTIONS

I bought the stock Roku at $33 in 2018, even before I knew what a Roku device was. I liked how the chart looked after hearing about it on CNBC many times, so I bought 300 shares. I sold 200 at a nice profit of about $50 and kept 100 shares for the long haul. Three years later it was trading at about $350 and I was pretty happy. The volatility on Roku was rather lofty, so you could sell a call quite far out of the money and make a couple of hundred dollars a week at that point. I sold a $400 call for around $3.00 with a little over a week to go, thinking I would make an easy $300. Three days later Roku was trading over $400 for no good reason and the option was at $25 with a few days left to expiration. I let it get exercised and felt awful about the $7,000 I just gave up when three weeks later it was trading over $475. A month later I was happy again as it dropped below $300 and I bought back the 100 shares, thinking I was genius. I lost the stock again, this time at $350 on another covered call. I felt worse than before when it rallied almost 200 points in the next few weeks, missing the whole move. But now that it's trading at $53, I am happy to have gotten out $300 higher.

BEST STRATEGIES FOR WRITING COVERED CALLS

Here are some of the best strategies for writing covered calls.

Avoid Very Strong Trends

Avoid writing covered calls on stocks in a strong uptrend unless you go way out in price. If not, be prepared to lose the stock. When a stock is skyrocketing, you are better off just enjoying the growth rather than giving up huge potential profits in runaway bull markets. Moderate uptrends are the best scenario for covered calls, as they allow for growth in the stock and some predictable targets.

Sell High Volatility

Covered calls work better with stocks that have high implied volatility (IV). High volatility lets you sell calls that are further out of the money and get a decent price, compared to a low IV scenario. (Though too high a volatile stock could mean it will reach your strike easier and you may get assigned.) I don't recommend covered calls on stocks with low IV. For example, I own shares of Coke. It has an IV of 14 and is trading at $61. A 10 Delta call with 48 days to expiration is worth about 17 cents. It's just not worth writing a covered call for the extra $12 to $15 you can potentially make on the stock, after slippage and commissions.

Picking the Best Strike Price

You can pick the best strike price in two ways. One is by looking at a chart; the other uses an option's expected range and Delta. I always look at charts before making any trade, no matter what strategy I am using. Others may never look at a chart. In the Exxon chart at its current levels, I may consider selling a call a little closer to the current price than I would have in late September, when it was at the trendline at around $85. At the trendline, there was a good chance of a big pop, and a call $10 away is more likely to get hit than when the stock is trading almost $15 above the trendline and could potentially see a pullback. I would even consider not doing anything if I thought a big rally could happen.

You can also use the charts to look for a target desired exit level and place the call there. That way there are no regrets if you get assigned—I wouldn't mind exiting at $110. Make sure it's a reasonable price or the option may not have enough value to make it worth selling.

Though charts give me a visual of what can happen. I also look to use Deltas that are outside one standard deviation from a stock's current price, as these are not as likely to get hit. I am assuming you remember that the one standard deviation level is the 16 Delta option.

There is no option at 37 days to expiration with a 16 Delta, but there is a 19 Delta call (110 strike) for about $1.10 and a 10 Delta call (115 strike) for about $0.55. It's up to you how conservative you want to be and whether you prefer more income with a greater chance of the stock being called or a smaller, safer profit. At the current level I am comfortable with the 110 strike, but I would be quick to get out if the stock rallied above that level. Normally though, I prefer to sell calls with a 16 Delta or less.

The exception is if I ever do a *buy-write*, where I am buying a stock and selling a call at the same time for a short-term trade, then I am content to sell a 40 Delta call and hope I get exercised. In Exxon there is a 47 Delta 100 call that would make about $410 in premium. If Exxon rallies above 100, I would make $567 ($157 on the stock and $410 on the call), which is 5.75% profit on the $98.43 trade in about a month. If the stock went down, I would have a $4.10 cushion on the stock price from selling the call.

Exiting Winners

Don't hold till expiration, when your option starts having very little value and is close to worthless. Get out. You are better off taking your profit and selling a further-out call for more value. If the option is worth little because the stock has dropped, sell one with a lower strike price and greater premium in its place.

Be Wary of Earnings

Know when earning reports are due, as options will increase in value then. This lets you go further out in strikes and still make the same dollar that you normally aim for. You may want to avoid selling calls around earnings if you are scared of losing your stock, as anything could happen. A great earnings announcement could move a stock 20%, blowing through your strike price.

What Time Frame to Use

Should you sell monthly calls and collect a fatter premium or sell weekly calls and get a greater daily time decay? You could make a case for both, and the answer comes down to your personal trading style. I like to sell options with about 14 days to go, assuming there are weekly options. If not, I sell the closest expiring contract. I normally buy the option back with five days to expiration and then resell the option that is two weeks out. In general, trading options with a week to go is risky, due to the Gamma risk involved. But being that I am selling options far out of the money and I am protected from a big loss on the option because I own the stock, I am willing to take that risk. The strategy means I can capture faster-decaying time premium while being able to adjust my option price every week. If you cannot watch the markets actively, you should stick with the "enter at 45 days and exit at two to three weeks" rule.

I'll compare the original covered call with shorter entry and holding time frames and repeating it using Table 13.1.

Scenario 1: 37 DTE 10 Delta call 115 strike sold for $0.55

Scenario 2: 37 DTE 19 Delta call 110 strike sold for $1.12

Scenario 3: 16 DTE 10 Delta call 110 strike sold for $0.37

Scenario 4: 16 DTE 15 Delta call 108 strike sold for $0.58

Assumptions

1. This assumes that Exxon's price and IV don't change.
2. Cover all calls with nine days to go using the equivalent nine DTE option as a price estimate.
3. The 115 call at nine DTE is currently $0.03, the 110 call is $0.10, and the 108 call is $0.19.
4. Keep selling 16 DTE for four weeks to compare it to the 28-day holding period of 37 DTE.
5. Assume you will keep getting the similar prices.

TABLE 13.1 XOM Covered Calls

	Scenario 1	Scenario 2	Scenario 3	Scenario 4
DTE	37	37	16	16
Strike Price	115	110	110	108
Delta	10	19	10	15
Premium Collected	$55	$112	$37	$59
Cover with 9 DTE	$3	$10	$10	$19
Profit	$52	$102	$27	$40
Holding Time	28	28	7	7
4 Week Total	$52	$102	$96	$160
Yearly Return	6.30%	12.40%	11.70%	19.50%

If you have the time to manage these trades, the shorter time frames provide better opportunities with smaller risks of being called. With the two 110 calls, you make about the same profit over a four-week period. The difference is scenario 3 has a smaller chance of being called as it would be harder for the stock to reach $110 in one week than in four weeks. The smaller Delta means a smaller chance of the stock being in the money. The trade-off is you have to make four trades over the time period as opposed to one.

In scenario 4, you would make much more than with the other three choices over four weeks. This is the reward for choosing a lower strike and a higher Delta. The option also has a better shot of being called. In the end, it comes down to risk levels. I would be comfortable with any of these options, but prefer the 16 DTE 15 Delta put.

I also like the fact that if the stock moves, you can sell a different strike the following week. You are not locked in, so you can try to maximize gains by selling a more appropriate strike if the market drops or rallies.

One last assumption is that my assumptions will actually happen. It's farfetched to think a stock won't move or that option prices will be the same every week. There will be times when you lose money on a call or lose the stock, or you may not trade for a period or two. Overall, using covered calls can gain you an extra 10% a year if everything works out close to what's expected.

COVERED PUTS

This a powerful trade for those who buy stocks and can also be done in IRA accounts. Covered puts, also known as secured puts, let you either buy stock at a cheaper price or make a bit income if you don't get the stock.

A covered put is a combination of a short put and available cash in your account. The cash is the sum necessary to buy the underlying stock at the strike price you choose. You would do this with a stock you want to own but that you think you can get at a better price. When it works out you actually get paid to buy the stock. The way it works is you sell a put below the current market price. If the stock rallies, you keep the premium on the put. If the stocks falls, you get to buy the stock at a better price than it's currently trading.

IF IT'S GOOD ENOUGH FOR WARREN BUFFETT . . .

Warren Buffett was once eyeing Coca-Cola, which was trading around $39 at the time. Instead of buying the stock, he sold 50,000 35-strike puts at $1.50, for a total of $7.5 million. This in effect let him buy Coke at $35 while keeping the $7.5 million. He would have kept the $7.5 million even if Coke didn't go down to $35, but the added bonus of getting the stock $4 cheaper than the current price didn't hurt.

I will stick with the same Exxon chart and options as an example. You might want to buy the stock but think it might retrace to the $90 level fairly easily. Instead of buying it at the current price of around $98, you can sell a –38 Delta 95 put for about $4.10 or a –25 Delta 90 put for $2.45. Both of these are 37 days to expiration, though you can choose a different time frame. If you sell the 95 put and the stock settles below that price at the option's expiration, you will be "put the stock." This means your put option will get assigned and you will have to buy the 100 shares of the stock at $95 a share. You also make $410 from the short put, so your price is essentially $90.90. I want to reemphasize that, in order to make this type of trade, you need enough cash in your account to cover buying 100 shares of stock. In this case, that's $9,500, which is a bargain compared to the current $9,800 selling price. It's really $9,090 you need, as you get to use the $410 from the short put toward your purchase price.

If you think the stock may go still lower than your original target, you can buy the put back instead of buying the stock. There is a decent chance that you will have made money on the put if the price of the stock hadn't dropped too much.

If you don't get the stock, you make around 4.5% on the idle money sitting in your account over 37 days, which is great as well. What is great about this type of trade is that it lets you benefit from multiple scenarios. A drop in implied volatility will suck value out of the option. If the stock moves sideways, higher, or only slightly lower but stays above $95, time decay will be on your side and you keep the $410. If it drops below the strike price, you get to own a stock you wanted to own anyway, but at a discount.

Risks Involved

Like any other trade, covered puts come with risks. First, if the stock tanks, you could be losing thousands before you even get the stock. This is why you shouldn't make this trade unless you really want to own the stock. The drop can also happen after you own the stock. The second risk is that the stock might also never go down. If two months later it's trading at $145, you've missed the whole move and a chance to make $5,000. Your consolation prize being the $410 in premium.

When to Use

The best situation for a covered put is a slightly bullish or neutral outlook. In both cases you keep the entire premium received, without the risk of missing a big move. You also have the chance of a slight pullback to get exercised. Trying this in a full downward trend can be costly, as the market can keep going lower and the stock can drop dramatically. As with any option-selling strategy, the stronger the implied volatility, the better the odds of success.

What Deltas to Use?

If you hope to generate cash without owning the stock, stick to the 16 Delta puts, just as you would with covered calls. You can always use technical analysis to determine retracement/support levels you think the stock will reach and place your put below that. In this example 16 Delta is the $85 put. This coincides with my trendline and is worth $1.45.

   If your goal is to own the stock, use strikes that have a higher Delta and are above those support levels. Look for a price the stock can hit. You can even do this at 50 Deltas to generate fatter premiums, get the biggest Theta returns, and give yourself a better chance of getting the stock if you really want to own it. You would buy the stock at around its current price, but with a nice premium of $520. When I want the stock I use a 35 to 40 Delta, which gives me a little bit of a pullback plus a decent premium.

Time Frames

As with covered calls, I prefer two weeks to expiration. However, if I want the stock, I don't get out of the option with a week to go. I would even sell 50 Delta puts with one week left to expiration if I really wanted to own the stock. This gives me a 50/50 shot at getting the stock, with a nice payoff if I don't get it and a chance to try again. You can also go to a safer, more controllable time frame of about 45 days if you want to collect a bigger premium and not have to worry about managing the trade as much.

THE WHEEL

The last strategy in this chapter is the *wheel*, which is basically buying a stock through a covered put, then selling the stock with a covered call. This can be done very short term, or you can hold the stock for months, waiting for high volatility to give you a better call premium. You could also sell covered calls on it continuously. I like to make this as a quick trade, selling the 50 Delta put to collect a nice premium while hoping the put gets exercised so I get to buy the stock. I then immediately sell the closest expiring 50 Delta call looking to get out with a small profit in the stock while collecting premiums on both sides of the trades.

As an example, if you sell a $97.50 put in Exxon for $520 (and get put the stock at $97.50), you can then turn around and sell a $97.50 call for about another $500, hoping to get filled, selling the stock at $97.50. You would make nothing on the stock itself but would earn $1,020 on the options if it worked out as planned. The risk is that you get the stock but it keeps dropping past your breakeven point of $92.30.

Wheel trades work well in flat to slightly upward-trending markets, when stocks aren't doing much. It's a different way to generate some return in your investment account that most traders ignore.

WAIT, I'VE GOT ONE MORE

If you own a stock you like and wouldn't mind buying more if it went down a little, you could combine selling a covered call and a secured put, in effect putting on a covered/secured *strangle*. This strategy lets you make extra cash flow through the covered call and the covered put. This works well in a flat market, letting you take in money on both sides. You either lose the stock at a higher price, buy more of the stock at a lower price, or pocket the premiums. (This trade assumes you have the buying power to purchase another 100 shares.)

FINAL THOUGHT

If you own stocks, writing covered calls and puts is something you should be doing to generate regular income. These strategies can let you easily increase your portfolio's return and are a great introductory course on selling options.

CHAPTER 14

Vertical Spreads

Moving along to multi-leg strategies, I start with a typical vertical spread, as it sets the groundwork for the other trades I'll discuss in the next few chapters. I spend a bit more time in this chapter than the others because the principles here apply to the rest of the strategies covered as well.

WHAT IS A VERTICAL SPREAD?

A vertical spread involves trading two strikes of the same option type (put or call) in the same expiration. The strikes will be laid out vertically on an option chain. Each option in the spread is considered a leg of the trade. One of the legs is buying an option; the other is a selling an option at a different strike price. An example of a vertical spread is buying a 50 Delta 100 call for $8.00 and selling a 30 Delta 110 call for $3.00, both with the same expiration.

There are four types of vertical spreads. I categorize them by directional outlook:

Bullish Outlook

1. Long call debit spread: buy the higher-priced call, sell the cheaper call.
2. Short put credit spread: sell the higher-priced put, buy the cheaper put.

Bearish Outlook

3. Long put debit spread: buy the higher-priced put, sell the cheaper put.
4. Short call credit spread: sell the higher-priced call, buy the cheaper call.

Some Key Things to Remember

Regardless of put or call spreads, when you buy the option with the lower strike price and sell the higher priced strike, the position is bullish. When you buy the higher strike price and sell the lower strike price, the position is bearish.

Buying the higher-priced option creates a debit spread. You pay money for the trade. Selling the more expensive option creates a credit spread. You will earn money for it.

All spreads have a defined risk and profit clearly established. Before you make the trade, you will know the trade's maximum profit and worst possible loss. There are no surprises.

The cheaper priced option is the spread's defining leg. In a debit spread, it decreases your total cost while putting a cap on profits. In a credit spread, it limits the potential risk and determines the maximum profit.

Spreads always have some directional bias, as one of the legs has a bigger Delta than the other.

You can't win on both legs. One leg of the spread will always be a loser and the other a winner.

ADVANTAGES AND DISADVANTAGES OF TRADING SPREADS

The pros and cons of spreads:

Some Advantages of Trading Spreads

- They lower risk, letting you sleep at night.
- They have a defined risk.
- They reduce the cost of trading options.

- They have a higher return on margin.
- They let you make more trades.
- They let you collect time premium without being naked.
- They provide some protection against time decay.

Disadvantages of Vertical Spreads

- They limit your potential rewards.
- The higher the probability of profit, the lower your rewards.
- They can lose money.
- They take longer to respond to market changes.

CREDIT SPREADS

I tend to trade credit spreads a lot as they offer diversity and a high probability of success. When used at proper Delta levels, they are income-producing trades with low directional risk that provide a wide margin of error. You can make them very directional or somewhat directional. You can also use them as hedging tools to alter your overall Delta exposure. Credit spreads are a great way to get time decay revenue, similar to selling an outright option, while giving you a defined, controllable risk. You can also use them to take advantage of volatility.

As opposed to selling naked options, credit spreads are a safer trade you can do in a much smaller account, as margin requirements are much smaller. If you want to sell speculative options, this is the way to start. I think of spread trades as going for singles, walks, and sacrifice bunts. These are not home run trades, but you won't strike out nearly as much. What's nice about a well-placed credit spread is that instead of predicting where the market will go, you are trying to predict where it *won't* go. (Your hope with credit spreads is that they expire out of the money and worthless, while time decay does its thing eating up all their value.)

DEBIT SPREADS

Even though I prefer trading credit spreads, it's probably easier to understand debit spreads, so I will start with an example of them first. Here is a long call debit spread that is directional in nature. Assume you are bullish on the Nasdaq 100 and want to put on a trade using QQQ to capitalize. QQQ currently trades at $269.11 and you think it will go above $280.

As you can see in Option Chain 14.1, you could buy a 43 DTE 49 Delta 270 call for $12.35. This is just out of the money, so that $12.35 is all extrinsic value. You would need a strong rally to make money on this trade if you held it until expiration. Even if QQQ rallied to $280, you could lose money on the trade, as the breakeven point is $282.35. You can't see it on this table, but the Theta is –14.23 and the probability of profit (POP) is 30% for a 270 call. You can alleviate some of this extrinsic value and cost by selling a higher call, in this case the 43 Delta 275 call for $9.84.

This would create a bullish debit call spread, as you want prices to go up and you are paying $2.51 for this spread ($12.35 – $9.84). The spread's maximum loss is the $251 you pay for it—much better than the original $1,235. This will lower your BE price by the amount you received by selling the call to $272.51. The new BE is the long strike plus the price of the spread.

The Theta on the 275 call leg is –13.62. The option chain shows Theta at –0.616 (bottom of option chain); that is combined Theta for both legs of this trade. Theta is still negative, so you are still fighting time decay. The effects of that decay, however, have dropped from –$14.23 a day to –61 cents a day.

A lower breakeven point moves the spread's probability of profit from 30% to 41%. This gives you a better chance of making money over just buying the 270 call. You do give up unlimited potential profits by trading the spread. No matter how high QQQ goes, the most you will receive on this spread is the difference in strike prices ($500) minus the cost of the trade ($251), or $249.

BREAKEVEN FOR SPREADS

Debit call spread: breakeven price is the long strike plus the cost of the spread.

Debit put spread: breakeven price is the long strike minus the cost of the spread.

Credit call spread: breakeven price is the short strike plus the premium received.

> **Credit put spread:** breakeven price is the short strike minus the premium received.
>
> Don't worry about remembering this. It will become second nature as you trade.

OPTION CHAIN 14.1 Call Debit Spread QQQ

Source: tastytrade

BULLISH CREDIT SPREAD

But what if you did this trade differently? Imagine that you are still bullish and think the stock's price will go above $280. You can get the same results using the same strike puts. Using Option Chain 14.2, this time you sell the 275 put for $14.68. For this single option to work out, you don't need a market rally. The stock price just needs to stay above its breakeven point of $260.30 at expiration.

On its own, this strategy has a POP of 56%. The max profit is at $275 and above, and that's the $1,468 premium you collected. Without a protective leg this trade is risky. It takes up a lot of buying power, and a big market drop can wipe you out. You decide to protect yourself by buying the 270 put for about $12.20, covering any downside move beyond $270. This means you would only be getting a premium of $248 ($14.68 – $12.20) to make this trade, lowering your max profit potential. Your max loss now is no longer unlimited. It is capped by the difference between the strikes ($500) minus the net premium you receive ($248), which is $500 – $248 = $252 max loss. The breakeven point on this trade is $272.52 ($275 – $2.48), with about the same Theta as before and a 41% probability of profit. I wouldn't make this trade either, as it relies on a directional move up to break even and does not collect any time value.

Comparing these two trades, you will notice they are pretty much identical. They both have the same chance of working out, with the same cost and maximum profit. This is not a coincidence; it's a result of *put call parity.*

When we're talking about spreads, put call parity means that a long call spread is synthetically the same trade as a short put spread and vice versa, when using the same strikes. They have the same results. Both trades have similar net Deltas, Thetas, breakeven points, risk profiles, profit/loss ratios, and probabilities of success.

OPTION CHAIN 14.2 Put Credit Spread QQQ

Source: tastytrade

"So," I hear someone thinking, "does it matter which one I use, if the results are the same?"

The answer is yes, it does matter. Remember that as options get deeper in the money, they tend to have less liquidity, and come with a higher risk of assignment (Chapter 20). In this trade I would consider making the debit spread, as the 275 call option is out of the money and thus lower priced than the in the money 275 put. It is not noticeable here, but if the trade were further away from at the money, you would start seeing a larger bid-ask spread on the higher-priced in the money put options.

Then there is the risk of assignment. As a general rule, stay away from selling in the money options to avoid the chances of getting assigned. There is nothing as exciting as looking at your account in the morning and noticing a $24,000 margin call because you are short 100 shares of Tesla, as someone exercised their right to sell you 100 shares. This only happens when a short option is in the money.

MONEYNESS OF SPREADS

In the trades I've just discussed, a difference is that the debit call spread is out of the money while the credit put spread is in the money. This is the opposite of where the spread must eventually be if you are to make money on either trade. I've used these spreads as an example—they are not ones I would make unless I was very bullish. The market has to rally to make money on either trade, and the probability of profit is lower than I like. The trades also have a negative Theta. Collecting time premium is a major reason for shorting options, but it doesn't work here, as I'll explain shortly. If you were extremely bullish you might do something like this to capture more premium, and then they become directional trades.

In general, the better trade is to sell an out of the money spread. At worst, sell a spread that straddles the ATM option. Out of the money credit spreads give you much more wiggle room. You can even be wrong in your directional outlook and still make money while also collecting time decay. Granted, you make less per trade, but you get paid much more often than with directional trades that start in the money.

When selling spreads, the further out of the money a spread is, the less it will be worth, but the better the odds of making money. You can potentially make more by selling in the money or at the money spreads, but then you are relying on some directional help from the market. When a short position is out of the money, the Greeks work for you. In the money, things are reversed and the Greeks will work opposite from how you want them to.

REASONS TO SELL SPREADS THAT ARE OUT OF THE MONEY

There are a number of reasons to sell spreads that are out of the money:

- The further out of the money your short option is, the higher your probability of profit.
- In the money options are higher priced with larger bid and ask spreads.
- There is less liquidity as you get further in the money.
- There is less risk of assignment.
- You don't have to be as right.
- You have Theta on your side.

VOLATILITY AND MONEYNESS

One reason you always want to short spreads when a stock's implied volatility is high is that it means you collect bigger premiums. This allows you to go further out of the money to collect the same amount as when volatility is lower. As an example, two stocks both trade at $100. Stock A has an IV of 20, while stock B has an IV of 60. You want to sell a put spread with strikes $10 apart and collect a premium of $350. With stock A you may have to sell the 100/90 put spread to get the $350, but because Stock B's options will be higher priced, you may get that $350 price by selling the further 90/80 put spread, giving you some extra buffer to be wrong if the stock drops. Yes there is more risk and movement in a higher IV stock, but that is rewarded with higher probability of returns. I would rather have the cushion of starting a trade $10 out of the money for the same reward. You also have the benefit of selling a higher IV and making money if it contracts.

OPTIMAL SITUATIONS

Here are some optimal situations for trading in spreads.

Trading Time Frame

Spreads tend to work best with the "45 DTE entry and exited with about three weeks left" guideline. It doesn't matter if you are short or long. Time decay and Gamma really make a big difference the closer you get to expiration. Spreads react more slowly to the Greeks than do single options. What you gain on one side is offset a bit by what you lose on the other, so time decay isn't as noticeable at first. Any trades longer than 60 days won't do much at first without a big price movement.

On the other end, if you let trades get too close to expiration—especially the big winners—they can burn you with a market move. It's easy for a trade that is almost at max profit to turn around and be at max loss in two days as the options approach expiration. It's just not worth the risk/reward and use of capital to hold it in the last two weeks.

Debit Spreads

Debit spreads tend to be more directional. Do them only on low-volatility stocks with an IVR of well below 50%.

Debits spreads work best if you buy the option with less extrinsic value and lower IV compared to the short option. This works because if the volatilities on the two legs come back to equal levels, either the long option gains value or the short option loses value. In either case, your position will see a net improvement.

By shorting the option with greater extrinsic value, you'll have time decay working on your side. The best scenario involves buying a slightly in the money option: around a 55 to 60 Delta and selling an out of the money option. Try to get the extrinsic value of the long option as close to or less than that of the short option. If you can get the net extrinsic value of the trade to be positive and there is no price movement, the long option will hold more value than the spread will lose, allowing for positive time decay. This removes some of the trade's directionality and increases the probability of profit. It results in a breakeven point below the current price (above for puts), making it easier to make a profit.

Look at the QQQ debit spread option chain (Option Chain 14.1) again, but this time look to buy the 266 call for $14.60 and sell the 271 call for $11.85. The spread would cost $2.75. The 266 call would have an extrinsic value of −1149 versus 1185 for the 271 short call, resulting in a positive extrinsic value of 36. This makes the trade more favorable compared to the 270/275 call spread from before. It now has a lower breakeven, going from $272.51 to $268.75. Its new POP is 55% compared to 41%. QQQ no longer has to rally to break even—now it only needs to get to $271 for a max profit of $225. When compared to the

270/275 call spread that needed to rally to break even and reach $275 to achieve the max profit of $249, you have a better trade.

If I had a greater directional outlook and wanted to make more on the trade, I would still buy a 55 to 60 Delta call, but would move the short call further out. I would pay more for this trade and give up the extrinsic value advantage for potentially greater gains. It's all a matter of your price target and profit goals.

Credit Spreads

I much prefer credit spreads, especially ones with high IVR. With credit spreads you want to sell an out of the money strike and buy one that's even further out of the money. The further out of the money your short option is, the higher the probability of profit.

The ideal situation is to sell a spread where you collect one-third the width of the strike prices, with the lowest Delta on the short option that matches this criteria. This means that if you short a $5.00 wide spread you want to collect at least $1.67 on the trade. This trade usually has a probability of success of around 65%. Volatility determines how low you can go. In a stock with low implied volatility, you may have to short the 50 Delta option to achieve this goal, while in a high IV stock you could maybe get the same results shorting the 30 Delta option.

If you are just looking for slow-moving, Theta-eating trades that rely less on direction, lower your short Delta to about 20 or below. Place these outside the expected range to increase your odds. This will give you trades that win around 85% of the time, with small winners that move slowly. I will discuss this strategy more when I get to iron condors.

For more directional trades with bigger rewards, stick to trades where the short Delta is between 35 and 50. These allow for a margin of error if you are wrong, but still make money on direction and time decay. At the greatest, you can straddle the 50 Delta strike with your options. These may need a little market move to get to breakeven and start having positive time decay. None of these are good or bad trades, just trades with different risk profiles. A good mixture of them in your account will help spread your portfolio risk and give you some directional bias if you want it. If I have a directional feel, I look to short the first out of the money option there is (around a 40 to 45 Delta). Then I buy the Delta that gets me a premium of one-third the trade's width. If volatility is too low, I may not be able to get that much. In that case, I would consider passing on the trade.

HOW WIDE TO MAKE THE SPREAD

This comes down to your risk tolerance. Spread widths of $5 are a good choice overall. The wider the spread (more risk), the more potential profit. Wider spreads will start to act more like naked positions, compared to tight spreads. They give the trade more room to breathe without the protective option fighting it so closely. This lets the Greeks work with fewer constraints. Larger spreads have bigger premiums, resulting in better breakeven prices with better probabilities of profit.

Wider spreads mean you'll receive more credit or pay more for a debit spread. They also have larger potential max profits and losses. If you widen a spread too much it will behave like a naked option, losing a lot of the protection that the second option gives you. The more you tighten the spread, the more similarly the two options will behave and the slower the spread will move. A 100/99 spread will not move much at all.

You can use wider spreads to reduce the number of contracts you trade and better your chances. If you short two $5 wide spreads at $1.75 each, your total premium is $350 and your breakeven point is $1.75 from the short strike price. If you instead you shorted a $10 wide spread, you would get around $350 total as well. Now, however, the breakeven is $3.50 from the short strike price, which increases your chances. Your total risk and rewards haven't changed. You still have a maximum profit of $350 and a maximum loss of $650. And you saved a small amount in commissions.

EXITING

Trades aren't meant to be held forever. In addition to having a set time parameter like exiting at 21 to 14 days before expiration for risk reasons, you should also set exit targets for both losing and winning trades. A good profit target is 50% of the premium received. You can aim for a little more, but typically the second 50% of profit will take longer to achieve than the first 50%. You are better off taking the 50% profit and using the money for a new trade with more profit potential.

For losers, you can set a target such as 100% of the premium received. I prefer to get out when both options go in the money. Try to avoid letting them get to max loss. If you can save yourself $35 on

100 losing trades a year, that's a vacation you could take. I will discuss exiting trades in detail in Chapter 20.

THINGS YOU SHOULD KNOW

Here are some things you may want to remember regarding spreads.

Risk and Probability of Profit

The higher the potential risk you take in a spread, the higher your probability of success will be. A trade that risks $450 to make $50 should have a chance of success close to 90%. One where you risk $50 to make $450 may have a 10% chance. By "risk," I mean maximum potential loss, not how risky a trade actually is. A credit spread with the short option at a 10 Delta is very likely to expire worthless, so it's not as risky as one with a 50 Delta. Your risk to reward involves risking $450 to make $50, as opposed to risking $250 to make $250 in the higher Delta trade. The first trade has a bigger absolute dollar risk, so it represents greater risk to a trader.

A Spread's Delta

A spread's Delta is the difference between the Deltas of the two strikes. It implies how much a spread will move for every dollar the underlying moves. The QQQ short 270/275 put spread from earlier has a bullish outlook, so its Delta will be positive. The option chain shows that the net Delta is 7, confirming this. Or you can do the math: long Delta (–51) minus short Delta (–58) = a Delta of 7. This means that if the QQQ moves from $269.11 to $270.11, the spread improves by $0.07. This is part of the slow-moving Greek effects of spreads.

A SPREAD'S DELTA

A spread's Delta is the Delta of the long leg minus the Delta of the short leg.

Call credit spreads and put debit spread are bearish position and have a negative Delta.

Put credit spreads and call debit spreads are bullish positions and have a positive Delta.

Spread Width and Delta

You can increase or decrease a spread's Delta by changing the width of the spread. If you want more directional risk, use a lower strike for your lower Delta option. You can also do this by moving the whole spread. Spreads have the highest Deltas when they are at the money and lowest as they move away in either direction.

Deltas Will Change

Though the spread currently has a positive 7 Delta, this will keep changing as you get closer to expiration. Options with a week to go have the 270 put with a 54 Delta; the 275 put has a 72 Delta, for a net Delta of 18. This spread is more sensitive to movement than it was at 43 days to expiration. Keep this in mind. It is a clue to how Gamma can hurt you as you near expiration.

Theta

As with all the Greeks, Theta reacts slowly as one option fights the other. In a spread, each leg has a different time decay. The ATM option is the one with the highest Theta. As a stock moves away from at the money in either direction, Theta shrinks. When trading credit spreads, one of the goals is to have a positive net Theta, so you can capture time decay. Set up the trade so the leg you are shorting has a higher Theta than the long leg. As long as the spread is out of the money, this will be the case.

A PROPER CREDIT SPREAD

Look at Option Chain 14.3, "MSFT Credit Call Spread." This is how I would prefer a credit spread to look. It uses out of the money strikes, shorting the 38 Delta call and buying the 30 Delta call. The Theta is now positive and the trade will benefit from time decay. Both of the options are out of the money, and the short 230 leg has a higher Theta than the long 235 call. The net Theta is 1.117 (at bottom of option chain), implying that you will receive time decay of $1.11 a day. That's not a ton, but it's better than losing money. If Microsoft rallies and the options go in the money, time decay will reverse, because the long option will then have a bigger Theta.

If you had shorted the 215 and bought the 220 strikes (which are in the money), the 215 call would earn less time decay than the 220 call is losing, giving you a net negative Theta of −0.123. This makes sense, if you think about it. Suppose the spread was $5 in the money with two weeks to go. Every day you hold it and the market doesn't move, the spread has a higher probability of expiring completely in the money at its full loss of $5.00. You should expect to lose money on it daily. The only thing that could help you at this point is a downward move in the stock. This is why shorting spreads that are already out of the money lowers directional risk and adds time decay. Once they go in the money, consider exiting them.

This trade has a nice setup that I would consider making without hesitation. It has a probability of success of 67%. The premium received ($158) is close enough to one-third the width of the strikes ($500), which I like to see. It also has about a $10 directional buffer to breakeven.

While a short option spread is out of the money, it is collecting time premium. Once it goes in the money, it is paying time premium.

MSFT	IV RANK		LAST		Change		Bid		Ask	
Microsoft	46.00		221.39		7.14		220.9		221.26	

				CALLS							
	Ext Val	Impl Vol	Vega	Gamma	Theta	Delta	Bid	Ask		Strike	
Dec 16th		42DTE					IV : 54.14%			+/- 29.36	
	3.24	0.36	0.20	0.01	-0.09	0.81	24.20	25.05		200	
	3.96	0.34	0.23	0.01	-0.10	0.77	19.50	21.20		205	
	5.61	0.35	0.26	0.01	-0.11	0.70	16.65	17.35		210	ITM
	7.29	0.34	0.28	0.01	-0.11	0.63	13.40	13.95		215	
	9.31	0.33	0.30	0.02	-0.12	0.55	10.40	11.00		220	ATM
	8.23	0.32	0.30	0.02	-0.12	0.47	8.10	8.35		225	
Sell 1	5.93	0.31	0.29	0.02	-0.11	0.38	5.65	6.20		230	OTM
Buy 1	4.35	0.31	0.27	0.02	-0.09	0.30	4.25	4.45		235	
	3.06	0.30	0.23	0.01	-0.09	0.24	2.97	3.15		240	
	2.09	0.30	0.20	0.01	-0.07	0.18	2.02	2.15		245	
	1.44	0.30	0.16	0.01	-0.06	0.13	1.39	1.48		250	

POP 67%	EXT 158	Delta -7.83	Theta 1.117	Vega -2.46	Gamma -0.01
	Max Profit 158	Max Loss -342		BP Eff 342	

OPTION CHAIN 14.3 MSFT Credit Call Spread

Vega

Vega and implied volatility will also play less of a role with spreads due to spreads' push-pull nature on the Greeks. But you can still benefit from implied volatility contractions by selling the higher Vega option. If you believe IV is high, you want the option you short to have the higher Vega. The ATM option will usually have the highest Vega and be most sensitive to changes in implied volatility. Vega decreases as you go away from at the money. Vega reacts opposite to this when an option is in the money. In Option Chain 14.3, this spread starts out properly, but if it ends up going in the money, the long call will be the most sensitive to IV changes. This will hurt your position if IV falls.

Logically this is true because once a credit spread is in the money, it must go out of the money to lose value and make you money. The odds of this happening are better as a stock gets more volatile and has a bigger potential to move. If IV falls there is less chance of a losing trading climbing out of its hole.

Credit Spreads are short Vega and benefit
when volatility goes down.

IV and Spreads

The further options move from the at the money price in either direction, the smaller the influence volatility has on an option's price. In Figure 14.1 you can see the effect of IV on an option as its IV shrinks. The top curve shows that option's price at a 45% IV. The bottom curve shows the same option's price if its IV dropped to 35%. You can see that the effect is greatest on a 50 Delta ATM option and lessens as it moves away in either direction. When it is at the money, the option may drop from $5.00 to $3.50, but while it's out of the money or in the money it may drop from $2.00 to $1.50. Think of it as if the top curve is made of a bunch of options, starting at 0 Delta on the left and going to 100 with 50 Delta at the top. The change in the two lines at every Delta would be the difference in the option's price at each Delta if IV dropped 10%. You can see that 50 Delta loses more than the 20 and 80 Delta options.

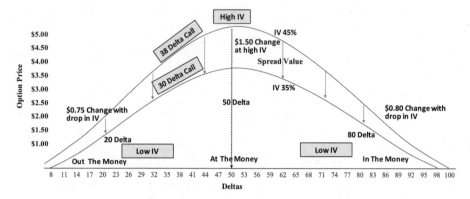

FIGURE 14.1 Spreads' Value Based on IV and Moneyness

The chart could also be used to compare the difference a change in volatility makes in the value of a spread. The top curve could be a 38 Delta call and the bottom one a 30 Delta call. The space in between is their spread price. The left side shows the value of a spread in a low-volatility environment. The middle shows that value as volatility increases, and the right side shows low IV again.

Combining these two thoughts should demonstrate why you should short spreads in stocks that have high IV. It's simply that you will get a much bigger premium, especially in the higher-priced option. If you had shorted with low IV you would start off with smaller premiums, and if volatility rose, you would start losing money.

Table 14.1 shows this more clearly. Going back to the MSFT spread at its current IV, the max profit is $158 with a breakeven of $231.58. If you made this same trade with higher or lower volatility, you would receive a different credit. At a low IV the trade is not worth making. You would be risking $390 to make $110. But at a higher IV you are only risking $300 to make $200. You will always have better odds because of the bigger premiums with any shorting strategy in a stock with a higher volatility.

TABLE 14.1 Effect of IV on Spreads

Short 230 Call	Long 235 Call	Spread	Max Profit	Max Loss	BE
High IV					
$6.75	$4.75	$2	$200	$300	$232.00
Current IV					
$5.93	$4.35	$1.58	$158	$342	$231.58
Low IV					
$5.10	$4.00	$1.10	$110	$390	$231.10

One last thought on volatility. Short put spreads benefit more from volatility, because as stocks go up, volatility tends to drop. Not only does the spread make money directionally, but as the stock goes up, it benefits from the help of a lower volatility. This inverse volatility to price movement won't hurt a call credit spread much, unless the stock's price moves sharply lower, causing a spike in volatility.

Extrinsic Value

When trading credit spreads, you should be keeping track of extrinsic value (EV). I always keep it visible in my positions page. Once a position has a very low extrinsic value, I exit it. Extrinsic value in a short position tells you how much more you can make from the trade. Once extrinsic value is close to zero, there is nothing left to capture and no point in holding a position.

When you are selling a spread, look to have your short option have a higher EV than your long option. This ensures that the short option deteriorates more than the long option, as long as the market behaves according to plan. Remember that if you short an out of the money option, it will only have extrinsic value. If it stays out of the money, all the extrinsic value will be eaten away and is yours to keep. Extrinsic value is always greatest for at the money options. If the short option goes in the money, it starts gaining intrinsic value at the expense of extrinsic value. If the position keeps moving and the long option gets to at the money as well, it will end up having more extrinsic value than the short option. If it keeps going further into the money, the position will worsen for you. This is usually the point where I reevaluate my position, as it means I am wrong in direction. I take a loss if I have to. If I like the position, I may consider redoing it at different strikes to be back on the right side of extrinsic value.

Gamma

Gamma is negative for credit spreads and positive for debit spreads. This is the opposite of Theta as you can't have both working for you. At the money options in the last two to three weeks of trading see an acceleration of Gamma that can easily move an option's Delta. When you are short an option that is slightly out of the money, the risk of it moving from in to out if the money is always there. With plenty of time, this doesn't affect your spread much. But when there are five days to go, it can turn a potential big winner into a big loser. To avoid this risk, exit with at least two weeks to go.

Figuring out Probability of Profit

It's nice to have a brokerage platform that shows you probability of profit, like tastytrade does. If not, you can roughly figure it out fairly easily, as I showed in Chapter 7, by finding the Delta of the breakeven price. This will tell you the probably of an option expiring in the money. For short positions, the formula is the Delta subtracted from 1. If that doesn't make sense, when you are short an option, you don't want it to expire in the money. If a call has a Delta of 0.15, it has a 15% chance of expiring in the money and an 85% chance of it not expiring in the money.

As an example, for a call spread, breakeven is the short strike price plus the credit received. Look at Option Chain 14.3 of MSFT again. The 230/235 credit call spread collects $1.58 in premium, so it has a BE of $230 +$1.58 or $231.58. You can eyeball the option chain and estimate that the Delta of an option with a 231.50 strike would be slightly less than the Delta of the 230 call, which I estimate at about 35. The probability of profit would then be about 65%, which is the same likelihood that the option will expire out of the money. You could get more exact with a calculator, but an estimate is sufficient, and is close enough to the actual 67% I get from tastytrade. You can also get an estimate by dividing the max loss by the spread width, or $342/$500 = 0.68, or 68%. This method assumes efficient pricing and can be used on any trade where you have defined risk and profits.

Return on Buying Power

When buying a spread, the margin requirement is typically the cost of the spread. When you short a spread, the capital requirement is the width of the spread and the buying power reduction is the margin minus the premium received. This is the money you are tying up. When selling options, calculate your return on buying power (RoBP) by dividing how much you made on the trade by how much initial buying power your broker required. Say you shorted the previous spread for $1.58 and got out a few weeks later at $0.75, making $0.83 on this trade. You used $342 in buying power. Your return on margin would be $83/$342, or 24%. If instead you had shorted the 255 call outright, your margin requirement would have been $6,639, and your max profit would be $595. Your maximum return would be about 9% of the buying power you used, with unlimited risk. The spread is a much better use of your capital, as it frees up so much more money for you to use to make more trades.

MAKING HIGH PROBABILITY CREDIT SPREADS

Here are some tips for making the best possible vertical spreads:

IV: Sell spreads when implied volatility is high, as you will get a better premium. If IV is low, consider buying spreads.

Delta: Aim for the Delta on your short option to be less than 50. The closer you get to 50, the more directional the trade will be. The lower the Delta, the higher the POP will be with smaller payouts. Look to buy the option that creates a premium that's at least one-third the width of the spread. Use the lowest short Delta option you can, for this increases your probability of success.

Time frame: Trade the monthly option closest to 45 DTE to expiration. Sell it before 14 DTE.

Target: A good target is 50% of premium collected.

Risk exit: When both strikes go in the money, you should cut your losses, or cut them at a predetermined dollar or percentage amount loss you are comfortable with. A typical set loss is double the premium received.

FINAL THOUGHT

Credit spread trades are a great way to start taking advantages of shorting options. These are high probability trades with modest defined risk. They're easy to get the hang of and can get you started trading the right way.

CHAPTER 15

Straddles and Strangles

S traddles and strangles are similar in nature, so I will include
them together. The only difference is where the strike prices are
in relation to the underlying price. These are the riskiest of any of
the common multi-leg short trades I discuss, as they involve selling
naked calls and puts. They also take up a lot more margin than regular spreads, and when you sell them the loss can be unlimited. These
trades are not for small accounts or the faint of heart. I have taken
quite a beating selling a couple of strangles over the years, but when
straddles or strangles are done in a large sample size over time, the
outliers aren't so bad. However, as I write this, I've seen some massive
earning moves this week, where the selling of a straddle or strangle
would have been painful. These are trades you may want to avoid
during earnings if stocks have been having 25% moves after an earnings release.

Short strangles do have some of the best overall back-tested results
over a large sample size, so you should consider them in a properly
sized account. In the next chapters on iron condors and butterflies, I
discuss how to put risk-defining legs on these trades to dramatically
lower the risk and reduce margin requirements.

BASIC DEFINITION

A straddle, like a strangle, is pretty easy to understand, especially compared to other trades. *A straddle buys or sells both a call and a put with the same strike price and expiration.* The strike price is usually the 50 Delta at the money options, or closest to it if price is not exactly at a strike. You can do straddles that are in or out of the money, but the most common is at the money.

With a stock trading at $85:

A long straddle would be buying both the 85 put and call.

A short straddle would be selling both the 85 put and call.

If you have a stock trading at $87 and the strikes are in $5 intervals (i.e., 85 and 90), you really can't do a straddle. You would have to do a strangle instead.

A *strangle* differs from a straddle in that it trades strike prices that are out of the money. Usually the strikes or Delta are equidistant from the current stock price. But you could have a biased strangle by changing the Delta of one the legs.

A long strangle would be buying the 80 put and 90 call.

A short strangle would be selling the 80 put and 90 call.

LONG STRADDLES AND STRANGLES

Like most of the trades I recommend you will be better off on the short side of these trades. When you are long a straddle or strangle, you have to pay for the trade. You are hoping for a big move that covers the price of both the options you bought. You are fighting time decay and price movement the whole time.

Long straddles and strangles have low probabilities of success, though they do offer defined risk and unlimited profit potential. They are long volatility trades that welcome volatility increases. If implied volatility increases immediately after buying them, the trade can show an unrealized profit as the premiums on both sides should rise in value.

You should only consider these trades during low-volatility scenarios where you expect an increase in IV or a big market moving catalyst that could move the stock significantly in either direction: an earnings release, a Food and Drug Administration decision, a Fed announcement, election results, and so on. To capitalize on this, you would buy both a call and a put to catch that move one way or the other. In a long straddle or strangle, the stock needs to make a move that is greater than the combined premiums of both legs. You are not the only person thinking this stock may have a big move, so premiums may be inflated and volatility will likely fall after the event.

Long Straddles

Long straddles tend to be a fairly relative expensive proposition because they involve buying the two at the money options that have the greatest amount of extrinsic (time) value in them. Long straddles usually have a probability of profit averaging about 46%, meaning a 46% chance of expiring outside the range of the combined premiums. This combined premium is close to an expected one standard deviation move from the current price. So, even if the trade reaches its breakeven level, it will most likely run out of steam and you may not get much follow-through.

In plain English, if a stock is at $100 and you expect a big move one way or the other, a straddle would buy the 100 call and the 100 put. If you paid $7.05 for one and $7.35 for the other, the straddle would cost $14.40, and you need a $14.40 move up or down to break even. That means that to make money at expiration, the stock has to either go below $85.60 or above $114.40 ($100 +/– $14.40). These are the breakeven levels. See Option Chain 15.1 to follow along.

Long Strangles

A long strangle has the same principles as a straddle, though it's cheaper and you may need an even bigger move if your strikes are too far out. In a strangle you buy out of the money puts and calls, again in the same time frame. Maybe buying the 110 call for $3.30 and the 90 put for $3.40, so you pay $6.70 total. It's a bit cheaper than the straddle, but now your breakeven points are further away, at $83.30 and $116.70 with a POP of 37%.

Strangles provide more leverage, as they are cheaper than straddles but will expire worthless more often, making it an even lower probability trade than a straddle. The breakeven levels are further away as the probability of profit starts at 46% with near the money options and shrinks as the Deltas get lower as you go further out of the money.

I am not going to spend more time on buying straddles and strangles because I never trade them. If you are inclined to buy them, just reverse everything I discuss about shorting them.

SHORTING STRADDLES AND STRANGLES

When it comes to straddles and strangles, I much prefer being on the short side of the trade. I don't normally trade straddles, as I find them a bit riskier, but I do a fair amount of strangles. Straddles and strangles eat up a lot of buying power, the same as shorting a put or call outright. Buying power can change once you're in a trade, if the market moves or volatility changes. If that happens and you're already maxed out on your buying power, you will get a margin call and will be force to either liquidate something or deposit money.

Strangles in particular have a very high probability of success, so professional traders like this trade. But they do have unlimited risk, so be careful in trading them. They can be a "get rich slowly and go broke quickly" situation if you let one big move get away. They do come with limited maximum gains, which is the premium received from selling them.

BOTH SIDES CAN'T BURN YOU

With all two-sided short trades, such as iron condors, you can only lose money on one side of the trade at expiration. If the call is in the money, the put side will be out of the money. One side will always be somewhat profitable, no matter how much the other side loses. Because of this, the margin requirement for a short straddle or strangle is not the margin requirement of a short put plus that of the short call. It's just the margin requirement of the largest side.

Short Straddles and Strangles Traits

Delta-neutral strategy to start, and you don't care what direction the stock moves.

Defined maximum profit with unlimited loss potential.

Collects premium in exchange for unlimited risk.

Short Vega benefits from falling volatility.

Long Theta benefits from time decay.

Short Gamma benefits from very little price movement.

Strangles have a high probability of success.

These are trades you want to make when you think the market is range bound. Your hope is for the options to expire worthless, and/or you believe implied volatility will fall or stay roughly the same. If you are wrong and the underlying stock moves significantly in either direction, you should get out quickly as there is no limit on how much you can lose. Actually, on the downside, the limit is that the stock can only go to zero, but that still could be a ton of money. Straddles and strangles tend to work because, in an efficient market, option prices reflect where the stock should be at expiration. It is more likely than not that the stock will not move past the trade's breakeven point. As I previously mentioned in Chapter 5, volatility tends to get overstated, so the stock may fall a bit short of where the options are pricing it to be.

STRANGLE GONE AWRY

I sold a strangle on Snap at earnings two years ago. You can see when in the circle on Chart 15.1. I don't recall the exact numbers, but with Snap trading at about $28.50 and earnings coming out, I sold a strangle outside of its predicted range: probably the 25 put and 32 call, strikes that were more than a 10% move away. I received around $200 in premium believing it would stay in that range. Instead, Snap was up 35% the next day and didn't look back for a year. I stayed in the trade longer than I should have, hoping for a pullback. Eventually I lost nearly $1,500 on the trade. This kind of loss can wipe out 5 to 10 good trades. Luckily, this was a low-priced stock, so it wasn't a horrendous loss, but over the years I have seen many ridiculous overnight moves in stocks. So take it as a warning and be careful. Big moves like this are more common than you think. Also don't forget, no matter how good your money management plan is, you need to stick to it all the time for it to work. I didn't in this example, and it came back to hurt me.

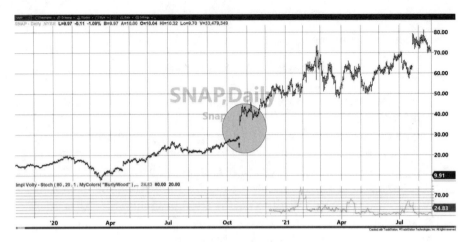

CHART 15.1 Snap After Earnings
Source: TradeStation

Short Straddle

A short straddle sells both the at the money put and call. The most money you can make is the total premium collected, if at expiration the stock settles at that price. Option Chain 15.1, Meta Strangle, is set up as a short strangle. If it were a short straddle, it would be selling the 100 put and call. As a straddle it collects $14.40 in premium, which is the maximum profit, that can only be achieved if the stock is at $100 on expiration. The breakeven levels on the trade are at 100 +/– the combined premium, so the low-side breakeven is $100 – $14.40 = $85.60 and the high-side breakeven is $100 + 14.40 = $114.40

BREAKEVEN FOR STRADDLES AND STRANGLES

Straddles and strangles have two breakeven points: one if the market rallies and the other on the downside. For a short trade to make a profit it needs to stay inside these points. For a long trade it needs to be outside the range.

Breakeven for put = put strike − premium

Breakeven for call = call strike + premium

The probability of profit for this straddle is 54%, as opposed to 46% if it were a long straddle, which tells you that shorting a straddle works more often than buying one. One problem with a straddle is that the max profit is only achieved at a single specific price. As the straddle moves in either direction, your profit dwindles until you reach the breakeven levels. (Payoff Diagram 15.1 later in this section shows a payoff diagram for both straddles and strangles.)

OPTION CHAIN 15.1 Meta Strangle

Source: tastytrade

Short Strangle

A *short strangle* is a better trade than a short straddle, at least in my opinion. Strangles have a wider profit zone allowing for more wiggle room for a stock to move. It also comes with a higher probability of making money. The trade-off is a much lower maximum profit potential. A short strangle uses strike prices that are out of the money from the current price. The call is above the current price and the put is below the current price. The goal and hope is to have the stock price settle in between the two strike prices. Unlike the straddle, where max profit depends on the stock settling at a chosen strike price, a strangle achieves max profit anywhere in between the strike prices. Both strangles and straddles begin close to Delta neutral, but the strangle has more room before a change in Delta hurts. The Meta position has a little call skew, so the net Delta is slightly negative, as you are shorting a bigger Delta on the call side.

The strangle shown in the Option Chain 15.1 Meta Strangle has a 77% probability of profit, using the 16 Delta, one standard deviation away options. Its max profit is only $279. That's much less than the straddle, but the strangle works more often because of its wider breakeven levels. Look at Payoff Diagram 15.1 for a short straddle and strangle. The strangle is the dotted line. Notice the wider payoff area compared to the straddle; the trade-off though is the much lower max profit. To be profitable, the stock would have to stay within the shaded area by expiration. I prefer the strangle as it's not so easy to pinpoint where a stock will be in the future and I prefer its wider profit area.

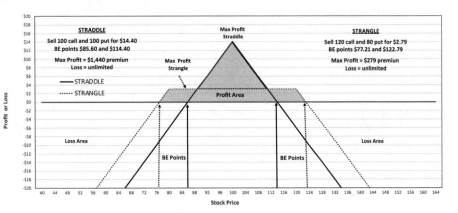

PAYOFF DIAGRAM 15.1 Short Straddle and Strangle

PROBABILITY OF PROFIT

You can estimate the probability of profit by finding the Deltas of both breakeven points and adding them together. Subtract from a 100 for short positions.

Probability of profit =
100 – (Delta of BE low side + Delta of BE high side)

SKEW AND DIRECTIONALITY

You don't always have to trade equidistant Deltas or strikes. If the option table shows skew to one side, you can adjust your strike on one side. Say there was a little more call skew in the Meta example, implying upside risk. The 120 calls had a 20 Delta trading at $2.00, and the 125 calls had a 13 Delta trading at $1.20. You could trade the strangle with the 125 call and 80 put to even out the trade's Delta.

You may also see times when both sides have an option with the same Delta but different prices. Perhaps the 20 Delta put is $2.50 and the 20 Delta call is $3.00. You could move the call to next lower strike to balance out the premiums and get an extra buffer on the call side. The net Delta would have a slight positive bias, but moving the strike makes it a little safer.

You can make a straddle or strangle directional by moving one or both strikes. If you tighten one leg you are willing to get paid more, believing the stock will likely head in the other direction. You also don't have to make the trade around the at the money price. If you believe Meta will drop to around $90 in a few weeks, you can place the trade so it revolves around that price. You could (for instance) sell the 51 Delta 100 call and –13 Delta 80 put for about $8.45, which will give you new breakeven parameters. If you did this, your position would no longer start at Delta neutral, but with a –38 Delta. You now need the stock to move into that price range to make a profit. I prefer to structure a trade around the at the money strike price, hoping that the stock stays within its expected range while also looking for volatility implosion. I will move a leg out if there is skew.

GREEK EXPOSURE

Because these trades have no protective legs acting as an opposite force, strangles and straddles are more sensitive to the Greeks than are other multi-legged trades. Straddles and strangles rely heavily on time decay and volatility to make them work. Ideally the gains made from Theta and Vega outweigh any loss caused by a move in the stock.

Theta

Not only does Theta work faster on straddles and strangles, but you get double the time premiums, because both options gain simultaneously from time decay. A short strangle always has positive Theta for the trade's whole duration. Even if one option is in the money and losing money, there will still be some extrinsic value left that can be recouped. The trade may still lose money, but if the stock doesn't get worse you could perhaps lose a little less. The META strangle has a combined Theta of 8.48, so it will gain $8.48 every day for now and pick up steam nearer expiration, assuming it stays near the money.

Vega and Volatility

Straddles and strangles are volatility trades. You want to short them when a stock has high implied volatility with inflated premiums, and when the implied volatility rank or percentile are high with a chance of getting lower. The Meta strangle has a combined Vega of –16.57, so it will gain $16.57 for every point that implied volatility drops. The higher the IV, the further out in strike prices you can go to collect the same amount of money compared to a trade with low IV. If the IV rank is too low, you may not receive sufficient premium to offset price movement past small breakeven points, making this a long run unprofitable trading strategy.

Delta and Gamma

Both straddles and strangles start with a net Delta very close to zero, as the call's long Delta cancels the put's short Delta. Once the market starts moving, you will see the Delta move. If you were short the Meta 80/120 strangle, you would start with a –3 Delta. If the stock moved to 90, the put becomes less out of the money, which is bad for your short put, and may have a –28 Delta. The call moves further out of the money and may have a 7 Delta, giving you a trade with a net 21 Delta. Since you are short, don't forget to reverse the Delta signs. Now you are rooting for a move back up to get you back to Delta neutral.

The Gamma (Γ on the bottom of Option Chain 15.1) in this trade is – 2.41; it tells you what I just wrote. A 10 point negative move changes the Delta by about 24 points, giving the position a +21 net Delta. Once you near expiration, Gamma increases sharply, and a 10 point move can easily turn a trade that is near a breakeven level into a loser. Gamma is always negative for short strangles and straddles, so they benefit when there is little price movement.

Reducing Risk

To reduce the outlier risk that a stock can represent, you can use ETFs instead of stocks for strangles. Whenever you have a naked position in a stock, you are at risk to company-specific events. Make sure you know when earnings are being released and avoid having your position on during that time—unless you are trading earnings, in which case enter the trade just before the market closes the day earnings are announced to get the highest implied volatility possible. In addition to earnings, other events can cause an outlier move in a stock. When Disney unexpectedly fired its CEO and replaced him with its old CEO, the stocked moved 10% premarket. ETFs take this single stock risk away, as it is not so easy for a whole sector to make a punishing move overnight.

You also reduce risk by selling when IVR is on the high side. Selling into high IV means getting richer premiums that make the probability of profit on a trade a little better. Do not sell strangles without knowing that IV rank is high. Be selective in your trades and you will be putting the odds in your favor.

Adjusting

If you sell the 80/120 Meta strangle and the stock rallies to $115, the 80 put will not have much value left in it. When this happens, you are better off buying the put back, as it has very little upside to give you. You could then sell a higher put, such as the 95, and receive a decent credit for doing so. This increases the trade's total premium and breakeven levels, giving the 120 call a little more breathing room.

BEST CONDITIONS FOR SHORT STRANGLES AND STRADDLES

Following are the best conditions for short strangles and straddles.

Stock Price

Straddles and strangles work best on lower-priced stocks trading in the $50 to $150 range, with a generally modest historical volatility. These typically don't have the potential to really hurt you. I wouldn't recommend trading a strangle on $400 stock with an IV of 90% that can move $50 in a day, unless you are a thrill seeker. I prefer selling a strangle in stocks with a more stable price and an IV of 40%.

Ideal Strangle Strikes

You can choose any strikes you like, with the caveat that the closer to the current stock price they are, the lower the chance of making money is—but your potential max profit will be greater. Using options with Deltas at or below a one standard deviation increases your chances of the market staying within the expected range and in between the strike prices. The best results come with the 16 to 20 Delta strikes. You may go up to 30 Delta (with a probability of profit around 60%) if you're feeling risky, but that's about it. The 16 Delta strike will give you around a 75% chance of success and the 20 Delta about 70%. Your probability of profit is reduced to about 55% as you reach the at the money level, where the trade then becomes a straddle.

Make sure you get paid. You don't want to short Deltas so low that you are not making much on the trade. Going too low means you are taking on a lot of risk for barely any reward. Never assume that strikes are too far away to be hit, because one day a strike may get hit that could wipe out a year's profit.

Trade Length

Strangles and straddles can be dangerous, so you don't want to hold them for too long. Like I've been preaching, enter with about 45 days to expiration and exit with around 21 days left. Straddles should be held for less time due to their tighter breakeven area. You can hold strangles a little longer. In either case, take your profit if your target is reached before a stock has a chance to move and turn your winner into a loser.

Exit Targets

More than any other trades, straddles and strangles should have exit strategies. As they are riskier, be quick to take a profit and manage your losses before they get out of hand. Exact max loss targets won't always be possible because a stock can gap open, especially after an earnings report, and leave you holding the bag. But learn from my Snap mistake and get out after a loss target level is breached and don't hope for a reversal.

Winners

Don't overstay your welcome with these trades. If you get a good profit quickly because IV drops right away, take it before it disappears. Profits in straddles should be taken quicker than in strangles:

Exit straddles at around a 30% to 40% profit

Exit strangles at around a 50% to 60% profit

Losses

Straddles: Take losses at 50% of total premium. If you receive $1,000 for the trade, don't lose more than $500.

Strangles: Take losses at 100% of total premium or when one of your strikes is breached.

FINAL THOUGHTS

Strangles and straddles aren't for the faint of heart, but strangles in particular are one of the best trades you can make. They offer a great probability of profit and increased rewards over shorting one side of the market. Short strangles on a one-off basis can hurt, but when done over a large sample size, they have some of the best results of any option strategy.

CHAPTER 16

Iron Condors

Along with vertical spreads, iron condors are what I trade the most. I will put one on directly as an iron condor or sometimes turn a vertical spread into one by shorting another spread on the other side of the stock price. This is a great way to keep my portfolio Delta neutral. It's also the way I am most likely to make an earnings play if I am not directionally biased, in which case I would use a diagonal spread. I am only discussing shorting iron condors because I would never buy one.

An iron condor can be viewed two ways: either as a strangle with protection, or as the shorting of both a call spread above the current price of the underlying and a put spread below the current price at the same time and the same expiration. The goal is to place the shorts at a distance the stock is unlikely to reach so that the stock stays between the two spreads, just like when shorting a strangle. These trades are great high probability trades that may not make much per trade, but do provide a nice return on equity without the unlimited risks of a strangle.

Here are some characteristics of iron condors:

Risk defined: Iron condors have limited gains (the credit received) as well as predetermined max losses (max width of spread minus credit received). You can control the amount of risk by adjusting the wings (the width). The wider the wings, the more risk but the greater the profit potential becomes.

Long Theta and short Vega: Like strangles, time decay and/or a drop in IV works for you.

Nondirectional: It starts as a Delta neutral position but can shift as the market moves. You can adjust an iron condor to be directionally biased by making one side closer to the current stock price.

Probability of success: When compared to a strangle, the iron condor has a lower POP, around 60% to 70% for the 16 to 20 Delta strikes, but it also comes with a limited risk.

Slow moving: Like spreads, because of its two protective legs, profits take longer to generate than with naked positions.

Low margin requirements: Due to the lower risk, iron condors have a fairly low margin requirement, allowing you to trade more expensive stocks that would be too costly in margin if done as a strangle.

IRON CONDOR IN DETAIL

Continuing with Meta on Option Chain 16.1, it's now two days after the strangle in the last chapter, and with the stock now down to $95.20 here is an iron condor trade. Looking at just the short options (115 call and 80 put) you can see it's the same as the strangle, except that I've lowered the 120 call to the 115 strike. Normally you would want to be equidistant from the current price, however I am looking to use as close to the 16 Delta option as possible; in this case the calls are one strike further OTM than the puts due to the skew.

As opposed to a short strangle that has unlimited loss and significant reduction in buying power, if you buy the 120 call and 75 put as protective legs to the strangle, the trade is now limited in how much it can lose. This, in effect, now makes your trade a short call spread with a short put spread, that's placed at a "safe" distance from the current price. Like a strangle, you want the stock to settle in between the two short legs. These protective options are similar to buying a higher strangle to protect your short strangle.

The breakeven points are calculated the same way as a strangle: adding the total premium to the short call strike and subtracting it from the short put. Or you can calculate it like the breakeven of two spreads, but using the total premium. In this case, the premium is $1.15, so the breakeven levels are now tighter at $78.85 and $116.15.

By making this trade versus a strangle, you are lowering your max profit quite a bit to only $115 instead of $279; however, you are now capped at $385 loss. The $385 is also the buying power reduction for making this trade, much lower than for a strangle. This will increase your return on margin and will allow you to have more capital available for other trading opportunities, leading to a more diversified account. As you will see in Chapter 19, a diversified portfolio of trades is one of the most important tools in being a winning trader.

I probably would not make this trade, as I prefer to see a higher percent of max profit to max loss. For a 68% POP, you should get close to a 32% max profit to spread width. At $115 to $500, the max profit is only 23%. Remember, try to get the profit ratio plus POP equal to or over 1.

Like spreads, a 1:3 ratio of max profit to the width of one of the spreads is a good target to shoot for; a max profit of $167 for the $500 spread width would make for a better trade. This is the same as the max profit being half the value of the max loss. In order to achieve that target, you would need to increase the Deltas a bit. If you were to narrow this condor to the 110 call and 85 put, still with $5-wide wings, then you would be getting a premium of $180-ish, which would give you the 1:3 premium to spread width. Meta had just had earnings and the IV has come down considerably, shrinking the value of the options so the premiums aren't worth as much; looking at a higher-IV stock, like I will in the coming pages, it's easier to achieve this premium.

OPTION CHAIN 16.1 An Iron Condor Not Worth Making

Source: tastytrade

THE PROTECTIVE WINGS

The protective wings are what defines the risks and rewards in iron condors. Making the best use of where you place them will have an impact on your trading. Here are a few things to keep in mind.

Max Loss and the Wings

The max loss will be defined by the width of the protective long options to the short options, in the same way as a credit spread. Since you can only lose on one side, it's just the spread of either side. In the Meta example, both the call and put side have $5.00-wide spreads. This trade has a max loss of $500 minus the total premium received ($115), or $385. If one side of the iron condor has a larger spread, then the max loss would be calculated from that side.

POP and the Wings

The probability of success on an iron condor will be less than that of a strangle because you are collecting less premium, which results in tighter breakeven levels. This means that it has a greater chance it may expire outside of those breakeven levels. One way to increase the POP and the max profit is by moving the protective wings further out. This gives you a bigger premium and more breathing room, but it comes with a bigger potential loss.

Narrow Wings

If you are looking to lower your risk and seeking a higher return on capital, you will want to use tighter wings. In exchange, you will be giving up premium so you won't be making as much per trade. You will also have a lower POP with a higher chance of reaching the max loss. Very narrow wings will reduce the effect of Theta and Vega on your trades, as the long and short options will have Greeks that aren't far apart and will almost cancel each other out. This will result in a slow-moving trade.

Wider Wings

When you expand your wings, you are getting bigger premiums and further breakeven points. You will also have larger max loss levels, but these are less likely to be achieved. As you widen your wings, you will also experience fewer losing trades due to the wider breakeven points. If you move the wings out far enough, the trade basically becomes a strangle, as you will have very little protection and the trade is unlikely to hit your max levels. In general, condors react slowly to Theta and Vega, but you can increase that response time by widening the spreads. This will also mean that if you are correct, you can reach your target profit sooner.

I am using $5 wings in the Meta example, but if you were to move the wings to 125 and 70, increasing your buffer zone to $10 on each side, the results would be a 70% POP and $187 max profit, with a max loss of $813. In my back-testing I have found that strangles will out-perform iron condors, so I don't mind the wider wings.

When starting out and still in the learning phases, I recommend using narrower wings to keep your losses low, especially in small accounts. Once you get comfortable trading, especially with portfolio management, you can expand your risk.

WIDER IS BETTER

I recall a tastylive.com study showing that on a 30 Delta SPY iron condor, a $1-wide wing would expire at max loss 61% of the time, a $5-wide wing 32% of the time, while at $10 wide it will only achieve max loss 6% of the time.

GREEK EXPOSURE

You might think, "sometime today, please." Compared to a strangle, an iron condor's Greeks are slow to react, especially when you have tight protective wings. If the legs are too tight, as in a $2.00-wide spread in a $400 stock, the Greeks will not do much until very close to expiration. Time decay will not move as fast for you, because while in a strangle you have Theta working on every option, in a condor the protective wings are long positions and will get hurt by time decay, albeit at a lesser pace than the short legs. This is still a time decay trade, but not as fast as a naked position. The same applies for the Vega; much of a drop in IV will be offset by a drop in IV of the wings. This means it's a slow-moving trade, and you may barely see any gains at first. If you use 45 DTE to make this trade you may not see a dramatic move in the first two weeks, even if the stock doesn't move. Its only when you widen your wings that you will see quicker moves; with narrower wings you will need to hold longer to see a substantial profit.

Theta

When an iron condor is working properly you will start to see Theta accelerate around the 30-day mark. Prior to that, time decay will be slow to react. The Theta of an iron condor works like that of a credit spread: it will have positive Theta as long as it stays out of the money, but then Theta will work against it if one of the sides moves into the money. Once it's in the money you will be losing a bit of time value every day until the trade goes back into the safety zone. This differs from a strangle, which will always have positive Theta.

You can see this in Payoff Diagram 16.1, where any price outside the short strikes puts you in the negative Theta/loss area. Increasing the size of the wings would move the breakeven points further away, reducing the chance of it reaching this negative Theta area, as it takes a little more price movement for the stock to get there.

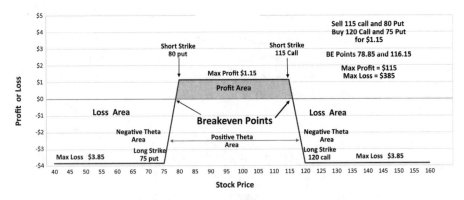

PAYOFF DIAGRAM 16.1 Short Iron Condor

Vega

IV works similarly to credit spreads. The closer to ATM the stock price is, the more aggressively each spread will react. Though an iron condor starts with negative Vega, and drops in IV help the position, it will also slow down and then reverse like Theta does if one side goes deep enough ITM. The net Vega on the position will tell you how much the position will move with every point change in volatility.

Gamma

Gamma is the same as for all previous strategies, so there is not much more to add here. Always remember, to reduce Gamma risk exit your trades with 14 to 21 days to expiration.

Delta

Iron condors will pretty much start as a Delta-neutral position, and won't stray too far from there until you near expiration or one side goes in the money. If one side starts gaining too much Delta, it means you have a bad position, and you should either get out or adjust the winning side to give you more Delta.

ADJUSTING

This is similar to strangles, in that if the market has moved far enough in one direction that the other side is worth very little, you should take your profits or adjust the winning side. If you want to earn more premium, then move that side a little bit closer; this will move the breakeven on the tested side a little further away. By the tested side, I mean the side that the stock price is approaching and starting to worry you. Alternatively, if you don't mind the Delta exposure you could keep one side open; the important thing to remember is to take off the side that has very little to gain.

BEST CONDITIONS

Following are the best conditions for iron condor trading.

Volatility

As with all shorting trades, you are looking for a high IV environment, one for better premiums and second to profit from if you think volatility will revert back down, or at worst stay stable. If IV keeps rising after you are in, it lowers your chances of making money. A rising IV will increase the expected range of a stock, making it easier for the stock to move outside the range of your breakeven prices. The key to trading high volatility is to try to sell when volatility is stable or falling, not just when implied volatility is simply "high." Though high IV will give you the best bang for your buck, if it keeps getting stronger, that's not a good sign for your trade.

Range-Bound Market

I always use charts looking for support and resistance levels that can help me find a range to place my legs. A range-bound market is best, but keep in mind that what is range bound today may not be in a month. After looking at the charts, I then look at Deltas and expected range to make sure they confirm my opinion.

Time Frame

Time frame will be the same as usual: 45 days to enter, and exit at two or three weeks. Though I won't recommend trading iron condors with little time left, there are some traders that will try to capitalize on the more rapid time decay. This is full-time trading, and you must be quick to exit should you get a large move. One way to trade short term is to trade a condor with two weeks to go at the beginning of the week and exit by Friday; stay away from risk over the weekend, and never hold into the last week. One risk with short-term trading is that to get any worthwhile premium, you have to place your trades close to the money. You may end up having to trade 30 Delta options or more to receive a decent premium, but this makes the trade Gamma risky. The only time I do recommend trading very short term is for earning trades—but when wrong, your max loss can be hit pretty quickly.

Exit Targets

You shouldn't let an iron condor fully decay; instead, aim to capture around 50% of premium received, or be out of it with about three weeks to go to reduce the Gamma risk. If you make 20% or 30% in the first week, that's a great trade, and you can take the money and find a new trade. None of these are set rules, but they are good back-tested strategies. Take a loss as you would a spread. When the stock goes outside one of the long wings and a side is in the money, your assumptions were wrong, and it should be a clue it's time to exit. In this example, it would be if Meta were to go above 120 or below 75.

Wing Sizes

Don't go too narrow; a one-strike protective leg on SPY trading at $411 is going to be a very slow-moving trade, which will have very little Greek exposure. Look to trade wings that are about 5% of the stock price. Typically, use $5-wide wings on stock up to and around the $100 range; you can go to $10 on stocks trading around $200 and so on. Don't go wider than you can afford or want to lose.

RETURNS

In the Meta example, the trade has a 68% POP with a potential $115 reward and a max risk of $385.

This 115/385 equals 29.87% return on margin, which is better than a strangle, which requires a much bigger outlay. If you can get closer to one-third the width of the strike price, then that return is 50% of your buying power used. Before putting on a trade, play around with the wings, or move the whole condor further in or out, to see if you can get a better risk/reward ratio compared to the probability of success of a trade.

Probabilities of Success Versus Risk/Reward

You can figure this out in a similar way to credit spreads, by calculating the Deltas of the breakeven points on each side, then combining them. In the Meta example, the $1.15 premium may move the Deltas by about 1 point on each side, so the breakeven Deltas would about 15 and 16; add these to get 31, then subtract from 100 to get a 69% chance of not expiring in the money. This compares nicely to the 68% POP used by the tastytrade platform.

Risk/Reward Method

In Chapter 7, I mentioned using the profit ratio (max profit/width of spread) to estimate POP; here, that ratio is 115/500, or 0.23; subtracted from 1, it estimates the probability of profit at 77%. The software POP of 68% suggests you should have a higher profit, closer to a 32% profit ratio. Try to get a POP plus profit ratio that adds up to close to or better than 100%, this will help put the odds in your favor.

A BETTER TRADE

Though the previous Meta example is a trade I wouldn't make, Option Chain 16.2 shows an NVDA iron condor setup that works much better. With the NVDA trade you are now getting more than one-third the width of the max loss, and the profit ratio is 181/500 = 0.362, which when added to the POP of 63% is pretty close to 1, making it a fair value trade. You are giving up a little probability of success, but you get a higher return for it and the strikes are still outside the expected range. As the title of this book implies, it is worth waiting for the high-probability opportunities to make a trade, rather than trading for the sake of trading.

| NVDA | IV Rank 31.5 | Last X Size 211.00 Q 2.36M | Chg -6.09 | Bid X 210.68 P | Ask X 211.00 P | Size 4x24 | Volume 42.9M | NASDAQ NVIDIA Corp | | Accounts ⌄ ‹ |

TRADE MODE: TABLE ⌄ | ANALYSIS STRATEGY: NORMAL | IRON CONDOR | GO ⌄ STRIKES: 20 ⌄ CONFIG

o Impl Vol	o Delta	Bid	Ask	⌄ Strike	40d	Puts	Bid	Ask	o Delta	o Impl Vol
⌃ Mar 17, 2023	o		Calls	40d						IVx: 57.4% (±28.19)
51.72%	0.16	2.58	3.05	255			44.80	46.30	-0.87	45.75%
51.62%	0.19	3.60	3.85	250			40.60	44.70	-0.84	46.77%
51.67%	0.22	4.45	5.55	245			35.50	40.40	-0.80	47.33%
51.84%	0.26	5.40	5.65	240			31.35	36.25	-0.76	47.64%
51.91%	0.30	6.60	6.70	235			29.55	32.30	-0.72	48.12%
52.19%	0.34	8.00	8.10	230			25.95	28.60	-0.67	48.54%
52.62%	0.39	9.60	9.75	225			22.60	22.80	-0.62	49.14%
53.08%	0.44	11.50	11.65	220			19.50	19.65	-0.57	49.71%
53.77%	0.49	13.65	13.80	215			16.65	16.80	-0.51	50.38%
54.40%	0.54	16.10	16.25	210			14.10	14.25	-0.46	51.06%
55.13%	0.59	18.80	19.00	205			11.85	12.00	-0.40	51.77%
56.02%	0.64	21.80	21.95	200			9.85	10.00	-0.35	52.55%
57.06%	0.69	23.75	26.10	195			8.10	8.25	-0.30	53.45%
58.11%	0.73	28.50	28.90	190			6.60	6.75	-0.26	54.32%
59.35%	0.77	31.50	32.60	185			5.35	5.45	-0.22	55.36%
60.31%	0.81	34.90	36.55	180			4.30	4.40	-0.18	56.19%
61.94%	0.84	39.60	41.35	175			3.40	3.50	-0.15	57.42%
63.65%	0.86	44.10	44.95	170			2.70	2.76	-0.12	58.53%
66.04%	0.88	46.35	49.40	165			2.12	2.17	-0.10	59.79%
68.25%	0.90	50.80	54.10	160			1.65	1.70	-0.08	61.05%

| POP 63% | EXT 181 | P50 75% | Delta 0.33 | Theta 2.331 | Max Profit 181 | Max Loss -319 | BP Eff 319.00 db ⌃ |

OPTION CHAIN 16.2 NVDA

Source: tastytrade

TRADING EARNINGS

Though you can use several strategies for earnings, the concept is the same: you want to take advantage of the impending volatility crush. It's now two weeks after the previous NVDA example, and earnings are being announced today after the close. I've decided to sell an iron condor on it as an example. As earnings approached, the volatility has become inflated. These same March 17 options now have an IV of 63%. The expiring contract with two days to go has an IV of 114%, as they are the options that will be the most affected by earnings. For a neutral strategy like this, or a strangle, you want to put on a credit-type trade outside the expected range of the earnings move. You could also use a straddle. The hope is that the price move will be less than expected, and volatility will come crashing down. What makes these trades attractive is that the credit received at earnings is much higher than it would normally be.

Trade Setup

With an iron condor, the ideal situation is to short the 16 or 20 Delta options, getting one-third the width of the strikes. Short the 16 Delta if you can get the right price. You want to sell the soonest expiring contract, which will see the biggest IV crush. Put on your trade just before the close and get out soon after the open the next day. These are very short-term trades, as you would only hold them for one day.

The first thing I like to do is get an earning's expected move for the stock; you can do this with the option table's expected range, the Deltas, or add up the at the money put and call. I also like to go MarketChameleon.com to get a detailed look at earnings expectations, including previous earnings moves.

Trade Details

Current price: $207.54

Expected next day move: +/–$13.95

Expected range: $193.50 to $221.50

DTE: 9

IV: 74.38%

Trade Setup

Sold 19 Delta 190 put and 18 Delta 230 call (the target I expect price to be in)

Bought 185 put and 235 call for protection

Credit received: $163

Breakeven: $188.37 and $231.63

POP: 65%

Net Vega: –3.49

I feel this is a safe range outside the expected move, and I am hoping it stays in that range and volatility comes tumbling down, at which point I will exit for a quick profit. Usually with earnings trades you should do them in the expiring contract for the biggest IV crush, but I choose nine days out as a price buffer in case of a big move, which has been happening to the upside recently. This would let me get out with a smaller loss if wrong.

Update, 4:30 P.M.
Earnings are out and the stock is up about 9%, trading around $225. Hopefully it sells off a bit premarket tomorrow, or at least doesn't go up any more so I can get out with small profit. I will update you in the morning.

Update, 10 A.M. the Next Day
Nvidia kept going up; it opened at $232.25, sold off for a few minutes, then rallied back up. I exited the trade at $3.20, losing $157 on the trade (actually it was $323 as I had two contracts on plus commissions and fees), knowing I was wrong. IV did come down to 54%, but this time price movement won.

UPDATE THREE MONTHS AND A WEEK LATER

You would think I learned a lesson on that trade. But I am editing this chapter three months later and just did another earnings iron condor on Nvidia a week ago. This time it went from $305 to $390 overnight. That's a ridiculous eight standard deviation move! Boy am I glad I didn't do a strangle. I lost $657 this time around, which is a reasonable loss for me. I have owned a good amount of the stock outright for quite a while, so overall I am OK with the small earnings lost.

Vega
The net Vega on this trade was –3.49; if the stock hadn't moved so extremely and IV had come off by 20% like it did, the trade should have dropped by about $70, which is the Vega times change in IV. The issue with this trade was that stock moved past my breakeven point, so the gain in Vega wasn't able to offset the directional loss. If there had been a smaller move, then IV would have dropped by even more, increasing the potential profits on the trade. You can see this volatility

crush in Table 16.1. Two things to note: first, the further expirations don't have as much of an elevated volatility, and second, they don't really drop off after earnings. The soonest expiring option is the one that will get you the most bang for your buck.

TABLE 16.1 IV Crush

	BEFORE EARNINGS		AFTER EARNINGS	
Expiration	DTE	IV	DTE	IV
Feb 24, 2023	2	114.15%	1	83.43%
Mar 3, 2023	9	74.38%	8	54.14%
Mar 10, 2023	16	69.21%	15	54.46%
Mar 17, 2023	23	62.97%	22	55.10%
Mar 24, 2023	30	62.60%	29	56.11%
Mar 31, 2023	37	61.01%	36	55.08%
Apr 21, 2023	58	56.82%	57	52.33%
May 19, 2023	86	55.82%	85	54.30%

And that is your typical iron condor earnings trade.

FINAL THOUGHT

Iron condors are a great risk-defined way to start taking advantage of neutral markets and volatility contractions. They are not as profitable as strangles, but that is the trade-off you make for limited risk.

CHAPTER 17

Butterflies

N ext up are butterflies, which I am breaking onto two types:

The basic butterfly

Broken wing butterfly

These are the trades that will make the most money if you can pinpoint where a stock will be in the future. Butterflies are one of the few trades you should make with less time till expiration, as they don't move much at all until they are close to expiration. These are trades that also work better with high volatility. Out of the two, the broken wing butterfly has the best potential, and it is the one I am more likely to trade and will discuss in the most detail, but they have the same principles, easiest to understand by starting with a basic butterfly. There is also an iron butterfly, which is a straddle with protective wings; it has the same relationship as an iron condor to a strangle, but I never trade these, preferring iron condors instead.

THE BASIC BUTTERFLY

A regular butterfly is not a trade I make often due to its low probability of success, though it does have a very high return ratio. These can be long shot trades that, if you can pinpoint where a stock will be, can be quite rewarding. It is a spread-type trade, falling somewhere between a straddle and an iron condor.

The typical butterfly shorts two at the money calls or puts (one or the other, not both), then buys one in the money option and one out of the money option; all three strikes are either puts or calls, it doesn't matter which. A butterfly would look symmetrical with the outer wings equidistant from the body of the butterfly (the two shorts). You can also think of a butterfly as a long and short vertical spread that both have the same short strike.

Like a short straddle, the max profit in a butterfly is at the short strike price and works best in a high IVR situation due to better premiums. Unlike other trades I've been mentioning, butterflies are made for a debit, usually pretty small, but have positive Theta and negative Vega like credit trades have. Butterflies can be counterintuitive as they are debit trades, and I have been stressing that you want to sell premium in your trading. The reason for this discrepancy is that a long butterfly is really a short trade as the two short options, or the body of the butterfly, are the defining part of the trade. The wings are still put on for protection, but since one will have a higher Delta and price, the trade ends up costing a little bit to put on.

Butterflies are risk and profit defined. You can only lose the price you paid for it, and your profits are limited by the width of the wings. They have a very low probability of success; depending on the width of the spreads, the probability of profit can be around 5% to 40%. They usually cost very little to put on. A $1-wide spread can cost $5 with a $95 max profit, while having a POP of around 8%. It is no better than buying a box in a Super Bowl pool or betting on a number at a roulette table. It gives you something to root for and has a nice payoff when it hits, though it's a long shot that you won't hit very often. If you widen the wings to the width of the expected range, the POP gets closer to 45%, with corresponding higher costs and profit potential.

THE CONCEPT

Option Chain 17.1 of Coinbase (COIN) is set up as a butterfly with directional bias, as it is how I prefer to trade butterflies. If you did this as an at the money butterfly, then you want no movement in the stock—but how often does that happen, especially in a high-IV stock? Either way, you are trying to pick where the stock will be as it nears expiration, with the end goal being to capture as much extrinsic value as possible in that time.

OPTION CHAIN 17.1 Coinbase

Source: tastytrade

If this were a typical nondirectional ATM butterfly, it would entail selling two 70 ATM calls and buying an ITM 65 call and an OTM 75 call. This could also be done on the put side with the exact same results; the primary goal is for the stock not to move much. In either case, the trade would cost about $17 with a $483 potential profit, including a very low POP as there is little chance of the stock being at $70 at expiration. You could also buy the 50 and 90 calls for a wider profit area; now you would be paying about $600 to make $1,400. I wouldn't make this trade, as the deep in the money options have too wide a spread. If this were your goal, you'd be better off with an iron butterfly; this would entail selling the 70 put and call and buying the 50 put and 90 call for protection. In this case, the results would be the same, but the iron butterfly allows you to buy a cheaper OTM put, with a tighter spread and more liquidity, and you would receive a credit instead of a debit. This is much the same as an ATM iron condor, with a probability of success of about 40%.

For a regular butterfly, the max profit is the size of the wings minus the debit paid, so ($5.00 – $0.17) × 100 = $483. If the stock was at $70 at expiration, the two short calls would be worth $0, and the long ITM 65 call would be worth $500, while the OTM 75 call would be worthless; combined, all the positions in the trade would be worth $500—not bad for a trade that cost you $17 to make. Any move in either direction past $70 cuts into that profit. At $71, for instance, the two short calls are losing $100 each (–$200 total), and the long ITM 65 call is worth $600, while the OTM 75 call is still $0. Now the trade's value is $400; this goes on until you get to the breakeven levels of $65.17 or $74.83. You can see how a butterfly reacts in Payoff Diagram 17.1.

BE = upper wing strikes minus the debit
and the lower wing plus the debit

This trade does have a small amount of positive Theta, which is always a bonus. The Delta is pretty much neutral, meaning you don't care which direction the stock moves, as long as it's a small move.

If you have a neutral outlook, it doesn't matter if you use puts or calls for your butterfly, as the pricing, POP, and profit or loss will be about the same.

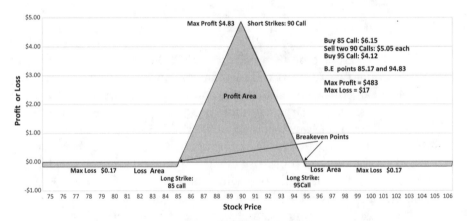

PAYOFF DIAGRAM 17.1 Butterfly

DIRECTIONAL BIAS

You do not have to trade a butterfly at current ATM strikes; if you have a bullish outlook on COIN, then you can center the butterfly around a target price like I did in Option Chain 17.1. Besides looking at charts to get a directional opinion, I let the options market pick my spot. What I am doing here is using the expected range based on the option pricing and centering the butterfly at the high end of that range. On tastytrade, the expected range is the ruler-looking strip to the right of the strike prices.

Though previously it didn't matter if you used puts or calls to make your trade, it does make a difference if you are making a directionally biased trade like this. Though the numbers work out the same whether using puts or calls, if given the choice, always trade out of the money options over in the money ones, especially for the short options. Again, the reasoning is better liquidity, tighter spreads, and most important, there is little chance of getting assigned. So if you are bearish, use a put butterfly below the market; if you are bullish, use a call butterfly that's above the current price.

In general, a butterfly like this will still have about a 5% to 8% chance of success and will cost almost nothing to make. This trade costs $17 to make with a $483 max profit. Even though you are bullish, the trade still has almost zero Delta exposure, so a price movement will not hurt your $17 much. This trade starts out Delta neutral and won't change a great deal until very close to expiration, which is the only time you will see a big profit on it.

THE WINGS

As the wings get wider, two things happen. First, the cost (the max loss) and the potential return both increase. The second is that the probability of success increases as well. The POP on a $1-wide butterfly will be around 5% to 7%, and you will probably pay 5 to 20 cents to put it on. That means you risk $5 with a potential to make $95. This is just a long shot of a trade. However, you can increase your chances of making money by expanding the strike prices. Widening the wings on the out of the money COIN trade to $10 wide will increase POP to 18%, and now you will risk about $82 to make $918, also still a long shot.

STRATEGY

The strategy of a butterfly is to guess where a stock will be at expiration, center the butterfly around that point, and hold till a day or two before expiration. If you see 25% of max profit before expiration, take it. You are best off trading butterflies with less than two weeks to go, as they don't move a lot further out in time.

BROKEN WING BUTTERFLIES

I don't trade straight butterflies very often due to their low chances; I rather trade broken wing butterflies (BWBs). A BWB differs from a straight butterfly in that the long wings are not symmetrical to the short options, instead skipping a strike or two on the further out of the money option. This makes the trade directionally biased and has more risk involved, but also gives you a credit. The lower Delta (further OTM option) is the one you will be moving to give you the credit on the trade. By doing so, you will dramatically increase the probability of success and will have no risk in one direction, making it a directionally biased trade. This is still a defined loss trade, albeit a larger limited loss, but it does give you a greater area to make a profit and has better Greek exposure, though still small compared to other trades. This is still a short Theta and Vega trade, so the higher the IV the better.

With a directional butterfly like previously discussed, you need the stock to be in a range to make money; if it lands outside that range on either side, you will lose (see Payoff Diagram 17.1). With the BWB, one side acts like a credit spread and would be all profit, regardless of how far the stock moved. It may be easier to see by comparing the payoff diagrams of the two. In Payoff Diagram 17.2, you can see that no matter how low the stock goes, it is profitable like a credit spread, while still having a lottery-like feel if you pin the short strikes. Compared to a regular butterfly, a rally above the breakeven point will see a larger loss.

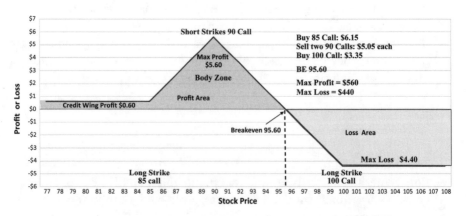

PAYOFF DIAGRAM 17.2 Broken Wing Butterfly

Using the same Option Chain 17.1 for Coinbase, the BWB would involve moving the cheaper option one strike away to a 100 call, paying $3.35 instead of $4.102 for the 95 call. This now gives the trade a $60 credit, which is yours to keep no matter how low the stock goes. The trade would now be long one 85 call, short two 90 calls, long one 100 call.

UNDERSTANDING THE BWB BETTER

Use Table 17.1 to follow along and compare a BWB to a regular butterfly. I find it best to think of a BWB as two spreads, an 85/90 debit call spread costing $110, and a 90/100 credit call spread getting $170, which nets $60 on the trade. It's the credit spread part of the trade that you would make wider to receive a larger credit; this bigger credit now finances the debit spread, which acts as some protection if the stock has a big rally. The short spread is the side that defines the risk; if the stock goes past the upper strike you will achieve the max loss.

TABLE 17.1 Butterfly to Broken Wing Butterfly Comparison

Regular Butterfly	Broken Wing Butterfly
+ 85 call = $615	+ 85 call = $615
− 90 call = −$505, Debit Spread = $110	− 90 call = −$505, Debit Spread = $110
− 90 call = −$505	− 90 call = −$505
+ 95 call = $412, Credit Spread = $−93	+ 100 call = $335, Credit Spread = −$170
Debit of $17: BE = $85.17 and $94.83	Credit of $60: BE = $95.60
Max Profit = $483 / Max Loss = $17	Max Profit = $560 / Max Loss = $440
POP 8%, Theta 0.19, Delta 0.61, Vega −0.12	POP 82%, Theta 1.0, Delta −3.54, Vega −0.71

Thinking of the credit spread first, you set up the trade like you typically would a credit spread using the 20 or 30 Delta as a good shorting spot. I used the 90 strike call with a 34 Delta; you can go lower, but then your credit gets smaller. In order to hit max profit on this credit spread part of the trade, you still want the stock at $90 or below. Above $100, the max loss on this spread would be $830 (the width of spread minus the credit).

On the debit spread part of the trade, you hope the stock expires at $90 or above, where it will have a max $390 profit; this side acts as protection for the bigger credit spread, reducing its losses if the stock rallies past $90. Now, the most the trade can lose is $830 – 390 = $440. In the next chapter, you will see that this is a ratio spread with protection.

At the peak level of $90 (the two short options), the max profit of the combined positions would be at $500 plus the credit of $60. The 90 and 100 calls are worthless, and the long 85 call is worth $500. This is the width of the narrower debit spread, then add the credit received of $60 to get max profit of $560. Once you get past the lower strike, the credit spread will make $170 while the debit spread loses $110, and you keep the difference.

Max loss of BWB = width of credit spread
– width of narrower debit spread – credit received

Confusing Directionality

The BWB can be confusing, as you are not sure which direction you are rooting for. I created this example with the short options centered at the 90 call, far above the current price of $71.42. Any trade you short, you want the stock to stay away from that strike; if Coinbase were to drop, your $60 credit seems more like a sure thing. But if the stock rallies to $90, you could make a max profit of $560 on it—however, if it keeps going you will eventually start to lose money. So what do you really want to happen? You should be trading a BWB for the smaller credit profit and not the peak area. The peak max profit is just a bonus that you will need to hold very close to expiration to achieve.

Though I made this example with a large upside buffer and an 80% POP, you can make it less directional by shorting the at the money options. This will increase the credit of the trade but lower your chances of success.

The Skipped Wing Size

The skipped wing is the side that defines the trade. There is no right or wrong answer; if you wanted to go for a bigger profit with more potential loss, then you can increase the width of it. This is a matter of personal risk tolerance, and how strongly you feel that stock won't move in the direction of that wing. I would typically set it up with wings that are $5 and $10 wide on stocks under $200. Ideally, you should aim for the debit spread side to be around 5% the price of the stock or the butterfly may be too narrow. If $10 is too much to handle, stick to lower-priced stocks

Probabilities of Profit

Overall, these trades have a very high POP: 65% when done near the money and 85% if shorting the 20 Delta options. The majority of that high probability lies in the small credit wing part of the trade. The body zone, where the max potential is, has slightly better chances than a regular butterfly due to the bigger breakeven—typically 15% to 20%. This is a long shot type of trade if you are going for the big payoff, but it can have great steady small returns if you miss in the right direction.

Breakeven Level

The breakeven level is calculated as follows:

Call BWB = (short strike + width of narrower spread)
+ credit received

Put BWB = (short strike − width of narrower spread)
− credit received

Profits Target and Exits

Keep in mind that there are two profit areas in a BWB—the peak butterfly type profit and the credit spread profit. Since these are slow-moving trades and you won't get anywhere near max profit until expiration, if you can get 25% to 50% of the max profit, or 50% to 75% of the credit profit, you should consider taking it. If the price of the stock goes against me to where the breakeven area is, I would get out, regardless of profit or loss; in this case it would be if Coinbase rallied up to $95.60. In the worst-case scenario, don't let the stock breach the lowest Delta skipped strike option.

Risk

BWBs do have risk on the broken wing side (short spread side) that you must be comfortable with, especially if you plan on holding close to expiration. You can control the risk when you put on the trade through the size of the spreads.

A FREE DEBIT SPREAD

If you had put this BWB trade on and Coinbase dropped 20 points to where the credit spread part of the trade was worth very little, you wouldn't have much more to gain from it. You could then consider taking off the credit part and leaving yourself with just the debit spread. As long as the credit spread captures more than the cost debit of the debit spread ($110 here) you can walk away with a tiny profit and have a free debit spread. To be clearer, if the 90/100 credit spread is worth $20 and you take it off, making $150 on that part of the trade, then you can't lose on the whole trade. The most you can ever lose with the 85/90 debit part of the trade is $110. You could leave it on as a lottery ticket to the upside if you wanted.

SOME NOTES

These are very slow-moving trades that react slowly to the Greeks, and you will only see real movement in last one to two weeks, so the exit early rule doesn't apply as much. These are trades you can put on with less than a month to go, even as few as one or two weeks or a couple of days.

A BWB is a trade that can be hard to understand at first, and the best way to get the hang of it is to make some trades and look at their payoff diagrams. I would start out using $1-wide intervals on lower-priced stocks where your max loss will be under $100. Eventually, you can aim for the debit spread side to be around 5% of the price of the stock. The credit taken in will still be very small until you start using wide strikes, but it's better to get the hang of the trade first.

FINAL THOUGHT

These are all low-probability trades with handsome payoffs, and they make up a small percentage of my trades. You could put on butterflies with a week to go (not something I would do with other trades), looking for a long shot. As part of my diversified portfolio, I usually do one or two BWB for every 10 trades I have on, to mix things up and occasionally get lucky. They are an alternative to strangles and iron condors for earnings plays, as long as earnings come in within the range you chose.

CHAPTER 18

Ratio Spreads

A ratio spread is similar to a broken wing butterfly, except that it is missing that lowest Delta option that was skipped in BWB. This means a ratio spread has no protection on that side. Since this trade is not buying that extra wing, it will also have a higher credit and wider profit area than a BWB. This is an undefined risk trade, with a very high probability of success through modest wins. The risk comes when the move is too extreme on the unprotected side of the short options, at which point it will act like a naked option. This is not for small accounts, as the naked short option aspect of a ratio spread eats up buying power.

BASIC DEFINITION

A ratio spread involves buying a call or put option, and then selling two (or more) lower-value options further out of the money. These don't have to be 2:1, but could be 3:1, 3:2, etc.; I will discuss the 2:1 ratio spread, as it is most typical. Selling more options than buying is called a *front ratio spread* (done for a credit); buying more options than selling is a *back ratio spread* (done at a debit). The easiest way to think of this is as buying a vertical spread that you finance with an extra short option, and get paid for doing. It has the characteristics of a broken wing butterfly, but with unlimited loss if it goes against you.

EXAMPLE

Option Chain 18.1 of EWZ MSCI Brazil ETF is currently trading at $30.55. First, look at it as a regular long 27/28 put spread, in which you would need EWZ to drop to below $27 to realize max profit, and below $28 minus the debit to receive any profit. A long put spread would cost $37, with a max profit of $63 and POP of 31%, plus a small negative Theta with a –5 Delta; this is not a trade I would make as I prefer shorting, especially because of the high IVR of 76.4 in this case.

With the ratio spread, you would short two puts instead of one and completely change this trade around; now it has a credit of $73, as you added an extra $110 in credit. It then reaches an 82% probability of profit, with a max profit of $173 and Theta is now in your favor. The downside is that because you are now short a naked put, the max loss is $2,527. This max loss could be infinity if this was a call ratio spread and the extra option was a short call. The buying power reduction in this trade is not all that much at $307.50, but it can be substantial in riskier higher-priced stocks.

EWZ	IV Rank 76.4	Last X Size 30.55 D 100	Chg 0.94	Bid X 30.54 P	Ask X 30.55 P	Size 98x126	Volume 22.8M

TRADE MODE

TABLE	CURVE	ACTIVE	GRID	CRYPTO	PAIRS	ANALYSIS

∧ Strike	Bid	Ask	○ Delta	○ Impl Vol	○ Vega
35d Puts	Dec 16 2022				IVx: 58.1% (±4.13)
22	0.11	0.24	-0.05	69.34%	0.01
23	0.23	0.26	-0.08	67.69%	0.01
24	0.31	0.42	-0.11	66.97%	0.02
25	0.46	0.58	-0.14	66.06%	0.02
26	0.76	0.79	-0.19	67.22%	0.03
27	1.06	1.15	-0.25	68.28%	0.03 S 2
28	1.44	1.50	-0.31	68.79%	0.03 B 1
29	1.92	1.98	-0.37	70.66%	0.04
30	2.48	2.55	-0.42	72.84%	0.04
31	3.00	3.35	-0.48	75.92%	0.04
POP 82%	EXT 73	Delta 19.16	Theta 2.528	Γ -4.32	
V -2.74	Max Profit 173	Max Loss -2,527	BP Eff 307.50 db		

OPTION CHAIN 18.1 EWZ MSCI Brazil ETF

Source: tastytrade

This trade does carry a 19 Delta, so it is directionally long bias because of the extra short put; however, your max profit of $173 would be if it goes down and "pins" the short put's level of 27, like it would in a BWB. At this level the shorts would expire worthless, while the long put would be worth $100 and you get to keep the $73 premium.

Looking at Payoff Diagram 18.1, you can get a better sense of how this trade works. To start with, the trade is made out of the money, and like a debit spread you need it to go past the long (highest Delta) option to start having profit potential, and to reach the furthest (lowest Delta) strike to achieve max profit. But unlike a debit spread, where you would make the same amount regardless of how low it goes afterward, if the market keeps dropping past this point you start giving up some profit, and then would later start losing because you are short an extra put at this level. The breakeven on this trade is $25.27 (the short put strike of 27, minus the credit of $1.73). Beyond this level is the danger zone of being short an extra option.

That was the debit spread part of the trade, but there is also the extra short 27 put option part of the trade, and this will give you an extra $110 credit to keep as long the stock stays above the strike you sold. This part of the trade is like a naked put. When combined, the two parts of the trade act like a broken wing butterfly with unlimited risk, because they do not have the extra protective wing below. Not having spent money buying an extra option, the naked option has some extra oomph, as this side of the trade has a greater credit.

The peak teepee-like zone is never the goal of the ratio spread; instead, the goal is for the stock never to reach that zone, and for you to just receive the credit. It's like a credit spread that has a buffer zone, where a stock can move against you a little and you will still be profitable. The max profit area here is part of that buffer zone; you want the stock to stay where it is or to rally. If the stock does go in that buffer area, it may feel good at first, but if it keeps moving, it can be painful. If EWZ drops to $20, for instance, then you are losing $1,400 on the two shorts, while only making $800 on the long one. It's a huge move for EWZ and unlikely for this ETF, but never underestimate that the worst could happen.

BENEFIT OF THE DEBIT SPREAD

As opposed to just shorting a naked 27 put that would have a breakeven of $25.90, adding the debit spread pushes the breakeven of the trade by $0.63 (the max profit of the debit spread) to $25.27. This then increases the POP by a few points, which would be even more substantial on a higher-priced stock with $5-wide spreads.

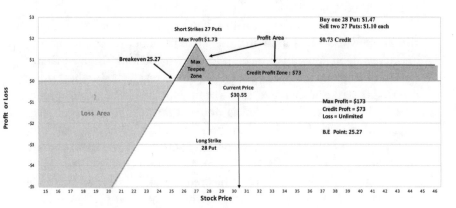

PAYOFF DIAGRAM 18.1 Ratio Spread

BREAKEVEN AND POP

The breakeven is calculated as follows:

Put ratio spread:
short put – the spread width – the credit received =
$27 – $1 – $0.73 = $25.27

Call ratio spread:
short call + the spread width + the credit received

The max zone (the teepee) will be the area between the long option and the short strike minus the spread width. For a call ratio, you add the spread width to the short option to get the far side. In this example it's $28 to $26; below $26 you have the buffer of the credit received ($0.73) before you start losing money.

The probability of profit using the Delta of the breakeven method would be about 85%. This is very typical for ratio spreads that use the 20 Delta option for the shorts. As you get closer to ATM the POP will lower to 70% to 75%, still a high percentage trade.

SLIPPAGE SUCKS

This is a trade I did put on, but was not able to get filled at $0.73, as EWZ moved after I captured the image of the options table. I had to lower my offer to $0.70 before getting filled. This is slippage in action, and it will affect your P&L and hypothetical results when back-testing or paper trading.

PLACING THE SPREAD

You should start out by selecting a spot for your short option, like any shorting trade. A 25 to 30 Delta area is ideal to receive the best value. If you go much lower, the credit received will be quite small and not worth making. The short option sets up the trade. You want the stock to stay away from this area to guarantee a profit. Next you add the debit spread. This is all done as one trade, but you can think it out from the credit side.

THE SPREAD SIZE

EWZ is a low-priced ETF, but in a higher-priced stock you normally use a $5 difference on a ratio spread. Widening the spread will increase the POP and the max profit, but will lower the total credit received. You want to make sure the debit spread is less than the price of the short option, to ensure you get a credit on the trade. Widening the spread will also lower the Delta exposure but won't affect the Theta much.

BUYING POWER

These can be expensive trades, taking up the same buying power as a short strangle or naked option. Each stock will differ; for example, Tesla requires $9,805, while Starbucks uses up $1,081. I recommend sticking to modestly priced stocks or ETFs to reduce some risk and lower the margin requirement. Make sure not to use up all your buying power by only putting on trades with naked options. They should only be part of a well-rounded portfolio of trades, but due to their high risk, don't load up on them, and never risk more than 5% of your total capital on any trade.

THINK BACKWARD

You need to think of a short ratio spread opposite to the way you would the debit spread inside the trade. It's the short option that you want to focus on. If you had a long debit call spread, you would want the stock to rally to achieve its max potential. Even though you would make the most if the stock rallied on a call ratio spread and settled at its peak max power, this side of the trade represents risk. Instead, you should want the stock to go into the credit zone of the trade that makes money from the extra short option. If you do get a rally, you have a nice buffer at first, but afterward you are exposed. If this is confusing, look at the net Delta of the trade; if it's positive, as in EWZ trade, you want the stock to rally so you get your credit.

A short ratio call spread wants the price to drop any amount, or to go up very little.

A short ratio put spread wants the price to rally any amount, or drop very little.

GREEK EXPOSURE

A ratio spread with its extra naked option will have a fair amount of exposure to the Greeks, much more so than trades that are fully protected. If done by shorting the 20 to 30 Delta options, it will have some directional bias, and have a net Delta somewhere between 10 and 25. This is a trade you want to make when IV is high to get a better premium on your shorts and capture any potential drop in IV.

Theta: positive—time decay helps

Vega: negative—a drop in IV helps

Gamma: negative—price movement hurts

EXIT STRATEGY

Ratio spreads are not home run style trades. When trading them, you are going for the smaller high probability credit they provide, and not trying to make the max profit at the peak of the triangle. With their dangerous naked exposure, ratios should be managed carefully and should definitely not be held close to expiration like a butterfly should. You should have two different exit targets, one for the credit zone and one for the max profit area. If the trade is going in the right direction and is in the credit zone, you should take a 50% to 75% profit of the credit. If it moves against the credit zone and into the max zone area where the shorts are, take a profit at 25% of max profit.

For a loss exit, look to get out if the stock reaches the breakeven price. It may or may not be a loss at this point, depending on IV and time decay, but it's a good area to exit and rethink the trade.

What's great about this trade is that due to the selling of far out of the money options, it can make money in either direction. Looking at the payoff diagram, you can see that in order to lose money, the market has to move a lot to get past the max profit point of $1.73; to get past the breakeven price of $25.27 requires a 17% move, so you have plenty of wiggle room to get out with a winner. If the market rallies, you have nothing to worry about.

TIME FRAME

Enter with 45 to 60 DTE and exit by 21 DTE, as you don't want to hold naked options close to expiration.

TAKE CREDIT WHEN CREDIT IS DUE

Not every ratio spread will have a credit, especially in low-volatility stocks. You only want to make this trade if you can get a credit; if you cannot, do not make this trade because you will give up the edge. Play around with strikes, finding strikes that give you a credit. This is not a set "buy a 40 Delta and sell two 20 Delta" trade; if you have to move your ratio spread a few Deltas to get a credit, do so. If you aren't getting a credit worth making, then skip it.

HELPFUL ADVICE

Due to the two profit areas, ratio spreads and BWBs are not so straightforward to understand. Simply reading how to make these trades will not help you grasp them; the only way to get used to them is to put them on with small low-value stocks and be diligent managing them. Making actual trades and monitoring them is definitely part of your 10,000 hours of practice. If you lose a little money at first, think of it as part of your tuition of trading that it takes to become an expert options trader.

FINAL THOUGHT

Ratio spreads, along with strangles, have some of the best back-tested results of any trading strategies. They have an incredibly high probability of success, with a very large profit area. Remember to go for small steady wins and control your losses. If your portfolio is large enough, you should definitely consider incorporating these into your trading.

MORE TRADING STRATEGIES

You can find a few more trading strategies at MarcelLink.com.

CHAPTER 19

A Well-Balanced Portfolio

K nowing how to optimally use a bunch of different trading strategies is not going to help you much on its own. It's not even knowing how and when to use them that will make you a winning trader. What really helps is knowing how to put everything together, making a diverse portfolio that can withstand whatever the market throws at you. Keeping a well-balanced portfolio is a major step in making sure you succeed in the long run.

DIVERSIFICATION SAVES ACCOUNTS

One concept you should adhere to is "Don't put all your eggs in one basket." Your best chance of succeeding long term is to make small trades over a large sample size. I am not just talking about making a lot of trades, but also about mixing those trades up, having different strategies, using different uncorrelated underlying stocks, using different time frames, trading in stocks with different volatilities, and not getting overly bullish or bearish, yet still having both directional and neutral trades.

I do know one thing for sure: anytime I took a beating, it was because "I knew" where the market was going and got too aggressively long or short without diversifying or hedging my opinion. Apparently

I didn't actually know where the market was going in the time frame it was supposed to go, and the outcome wasn't great if I was overexposed too directionally. It is hard to fight that feeling of being smarter than the market, but it is something you need to do if you want to be a high probability trader.

Unfortunately, the smaller your account, the harder it is to be diversified, but try as much as possible. If you only have $2,000 and can only afford five positions, do not make them all put credit spreads using SPY, SPX, QQQ, IWM, and APPL that expire at the same time with nearly identical Deltas. This is really just one big, very correlated, bullish position. It is not a diversified portfolio. If you are wrong you will be taking a break from trading due to an unexpected lack of capital. Instead, mix things up so you can be around another day.

Being diversified is not an excuse to trade more and more positions or greater size. Regardless of how diversified you are, there is still always the risk of some market-moving black swan event, such as the Covid-19 pandemic or Russia invading Ukraine. Your ultimate goal is to reduce risk as much as possible while still giving yourself a chance to make money.

A MANAGEABLE PORTFOLIO

Don't overdo it. I keep somewhere between 10 and 20 option positions at once. This may be too high or low for others, but it's a balance I can manage. If I keep more than 20 positions on at once, I find it harder to stay focused. If you are starting out, keep to a maximum of 6 to 10 positions before expanding to more. Having only two or three positions on doesn't give you diversity, so find a good mix. Don't trade for the sake of trading. Once you have your core set of positions, don't add more without taking others off. I don't like to keep adjusting losers, hoping they come back. It takes too much energy and keeps me from making better trades. I'd rather cut those losses instead of piling on new trades on top of them.

MIX UP THE THINGS YOU TRADE

Keeping your account well-balanced means that you are not dependent on the overall market direction. When I first started writing this book, we were in the midst of the strongest market I had ever seen.

The moves were insane. Some stocks went from $20 to $400 in a year for no reason, seemingly without a down day. Yet the market turned on a dime, and this year those stocks are back at $20 or below. Even the "safe" stocks, such as Microsoft, Amazon, Apple, Home Depot, and Disney, lost from 30% to 50% of their value. Not all stocks did poorly, though. Energy, pharmaceutical, and consumer staple stocks went up during this period. By having a mix of uncorrelated stocks with different strategies and trying to stay as Delta neutral as possible, you can make money regardless of the market's general moves. This will always be the safest strategy. If your strategy had been to only buy QQQ and Tesla calls last year, you would not have been a happy camper.

You should have a list of 30 to 50 favorite things you like to trade. My go-to list includes AAPL, MSFT, TSLA, NVDA, META, MRK, HD, KO, NKE, UAL, JPM, CRM, WMT, DIS, GLD, EWZ, SLX, XOM, XLE, IWM, SPX, SPY, QQQ, TLT, and EEM. This is a good mix of stocks, indices, and ETFs. It covers a lot of sectors that don't all move in sync.

As you assemble your own list, consider liquidity and implied volatility first, then how they correlate to each other and to the S&P 500. Knowing the correlations keeps you from piling on too many similar trades. As an options seller, the goal is to collect premium in high implied volatility options, not to worry so much about direction. The more uncorrelated you are, the better you reduce directional risk. Three semiconductors stocks can trade identically, but Exxon, JPM, and Campbell Soup likely have little relationship to each other and trade independently. That spreads your risk. This doesn't mean that when one goes up, the other must go down, but that they are not influenced by the same things, have no effect on each other, and will behave differently when the whole market moves. You will still have risk if the Dow drops 1,200 points in one day, but in the long run a diversified portfolio of different underlying stocks shouldn't have moves that are as violent as those of a lopsided portfolio.

USE DIFFERENT STRATEGIES

Not every strategy is suitable for every stock, every time. Using different strategies under different conditions opens up more possibilities. I do have favorite strategies, tending to trade more credit spreads and iron condors than anything else. Still, I always add most of the

other trades I have mentioned in this book. I am not a fan of straddles and straight butterflies, but I do a decent number of broken wing
butterflies, ratio spreads, a few calendars and strangles, and will occasionally buy single options if implied volatility is low.

Though strangles have a great overall rate of return, I would never
make them the only trades in my account. I do not want that much
undefined risk. But when I have 10 other trades going, the risk of two
or three riskier option positions diminishes drastically, bolsters my
diversity, and improves my overall chances of making money with
their high probability of success.

If you have the capital, consider putting on one or two undefined risk trades to increase your overall chance of success and for the
extra time decay they provide. You will be limited by your capital and
the options trading level restrictions on your account. If you cannot
afford to toss in undefined risk trades, stick to ones you can do. People
may get scared about having undefined risk trades, but anyone who
buys stocks always has large downside risk. I am even OK with having
a naked put or call on for a short period of time. This is a great way to
quickly fix a portfolio's Delta and get some time decay. Just remember
that naked positions are more Greek sensitive, so they move faster.

If you like to make earnings trades, don't have too many on at once,
as they can be dangerous. I may make five to ten a week if conditions
are right, but rarely more than two with earnings announcements on
the same day. I mostly use a mix of iron condors and diagonal spreads
for these trades, depending on my outlook.

A good diversified portfolio has bullish and bearish trades, along
with nondirectional Theta trades and some implied volatility plays.
Having a mix of strategies like this lets you take advantage of different market conditions. You can even have the occasional home run
looking long put or call, as long as it's a small part of the portfolio. If
you are risk averse, throw in deep out of the money protection puts as
well. This lowers your overall performance in regular markets, but if
you do get a giant unexpected drop, you will be very happy you have
the protection.

DIVERSIFY OVER TIME

Don't make trades that all expire at once. A balanced portfolio should
have different expirations and holding times. A majority of the trades
should have options that start with 45 days to expiration. That doesn't

mean you can't have other trades with longer and shorter time frames. If I make earnings trades, I usually do them in the expiring weekly contract. I typically trade butterflies with two to three weeks to go. On trades where I am short Theta, such as buying a call, I prefer to go out two to three months, to avoid big time decay. For the most part I use monthly options, but on very active markets the weekly options that fall in between the monthlies are also fine.

Avoid having too many trades expiring at once. Throwing in the weekly cycles lets you avoid the need to exit too many positions at same time, instead spreading out your exits over time. Spreading out your time frames, especially as they get closer to expiration, keeps you from getting hurt as much if the market makes a move against you. Having trades that expire in two, three, four, and five weeks gives you an added safety buffer, because your further-out trades won't feel the same pain that the trades closer to expiration feel.

In a diversified portfolio I may have one or two somewhat directional trades, like selling slightly out of the money vertical spreads or a broken wing butterfly in the stock indices with three to five days to expiration, getting out in day or two. I say, "somewhat directional," but I am also trying to collect premium. For the most part, these are speculative trades with a buffer. These trades have high Gamma risk, but since the rest of my trades have low Gamma risk, it balances out. I feel I can afford the risk.

DIRECTIONAL BIAS

It should be obvious, if you want to reduce risk, don't have 10 positions that are short vertical put spreads, broken wing butterflies, and ratio spreads, all hoping stocks go up. Even with 10 uncorrelated stocks, it's still very directional and you can get hurt with a macro moving event. Throwing in some short vertical call spreads or turning put spreads into iron condors gives you some protection against a major overall market move.

If you only want to make directional trades, you should find things you think may be going down as well as up. For example, you can sell a bullish vertical put spread on Microsoft and sell a bearish vertical call spread on Exxon. Having trades on both sides of the market should reduce your overall risk. You can have some directional bias in individual trades but should aim to have little directional bias in the total trades for your portfolio. You can trade with a bias if you want, but this book is about trying to get an edge by selling premiums and high implied volatility situations for a profit, instead of trying to guess where a stock is going.

MONEYNESS

Mix up the Deltas you use to get an overall better return. If you trade spreads and every trade is made around a 20 Delta level, you are getting a high probability of profit on every trade but never making a lot on any trade. Throw in some trades that are made at 40 or 50 Deltas. They will pay off more and help balance out your portfolio. You don't need every trade to have a POP of 75%, risking a lot with little potential profit. One big market move can mean you lose big on all of them. Stick mostly to your comfort level, but toss in a lower POP trade here and there for an occasional bigger win. Maybe do an at the money vertical spread that may have a 50% chance or a butterfly that has a low chance of success but pays big.

The Deltas you use on a trade affect your directional bias. By changing your net Delta on a trade, you become more or less bullish or bearish. You can do this by moving strikes around or widening a spread. You can trade the same stock with the same type of trade and in one case be very bearish and the other be slightly bearish to neutral. If a stock is at $141 and you sell a vertical call spread that is at the money, such as selling a 140 call and buying the 145 call, you need that stock to drop to $140 to achieve max profit. But if you sold an out of the money spread, such as the 145 call, and bought the 150 call, then though you still prefer the market to drop, you can still make the max profit even if the stock rallies to $145. This trade will rely less on a market move than the first one. If you increase your spreads to $10, your Deltas, maximum profit, and maximum loss also increase. This comes in handy when trying to balance your portfolio.

TRADE STOCKS WITH
DIFFERENT VOLATILITIES

Don't just trade all stocks with ridiculously high implied volatility, as their potential to make big moves can be costly. I am not referring to implied volatility rank, but to a stock's actual implied volatility. Making all trades in stocks with a 90% IV can be dangerous. In the majority of trades I make, the underlyings have IVs in the 25% to 60% range. That keeps it a bit diversified without extreme outliers. I do make some trades with both higher and lower volatility to mix things up, as these stocks and options act differently form one other.

As most of your trades should be made in high implied volatility ranked stocks, it's a good idea to toss in some trades that work best with low IV ranked stocks. Trades such as a calendar spread or buying a call or put outright in stocks with a low IVR will benefit if volatility goes up. Anything that can make money while protecting you from conditions you don't want will diversify your portfolio.

CAPITAL ALLOCATION

Keeping the capital required per trade fairly consistent over all trades will help in keeping a diversified portfolio. Don't trade five contracts on one spread that risks $1,500 when all your other trades are single lots that risk $350. This won't be as easy when you're doing trades with undefined risk, but set a reasonable maximum loss per trade and keep it consistent throughout.

A PROPER PORTFOLIO

A diversified, balanced portfolio incorporates a good mix of diverse stocks and ETFs, strategies, Deltas, POP, IV, DTE, and capital allocation. It should have trades that are neutral, bullish, and bearish. Once your positions are on, you should to some extent consider them as one position. This will help you keep your net Delta, Theta, Gamma, Vega, and risk in line and easily adjustable.

KEEP YOUR GREEKS IN CHECK

A few tips to help you keep a balanced portfolio that helps reduce risk.

Delta

Keep your portfolio close to Delta neutral. Unless you are a directional trader, keep your portfolio's Beta-weighted Delta between plus and minus 0.5% of total capital; plus or minus 0.2% to 0.5% is best. This allows for some directional bias but still keeps it fairly hedged. To stay actually neutral, you need to stay within plus or minus 0.2%. This means with a $10,000 account, keep your Beta-weighted Delta to about plus or minus 20 to 50 at most. Above that you put yourself at risk of a big move. I will explain Beta weighting later in the chapter.

ALWAYS KEEP LEARNING

This little piece of information (keeping Beta-weighted Delta to plus or minus 0.5% of total capital), along with Theta limits, is something I had never thought about and only learned from watching a tastylive video. Before that, my Delta limit was just a random amount of Delta I thought was reasonable to have, but I never quantified it. I have been using these guidelines since, and it makes it easier to see if I am too directional or not. Apparently in the past my estimate was a little high.

Theta

As with Delta, keep Theta in the 0.2% to 0.5% range of your total account. This may seem counterintuitive, as you want to rack up time decay. But the more Theta you have, the more Gamma risk you also have. Eventually too much positive Theta can hurt you if you are wrong on direction. Theta increases as you get closer to at the money, but an at the money option has more of a chance of being in the money than one with less Theta that is far out of the money. The at the money options will also have the greatest Gamma, which is the trade-off to having a larger Theta. So building a portfolio that takes in as much time decay as possible just means more Gamma risk. Don't go Theta crazy. To make things easier, keep both Theta and Beta-weighted Delta around the same percentage of your capital.

Gamma

Gamma is important when you want to stay Delta neutral. Keeping Gamma low will help you stay Delta neutral, regardless of what the market does. If Gamma is low, then the total Deltas won't move as much when stocks move, making it easier to stay neutral. If total Gamma is too high, a market move can easily push your Deltas out of whack. Luckily, you don't have to worry about another number here. Just keep your Theta within safe levels and your Gamma risk will also be good.

STAYING DELTA NEUTRAL

Keeping Delta neutral on either a position or portfolio eliminates a lot of the risk that comes from price moves in the market or underlying stock. Instead, the Greeks and volatility become more important. A great example is an at the money calendar spread where you buy a 50 Delta 45 DTE call while also selling a 50 Delta 21 DTE call. Price movement will not help this position, but time decay and volatility will. When trying to stay Delta neutral, the total Delta of all the options in your portfolio should be in the −0.2% to 0.2% of total capital range. The number will never be exactly zero, as Deltas move, but close to zero is close enough.

A Delta neutral position doesn't mean you are protected from a price move. Instead it means you don't care which direction the market moves and that a big move won't hurt all your positions at once. By staying Delta neutral you are hoping that the future price movement of a stock will be less than what the options are predicting the expected range will be.

A short Delta neutral position will start out like this:

Long Theta: time decay = good

Short Vega: drop in IV = good

Short Gamma: big move = bad

Delta Hedging for You and Me

Unlike market makers with a lot of money and technology behind them who constantly stay Delta neutral by buying and selling stocks or other options as a stock moves, Delta hedging for a retail trader doesn't need to be very elaborate. Look at your Deltas before the market closes and make some adjustments if needed. This can be done by position or for your entire portfolio, using current or new positions. I sometimes use futures to accomplish this overnight when I am too directionally biased. It sometimes feels like having two kids playing against each other in a ball game. You aren't sure who to root for. You don't want to lose on your hedge, but if your hedge works, your other positions lose. You just need to think of your hedge as an insurance premium to keep the rest of the portfolio balanced.

Deltas Will Move

Delta neutrality is an ongoing process, and you should stay on top of it, especially if you have options nearing expiration. What is Delta neutral today may not be tomorrow, as Delta constantly changes. A 20 Delta strangle (for instance) that starts out neutral moves as soon as the stock moves. As the stock moves, one side of the trade gets closer to in the money and its Delta goes up. The other side's Delta decreases as it gets further out of the money.

Look at Target in Option Chain 19.1. If you had a strangle using the 21 Delta 155 put and 22 Delta 190 call, it would be a roughly neutral trade with a net Delta of –1. A $5 rally would change this quite a bit. The call would probably have a new Delta of 35 and the put a 16 Delta, and soon enough your strangle has changed to a –19 Delta. One way you can adjust this is to cover the lower Delta put (the side making money) and move it closer to match the call's Delta, collecting more premium in the process.

Heck, price doesn't even have to move to move Deltas. As options near expiration, their Deltas move on their own, making them even more sensitive than normal. It's just one more reason to exit earlier.

Reducing Delta in Individual Positions

You can reduce your Delta risk on any given trade by adding something to that trade. Look at Option Chain 19.1 again. With Target trading $172.40, if you are short a 180/190 call spread, it has a net Delta of –16. Maybe you were originally bearish and now you are neutral or just want to reduce risk in general. You could do this and get the Delta close to zero a couple of ways. The simplest is to buy the 195 call with a 16 Delta. This gets you to zero Delta but costs you $165 and increases your maximum loss by that amount. You could also sell the 16 Delta 150 put for about $233, but that takes up about $2,000 in buying power.

My preferred method is to turn the trade into an iron condor by selling a 165/155 put spread and picking up about $275 in credit. This will pick up 14 Deltas, leaving you at only –2 net Delta. You could also short the 170/160 put spread that is worth 16 Deltas, but it is too close to the money for my liking.

Regardless of what you choose, the bottom line is you are reducing your Deltas and market risk. Neither are you tied to using the same expiration. You can reduce your Deltas by trading something in a different expiration and making a sort of calendar iron condor trade.

TGT	IV Rank 65.0	Last X Size 172.40 Q 100	Chg -4.36	Bid X 172.37 J	Ask X 172.41 P	Size 1x2	Volume 1.34M	NYSE Target Corp		Accounts ∨ ‹

TRADE MODE: TABLE ▾ ANALYSIS **STRATEGY:** SHORT PUT VERTICAL GO ∨ **STRIKES:** ALL ▾ **CONFIG** ▼ ⚙

o Impl Vol	o Delta	Bid	Ask	∨ Strike	Bid	Ask	o Delta	o Impl Vol
⌃ Mar 17, 2023			Calls	39d Puts				IVx: 40.1% (±15.84)
35.16%	0.11	1.04	1.08	200	28.95	29.30	-0.86	38.89%
35.17%	0.16	1.59	1.65	195	24.50	24.80	-0.82	37.98%
35.37%	0.22	2.41	2.49	190	20.25	20.60	-0.76	37.55%
35.73%	0.30	3.55	3.70	185	16.50	16.70	-0.69	37.50%
36.40%	0.38	5.15	5.35	180	13.10	13.30	-0.61	37.79%
37.24%	0.48	7.25	7.45	175	10.20	10.40	-0.52	38.68%
38.27%	0.57	9.85	10.05	170	7.80	7.95	-0.43	39.62%
39.59%	0.65	12.95	13.15	165	5.85	6.05	-0.35	40.91%
40.83%	0.73	16.40	16.65	160	4.35	4.45	-0.27	42.17%
41.80%	0.80	20.15	20.45	155	3.15	3.30	-0.21	43.66%
42.73%	0.85	24.15	24.55	150	2.29	2.36	-0.16	45.17%
43.20%	0.90	28.50	28.90	145	1.64	1.69	-0.12	46.83%

POP 69%	EXT 280	P50 78%	Delta -16.20	Theta 2.393	Max Profit 280	Max Loss -720	BP Eff 720.00 db ⌃

OPTION CHAIN 19.1 Target

Source: tastytrade

PORTFOLIO DELTA NEUTRALITY

Overall I do take some directional risks on individual trades. It's OK to have a long bias in oil and banking stocks and a bearish outlook in the Euro currency and tech stocks. But I care about making sure my portfolio as a whole is not overly biased. The simple way to do this—but not the best—is to have the Deltas of all the trades add up to close to zero. If you are short a call spread in one stock with a –10 net Delta, then short a put spread in another stock that has a positive 10 Delta. Whatever software you use to trade should be able tell you your portfolio's Delta or Beta-weighted Delta. If not, find a different broker.

BETA WEIGHTING

I said the method above is not the best way because not every stock is created equal. One hundred shares of TSLA moves very differently than 100 shares of Wells Fargo, Ford, or gold. Trying to offset one trade's Delta with another's will be useless unless you can correlate them. Being long 50 Deltas of Apple may mean a $250 move on a typical big day, while being short 50 Deltas of Ford could offset that by maybe $25. You would need 500 Deltas worth of Ford to be neutral with these two positions. Beta weighting is what lets you compare things evenly: apples to apples, not apples to cars.

You will see Beta as β. Beta weighting is what lets you compare all the stocks in your portfolio against a common denominator: most commonly the SPY ETF. The SPY (SPDR S&P 500 Trust ETF) is designed to track the S&P 500 stock market index; it is the largest and oldest ETF. You could change the weighted security to anything you want. Instead of SPY, you could Beta weight everything to live cattle. That won't do you much good, but it's a choice you have.

Beta weighting lets you see how correlated and fast a particular stock's move will be in relation to the market in general. Ford has a Beta weight of 5.12 and Apple 46.2. This means for every $1.00 move in SPY, 100 shares of Ford will move $5.12 in value while 100 shares of Apple will change by $46.20. You can see more precisely that you need about nine times as much Ford to offset Apple.

Knowing how stocks compare to each other and the S&Ps is an invaluable piece of information. Knowing your Beta weight tells you exactly how long or short you are and shows your total risk exposure as a whole, in a snapshot. This gives you a benchmark to quickly check how directionally biased you are and how much you need to fix it to get back to neutrality.

If you are too Delta positive for your liking, you can add some negative Delta (and vice versa). Some traders like to be bullish and others bearish, but knowing your limits can keep you in check. If you know you are OK with a net long position worth 40 SPY—at around $400 a share that's the same as being long $16,000 of the SPY—and your account starts showing a 50 Beta-weighted Delta, it is time to either unload something or put on some negative Delta trades. This is where keeping your Deltas to within a range of –0.5% to +0.5% of your total capital comes into play. This means with a $10,000 account, you should at most be long 50 Deltas of SPY ($20,000 worth), risking $200 per 1% move in the SPYs. Staying under +/–0.2%, or $8,000 worth of SPY, may be more reasonable based on your risk levels. You can have your own ranges, but now you know how to measure and control directional risk.

ADJUSTING THE PORTFOLIO

First, I like to look at each of my positions and see how I can adjust them to lower my Delta. Maybe I take profits on a few of the winners. If this doesn't lower my Deltas enough, I can add some opposite-Delta trades. Instead of adjusting a bunch of individual positions, the easiest way to do this is to use the SPY options to make a trade that will get you closer to Delta neutral. You could even trade the SPY outright if you have the capital.

For example, maybe you are short or long too much Delta, but like your individual positions as they are. You may be nervous about an upcoming unemployment report or Fed statement. A quick SPY or E-mini futures trade can easily get you close to Delta neutral. I tend to do this with futures contracts for simplicity and because I can trade futures 24 hours a day. You don't have to use SPY. You could also use QQQ, IWM, AAPL, or anything else. I recently hedged by shorting the Euro FX futures, which in one click dropped my Deltas by 150.

A LITTLE BIAS IS OKAY

Over the long run, the stock market tends to go up. Yes, there will be down periods; 2022 has been an example of that. But over the course of 40 years in trading, a little bullish bias will be rewarding. Just be careful not to get blown out in those down periods.

A LITTLE MORE ON CORRELATIONS

You can compare any underlying to any other ETF, stock, index, or future to get exact correlations between them. Correlations are different than Beta, as they tell you how one market or stock relates to another. Two oil drillers will most likely be highly correlated, while a drug company and a steel producer may have little correlation.

A strong correlation is 0.80 to 1.00, a mild correlation is 0.40 to 0.80, and 0.0 to 0.40 means no to very weak correlation. Correlations and Betas can also be negative. A negative correlation to SPY just means a stock moves opposite the SPY. The VIX, which tends to move in a different direction than the stock market, currently has a −0.68 correlation to the SPY and −26 Beta weighting.

It's easy to see correlations if you plot them on a chart. In Chart 19.1, you can see that Roku and Eli Lilly have a correlation of 0.04, which is close to zero. Sometimes they move in sync, as in late April and early May. They then went their separate ways for a bit, then in July they both traded sideway or slightly down before going in different directions again in mid-September. If I had matched LLY with another drug company, such as Merck, their charts would have a much tighter overlay, as they have a stronger correlation: about 0.80. They still move a little independently of each other at times, but in the same general direction.

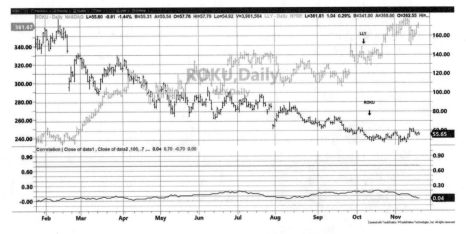

CHART 19.1 Roku-LLY Correlation
Source: TradeStation

FINAL THOUGHT

Keeping your options portfolio diversified with a mixture of everything is a big part of success. Have neutral, bullish, and bearish trades with multiple expiration periods, over a diversified group of underlying stocks and ETFs while using multiple strategies. Diversity along with keeping your trading size small is what will keep you in the game, even in the roughest of times. That is, unless of course you have the holy grail of systems. Then you can go nuts.

CHAPTER 20

Exit Strategies to Maximize Results

Y ou can be the best analyst in the world, able to pick market direction at ease, putting on one great trade after another, but this won't make you any money. You only make money when you exit a trade. Knowing how and when to exit a trade with both a winner and a loser is the difference between being a winning and a losing trader and should not be overlooked.

KEEP THOSE EMOTIONS IN CHECK

As you contemplate putting on a trade, you should also have its exit plan thought out, win or lose. This removes emotion and makes your exits more systematic. It is very easy to convince yourself that you can squeeze another $35 out of a trade, or that you are correct and the stock market is wrong (but the market needs a few more days to realize it is wrong), or that a trade will come back to where it was two days ago. Even worse is freezing up when looking at 10 losing positions and not being able to mentally take a loss.

Greed, fear, revenge, boredom, doubt, anger, depression, anxiety, ego, pride, and hopefulness are emotions that will hurt your bottom line. Keep them from controlling your decisions if you want to succeed. The best way to do this is with a predetermined exit plan.

Newsflash: a stock can keep going down day after day after day while its implied volatility explodes, no matter how much you "know" or hope it will reverse tomorrow. Many traders are too quick to cut winners but don't know when to take a loss. They end up watching trades that should have lost $250 go to their max loss. Then there is the dreadful situation when a trade is really working for you—it's up $300 out of a potential $350—but greed makes you hold on for $10 more. Then things change and you freeze with fear of losing your profits. Now it's a day before expiration and you are down $190. Next thing you know you are angry, depressed, and anxious to make it back on the next trade, so you trade double your normal size in revenge. Yeah, you are better off keeping those emotions in check.

HAVING AN EXIT PLAN

You should have some sort of market assumptions when putting on a trade. These might include:

Nike won't move more than one standard deviation in the next 30 days, and its implied volatility will come down from 44% to a normal level of 35% in that time frame.

The SMH ETF will rally a bit or not go much lower than its current price of $215.68 in the next couple of weeks, and its IV should come down from 38.4%.

Tesla will go back to $250 in six months.

When you make an assumption and choose the most appropriate trade for it, you should be plotting your exit plan as well.

In the Nike example, if I look at the option chain and see that earnings will be coming out in three weeks, I will scratch that trade idea. It's too risky, and the IV will most likely go up as the stock nears earnings. It is OK to bypass riskier trades while waiting for the high probability opportunities.

With SMH, I decide to put on a simple credit put spread with 39 days to expiration, selling the 40 Delta 210 put and buying the 34 Delta 205 put for a $185 credit. I am looking for a rally, but a small slow move down to $210 wouldn't be the end of the world. At the same time, I am thinking about how I will get out of the trade, regardless of what it does. There is always the strategy of holding the trade to the end, knowing the max you can lose is $315 or gain $185 at most.

Instead, I prefer to manage the trade. Here are just a few examples of what you can do. Everyone has different risk parameters, and you can adjust to what fits your own.

You can visualize the trade with the help of Trade Analysis Graph 20.1, which is a profit/loss analysis of SMH from tastytrade's platform. The current price of $215.68 is the small circle. The two shaded areas are the profit and loss if held to expiration, and the upwardly slanted line is what the theoretical P/L would be at 21 days to expiration. The platform lets you easily change the days to expiration as well as implied volatility, so you can see what your trade would be worth in the future at different volatility levels and at any time before expiration. This differs from the payoff charts I created, which only showed the profit or loss at expiration. I used 21 days to expiration as this is when I begin to target getting out of a trade. Any good software should let you do this. I find tastytrade the easiest to manipulate.

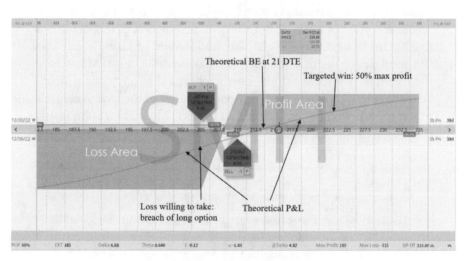

TRADE ANALYSIS GRAPH 20.1 SMH
Source: tastytrade

THE LOSING SIDE

Look at the loss side first, as controlling losses is more important than profits to your bottom line. You can set exit strategies for winning or losing trades several ways: price targets, price action, change in conditions, or time. No matter which you choose, it's important to have an idea before you get in.

Set Dollar Amount

One option is to set a loss based on the trade's price. In this case, you received $1.85 credit. You can decide to take a loss and get out if the spread goes to $3.00. Common loss targets are 100% of the premium received or 50% of the cost of a debit trade. You can set any amount you like. This is acceptable and better than nothing, though it isn't my preferred method. Sometimes these numbers can be random and fall within the normal range of trading. If you chose this method, you could enter a stop and not worry about it.

Price Action

I prefer to base my exits on technical analysis and other trade-based factors, not on the option's price. I made this trade thinking SMH would not go down below a support line I drew at $208. This is 7 points from the current price and also coincides with the expiration breakeven price of $208.15, but that's just coincidence. If SMH drops to $208 in the next three weeks, this trade would be losing about $50. (It's hard to see because the diagram has no scale, but that is where the theoretical price would be on the chart.) If at any time it drops below that level and breaks my support line, one of the reasons I made that trade is no longer intact, and I would exit. There is no point losing more than necessary, hoping SMH goes back up.

A MORE ACCURATE BREAKEVEN

$208.15 is just the breakeven at expiration, and since you shouldn't be holding until then, it's not an accurate number. A more realistic breakeven at 21 days to expiration would be closer to $213, according to the trade analysis graph. That's where the theoretical line crosses into the positive zone.

Greeks

Another method you can employ is having targets for your Greeks. I keep a very close eye on a trade like this when the short put goes in the money (50 Delta). If the long put goes in the money, I exit and take my loss. You can also get out at a target Delta, such as 40 or 60. I also use a parameter that if net Theta goes negative, I get out. If a reason I made the trade was to collect time decay and it stops doing that, I don't want to be in the trade anymore.

Volatility

Another thing you can do is have a volatility mental stop. If implied volatility reaches that target, you exit. This trade currently has a 38.4% IV and I am looking for IV to drop. You can say that if it goes up to 45%, you will no longer be in the trade, as your assumption that IV will go down is wrong.

Nothing at All

If you put on a very cheap debit spread or a butterfly that cost $12 to make, most of the time you can just it let ride. Even with a tight credit spread, if the most you can lose is $40, you won't get hurt much by holding it, so you can let it ride.

Sometimes the market just goes haywire or earnings drop a stock $25 overnight. There's not much you can do here but lick your wounds. Your spread may be so close to max loss that getting out doesn't really help you. If there is still time left you can hold and hope for a miracle. But don't hold too long, because as you get closer to expiration, there is a chance that an in the money option will get assigned.

THE WINNING SIDE

It's just as important to have an exit strategy when your trade is making money as it is when it's losing. More times than you would like, a winning trade can become a heart-wrenching loser. Greed can take over when you are making money and blind you. You can hold a winner for weeks, gaining 95% of its maximum profit. The options may seem to be safely $5 out of the money with two days to go to expiration, and you don't exit because you don't want to give up that extra nickel you can make on the trade. Then bang! The trade moves $8 in those two days. You freeze and end up with a max loss. This is the infamous Gamma risk at work, which I will thoroughly explain once and for all in a bit.

Getting out of a trade early lets you lock in profits and put on newer trades with higher profit potential. Here are some strategies I like to follow.

Profit Target

When you put on a trade, your intention should not be to hold for the maximum profit and/or until expiration. Instead have profit targets. I've mentioned them for various strategies already. A good rule of thumb is a target of 50% of a trade's max profit. Some strategies move slower, and if you get a 25% profit in a week that could be a target.

Time

In any premium-collecting trade I make with more than 30 days to expiration, I am out by 14 days to expiration. I start looking to exit with a profit at 21 days to expiration, but I am a little flexible, based on how a trade stands given my other exit criteria and directional outlook. Usually if a trade starts with 45 DTE or more, I use 21 DTE as my exit point. For trades with fewer than 40 days left, I may go closer to 14 DTE as my exit time frame. This applies to winning or losing trades.

If I'm putting on a trade closer to expiration, I have different considerations. Many traders day trade using options that expire in a day. That's not me. However, I will put on a speculative trade and use an option with a week to go, knowing I will get out with two or three days left to expiration. This isn't every trade I make. It's part of my overall trading plan with a small percentage of capital. If I do covered calls with 14 days to expiration, I get out with 5 days left.

Price Action

The above are profit and time targets, but you can use market conditions to exit trades. If you are making money and things change so that you are no longer bearish or bullish, it's OK to get out before a target is met.

STICK TO YOUR PLAN

It's not just that you need an exit plan to help limit losses and take profits off the table. You also need the discipline to actually follow through on that plan and close out your positions. This is a business, and you need to put the work in if you want to succeed. If you have 47 positions on at once, it isn't going to be easy to manage them. If you only have 10 positions on, then it's fairly easy to manage them on Excel or in a notebook, keeping exit notes that you can follow. If you do keep track of your trading, you can go back and review what you did right and wrong.

Thinking out an exit plan will also keep you from putting on trades for no real reason. You don't want notes that say, "Sold SPY strangle because—not sure why I actually did it, but I was bored and saw it on my Twitter feed, exit strategy = nothing planned."

WHY YOU SHOULDN'T HOLD TO EXPIRATION

Holding to the last minute could lead to bigger potential profits, but it adds more risk than it's worth and opens you up for big profit and loss swings. Here are a slew of reasons why you should manage your trades before they expire.

You Have Nothing to Gain

If you have a trade on that has acted quite well—for instance, selling a 110/115 put spread for a $180 premium with a max loss of $320—and the stock has rallied a lot going from $120 to $163 with both legs of the spread being worth 1 to 5 cents, you really have nothing left to gain. You have captured 99% of that trade. This position has no extrinsic value left, so it's pointless to hold it looking for more. You no longer have the same risk/reward ratio you had when you originally made the trade. Now all of your risk is on the downside.

Ask yourself if you would put this trade on now, risking $495 to make $5. The answer should hopefully be no. Yes, the chances are huge that it will expire worthless for a max profit, but the max loss from this point is not $320 anymore—it is now $495. The same thought process should run through your head when you've captured 75% of the profit. The more profit you take, the more risk you have of giving money back. Once a trade has worked and you've done well, there is little point in waiting two more weeks to make little bit more. Congratulate yourself and move on to another trade.

This is especially important in unlimited loss trades. When most of the premium has been captured, you need to exit. Nothing better can happen at this point, and you could really get hurt if something goes haywire.

Tying up Capital

Holding a trade with little potential to make more money or one that isn't working as planned is a bad use of capital. If you have limited trading capital and (per your trading plan) should only be putting on eight trades at once or are near your maximum buying power, why would you want to tie that up? Free up the money and find a better trading opportunity, one with a bigger profit potential. Everyone should think in these terms, not just those with small accounts.

One Less Thing to Worry About

If you tend to keep too many positions, you will not be able to focus properly. By getting out of trades earlier you can limit the number of positions you have and better monitor your portfolio. The last two weeks of trading before expiration can be the most dangerous time of the trade. This is the time you would need to be more on top of positions. Exiting early frees you of this stress allowing you to focus on newer trades.

Increased Rate of Return

If you use $500 in buying power on a trade and get out two weeks later after making $100 on the trade, that's a 20% return—not too shabby. If you hold it for five weeks and get $200, that 40% return may sound even better. But the returns aren't better when you annualize them. Both the annualized return on capital and profit per day tend to be lower the longer you hold trades.

The two-week trade yields close to a 500% return annualized (25 two-week periods = 20% × 25 = 500%; I use a 50-week year to make the math simpler). The five-week trade yields a 400% return. Looking at it on a per day return, using 5 trading days per week, $100 over 10 days returns $10 a day, while $200 over 25 days returns $8 per day. In both cases taking a quick profit earlier creates a better return on your money.

Making It Easier to Exit

When an option gets too far either in or out of the money, it can become harder to trade. In both cases there will be very little volume, making it harder to get filled. You will feel lonely when nobody wants to trade with you at a decent price. This is especially true on deep in the money options, which normally have a very wide spread, making it even tougher to get a good price. Look at Option Chain 20.1 of Apple and both the very high and low Delta options. Look at either the puts or calls—it doesn't matter. Volume distribution almost follows a bell curve, with barely any volume at the extremes. The wider spreads for the deep in the money options compared to very tight spreads near the money won't help you much either. You can avoid the problem by getting out earlier.

LESSONS LEARNED

I once had a $5-wide credit spread in a low-volume stock (Shake Shack) that I let get too far away, hoping it would come back for a profit or smaller loss. It didn't. With a week to go, I put in limit orders every day, trying to get out at a reasonable price—$4.25, then $4.50, $4.75, $4.95, even $5.00—but never got filled. I was only able to exit by doing each leg separately, eventually paying a total price of $5.20. This was a trade that I thought my worst-case scenario was exiting at $5.00, I ended up paying more than it was worth. Always trying to learn from my mistakes, my three takeaways here were:

1. Don't trade low-liquidity options.
2. Get out before it gets too late.
3. Take a smaller loss early over a bigger loss later.

Symbol	Description	Last	Net Chg	Bid	Ask	Hist Vol...	Beta Weighting	Account
▽ AAPL	Apple Inc	177.76	0.46	177.75	177.76	21.84 %	☐ SPY	All Accounts

Spread Single · Filter Spr Width:5 · Strikes 20 ·   Click to: Trade ·

	CALLS					PUTS				
Pos	Prev Volume	Delta	Bid	Ask	Strike	Bid	Ask	Delta	Prev Volume	Po
◢ 02 Jun 23 (1d) Weekly									29.32%	↑2.68
	59	0.98	22.00	22.70	155	0.01	0.02	0.00	385	
	8	0.96	19.55	20.45	157.5	0.01	0.01	0.00	106	
	66	0.93	17.25	18.15	160	0.01	0.02	-0.01	397	
	23	0.95	14.55	15.40	162.5	0.01	0.03	-0.01	156	
	1,793	0.95	12.05	12.85	165	0.01	0.03	-0.01	4,119	
	114	0.95	9.55	10.30	167.5	0.03	0.04	-0.02	2,405	
	2,395	0.86	7.35	8.30	170	0.03	0.06	-0.03	11,399	
	2,222	0.82	4.90	5.75	172.5	0.11	0.13	-0.08	14,434	
	8,157	0.73	2.81	3.05	175	0.38	0.42	-0.22	53,839	
	44,895	0.48	1.30	1.37	177.5	1.20	1.31	-0.53	67,210	
	144,550	0.23	0.48	0.50	180	2.83	3.00	-0.85	20,852	
	36,994	0.10	0.17	0.19	182.5	4.70	5.35	-1.00	1,459	
	27,332	0.04	0.07	0.09	185	6.60	8.35	-1.00	331	
	5,288	0.02	0.03	0.04	187.5	9.05	10.80	-1.00	69	
	3,883	0.01	0.02	0.03	190	12.40	13.20	-0.97	59	
	1,582	0.01	0.01	0.02	192.5	14.60	16.20	-0.95	5	
	959	0.01	0.01	0.02	195	16.45	18.65	-1.00	3	
	31	0.00	0.01	0.01	197.5	18.50	21.20	-1.00	0	
	21	0.00	0.01	0.01	200	22.10	23.30	-1.00	30	

OPTION CHAIN 20.1 Apple Volume

Source: TradeStation

Lowers Assignment Risk

I've mentioned getting assigned a few times, but haven't explained it, so here goes. Assignment is when you are short an option and a buyer decides to exercise their right on that option before it expires. Your brokerage firm does the assignment randomly from a pool of short option holders. Assignment typically happens when an option is in the money with little extrinsic value remaining, and somebody who is long that option decides they want to buy or sell the stock. Assignment is most likely to happen as you near expiration or when the option is so far in the money that it has no extrinsic value. The best way to avoid assignment? Don't be short any option in the money in the last two weeks before expiration.

GETTING ASSIGNED

Suppose you sold a 195 call on a stock that is now trading at $200. Anyone who is long the same option can decide they want to buy that stock at $195. Your broker randomly selects you and forces you to sell them 100 shares. Your option position is then converted to being short 100 shares of the stock. If you had been short a 210 put, then someone has the right to sell you 100 shares at $210. You would then be long the stock at $210.

If you are in a credit spread and the short leg is in the money, you run the risk of being assigned as you near expiration. If this happens to you for the first time, you may have a panic attack when you look at your positions in the morning. You will see two things. First, if you had had a 210/205 put credit spread, what used to look like being short a 210 put and long a 205 put would now look like you're long both a 205 put and 100 shares of the stock from $210.

The second thing you will notice, actually you will notice it first, is a $21,000 margin call: the cost of holding those shares of stock. The margin call only happens if you don't have the capital in your account; if you do have it, then you'll just have a buying power deduction. Either way a little panic may set in, but don't worry; in reality nothing has changed. If you have the buying power, you can keep this trade on. It has simply shifted from a spread to a stock with a protective put. The only difference would be to your benefit if the market started to rally, as you are not locked into the maximum profit you could have made on the short put. On the downside, you are still risking the same $500.

You'll probably get assigned at some point. Your best move in this instance is to get out of the position entirely by closing out the shares and selling your long option. If you really liked the trade, begin from scratch with longer expirations.

If you have a spread on with a short option that is in or near the money and it's an hour before it expiration, your broker will help you out by liquidating it for you at the market, ensuring a bad fill. But as you know, you shouldn't be holding trades until the last hour before expiration, so I am sure this will never happen to you.

GAMMA RISK REVISITED

Gamma is the risk that options prices will become more sensitive to movements in the price of the underlying stock. This sensitivity amplifies as you get closer to expiration. I have mentioned Gamma risk many times, and I will try to drive the point home now.

The easiest way I can explain it is, when you are short an option that is out of the money, you don't want it to move in the money. All you need is for it to stay out of the money with a Delta less than 50. A higher Gamma means that a move in the stock's price will affect an option's Delta and price more than when Gamma is low. A higher Gamma makes it more likely that an option's price and Delta will move against you. They can also move in your favor, but if you are already out of the money and there is only 50 cents left to be made, why take that risk? The chances are 50/50 that if it moves, it will move against you. Why risk turning a winner into a loser?

If you look at Option Chain 20.2 of Pepsi, you can see that, as the options get closer to expiration, the Gamma almost doubles every month, especially for the options closest to at the money. The extrinsic value also decreases. At the same time Theta, Gamma's flip side, is also gaining speed, though at a slightly slower pace than Gamma. The higher Gamma means that smaller price changes can move an option around more as it becomes more sensitive. At the money options have the most Gamma risk because a small movement in either direction sends the contract in or out of the money.

If you were short a 185 call with Pepsi at $184.22, it would be worth 90 cents with 5 days to expiration and $4.28 with 54 days to expiration. As long as it stays below $185, you are doing great. If suddenly the stock rallied up to $190, which is very reasonable, the five DTE call would be worth at least $5.00, while its Gamma of 0.125 may cause the Delta to jump from 41 to 93. The 54 DTE would trade at about $8.00. With a Delta jump of 52 to about 72 as it has a much smaller Gamma of 0.038.

This $5 move would cause the Delta of the option with five days to expiration to go up almost three times more than the 54 DTE option, which is the difference in the Gammas. You can't just multiply Gamma by the price move to get a new Delta as for every dollar increase out of the money, the Gamma slows a bit. I am estimating it looking at the 180 calls that are $5 further in the money.

Symbol		Description		Last		Net Chg		Bid
▽ PEP	▾	Pepsico Inc		184.22		-0.86		184.1:

Spread	Single	▾	Filter	NONE	▾	Strikes	8	▾				

					CALLS						
Pos	Imp Vola...	Vega	Extrinsic	Theta	Gamma	Delta	Mid	Bid	Ask	Strike
⊿ 02 Dec 22 (5d)	Weekly									
	~0%	0.00	0.09	-0.02	0.000	1.00	9.20	8.70	9.70	175
	18.86%	0.03	0.21	-0.06	0.026	0.95	6.82	6.35	7.30	177.5
	15.63%	0.04	0.31	-0.08	0.054	0.89	4.43	4.20	4.65	180
	15.74%	0.08	0.84	-0.13	0.098	0.69	2.46	2.20	2.71	182.5
	13.60%	0.09	0.90	-0.12	0.125	0.41	0.90	0.79	1.00	185
	14.41%	0.06	0.29	-0.08	0.075	0.16	0.29	0.23	0.34	187.5
	15.77%	0.03	0.09	-0.04	0.032	0.06	0.09	0.08	0.10	190
	19.35%	0.02	0.06	-0.03	0.017	0.03	0.06	0.05	0.07	192.5
▸ 09 Dec 22 (12d)	Weekly									
⊿ 16 Dec 22 (19d)										
	~0%	0.00	0.36	-0.02	0.000	1.00	9.48	9.00	9.95	175
	10.78%	0.05	0.51	-0.03	0.025	0.94	7.12	6.75	7.50	177.5
	12.62%	0.12	0.99	-0.05	0.051	0.81	5.10	4.80	5.40	182.5
	13.11%	0.16	1.76	-0.07	0.066	0.65	3.38	3.10	3.65	182.5
	12.99%	0.17	1.99	-0.07	0.072	0.47	1.98	1.89	2.08	185
	13.14%	0.15	1.08	-0.06	0.062	0.30	1.08	1.03	1.12	187.5
	13.53%	0.11	0.56	-0.04	0.045	0.18	0.55	0.52	0.59	190
	14.70%	0.08	0.33	-0.03	0.030	0.11	0.33	0.27	0.39	192.5
▸ 23 Dec 22 (26d)	Weekly									
▸ 30 Dec 22 (33d)	Quarterly									
▸ 06 Jan 23 (40d)	Weekly									
⊿ 20 Jan 23 (54d)										
	~0%	0.00	0.91	-0.02	0.000	1.00	20.02	19.70	20.35	165
	12.55%	0.06	1.19	-0.02	0.009	0.96	15.30	15.00	15.60	170
	15.89%	0.18	2.14	-0.04	0.022	0.83	11.25	10.80	11.70	175
	15.41%	0.25	3.31	-0.05	0.032	0.70	7.43	7.15	7.70	180
	14.59%	0.28	4.28	-0.05	0.038	0.52	4.28	4.00	4.55	185
	14.10%	0.26	2.13	-0.04	0.036	0.33	2.13	1.99	2.27	190
	13.87%	0.18	0.92	-0.03	0.026	0.18	0.92	0.88	0.96	195
	14.32%	0.11	0.41	-0.02	0.016	0.09	0.40	0.36	0.45	200
▸ 21 Apr 23 (145d)										

OPTION CHAIN 20.2 Pepsi Gamma

Source: TradeStation

The option with 54 days to expiration can handle a $5 move against it, especially if this was part of a spread where it has plenty of time to work itself out. With five days to go, you don't have this luxury, and it is less likely that the trade would come back to being in the money and profitable. Ignoring Gamma risk could take a trade that was $0.90 away from expiring worthless to one with a very good chance of biting you in the butt. It's just not worth the risk to have a profitable trade go bad over a relatively small move. You are better off getting out early and moving on.

GAMMA AND EXTRINSIC VALUE

You can think of Gamma risk in terms of extrinsic value risk: the less extrinsic value you have, the more you are at risk. Extrinsic value is Gamma protection. When you short an option, you are shooting to capture the extrinsic value. If you shorted the 54 DTE 185 call with extrinsic value of 4.28, your hope is for it to expire worthless. You would keep the $428 as long as Pepsi stays below $185. If it doesn't, you have a buffer to $189.28 to at least break even. As time goes by (I watched *Casablanca* with my son last night, so that was in my head) and that extrinsic value gets eaten away, you should think of it as a new position. When it's worth 90 cents, as at five DTE, forget about any paper profit you may have. From this perspective, the breakeven point is no longer $189.28. If you let it go to that, you'd give away $3.38 from the 90-cent current value.

With five days to expiration, the 185 option currently has no intrinsic value—only 90 cents of extrinsic value. Should the stock rally to $190 a day or two later, the option may be worth $5.25. It might have 25 cents of extrinsic value left, but would have gained $5.00 of intrinsic value. For it to now expire worthless and you to achieve max profit, it must first go through that $5.00 of intrinsic value. The 54-day trade, on the other hand, has $4.28 of extrinsic value and would also gain $5.00 of intrinsic value. It will have given up some extrinsic value for the intrinsic value it gained, but still has quite a lot left: at least three-plus dollars of extrinsic value will remain. Which one would you rather be short?

You can also look at it from another angle. With a move to $190, the shorter term option would quadruple in price, while the longer option wouldn't even double. That's a much more volatile move that you can control by getting out of an option before it nears expiration. This becomes even more pronounced with one or no days to go.

It isn't easy to fully understand Gamma or predict exactly how it will affect you. At minimum, you should understand that if your position is out of the money, the closer you get to expiration and the cheaper the option becomes, the more risk to potential reward you face.

STOPS

Stops can save you from taking major losses or letting big profits slip away. They can keep you from freezing up and watching losses grow and grow. However, I am against using stops when trading options, especially on risk-defined trades, as their protective legs give them a kind of built-in stop. I do use stops when I trade futures and in my stock portfolio.

Though I wouldn't place stops in options trades, I still stick to predetermined exit levels. I prefer to use a stock's price or volatility action as my stop trigger. I set an alert and then manually exit a trade when it hits that level. I also pay close attention to a trade if I am down 100% of the premium collected. That doesn't mean I will get out. I just start looking at my charts to see if the reasons I made the trade have changed. If I still like my parameters, I give the trade room to work.

The problem with stops in options is that they can have wide spreads and be thinly traded when they're too far in or out of the money. That can lead to unexpected and bad fills, especially when multiple legs are involved in a trade. You can easily get filled on a stop at $3.00 when a spread's theoretical price is $2.50, if the spread is wide enough. This gets amplified when options are in the money and you need the stops most, as in the money options tend to have the widest spreads.

If you are trading with proper position sizes, you should be able to afford your max loss on a trade and won't need to place stops. You will also have plenty of time to react to a market move, as options move slower than the market. But if you have a $5,000 account and are making 10 trades that risk $500 per each trade, you might be biting your nails if you are down $1,800 on a big move. Then yes, a loss will hurt you. The lesson here is to trade what you can afford to lose.

WHEN TO USE HARD STOPS

If you must, you should only enter stops on naked options or any other unlimited loss position that can really hurt you. Make sure you're in stocks or ETFs that have very high liquidity and tight spreads, such as AAPL, QQQ, SPY, MSFT, etc. If you do use stops, you don't want to make them so tight that a typical standard deviation move in a stock will get you filled.

You should give your trades room to work. Many of your trades will be losers at some point. This is normal, and by not letting them play out you won't have many winners. If you randomly place a stop at a $150 loss or 100% of the credit received, you will get stopped way too often and lower your overall chances of making money. Even if you have stops, they won't protect you from an outlier event like Covid where stocks open down 10%. You will get filled at a price that's much worse than where you placed your stop. Some folks don't have the discipline to get out, so they need stops. But if you do not have discipline, you should not trade unlimited loss option positions.

LEGGING OUT

Legging out means breaking up a position, such as a spread, strangle, or iron condor, etc. that was put on as one trade, but exited as separated trades. When you put on that trade, the other half of it was meant to protect you by reducing your Delta risk. When you take that off, you lose your protection. If you start playing around with one leg as the market rallies or drops, you can go from defined risk to unlimited risk while exposing yourself to one side of the market. You will also see a change in your buying power available, plus you are changing your trading strategy mid-trade. Instead of trying to capture extrinsic value, you are now trying to time the market, and very few people are good enough to do this consistently. In general you should get out of a position the same way you got into it and avoid putting yourself in unlimited risk situations. Yet there are times when I would say it's better to leg out of each position:

1. If your options are so far out of the money that they are almost worthless, you can exit the short position and leave the long leg, which might be worth a penny or two, as a lottery ticket in case the market dramatically reverses. Even so, if you can get $10 or $20 for it, I would take the money. When you do a thousand trades a year, that can add up to quite a bit of money.
2. When one side of an iron condor, strangle, or butterfly is far out of the money and not worth much, it's OK to remove that

leg. It now offers very little to the trade. You could then put on a newer leg closer to the money. This would even out your Deltas on the iron condor and bring in some more premium. You could also decide to just lock in a profit on one side and leave the other side on for a potential reversal. This would change your original market-neutral position to bullish, but things change and you should be able to adapt. Just keep to your other exit parameters for this leg of the trade. What you should never do is get out of the side that is losing money and leave the other side alone. The stock can easily turn on you, and then you would lose money on both sides of the trade.

3. There will be times when you try to get the midpoint price or are even willing to go to the bid and ask price but you will not be able to get filled or will be stuck with a horrendously bad fill. In this case, I am okay with legging out of the trade. I would first get out of the short option, to avoid any margin requirements. When filled, immediately get out of the other side. I am most likely to do this with iron condors and butterflies, as their multiple legs can make it harder to get filled at a good price.

SCALING OUT

You don't have to exit your whole position at once. Depending on your buying power and whether the trade size fits your risk plan, you can trade in multiples of two or three contracts. In this case you can take a partial profit at one target (perhaps 25%) and then another target (maybe 50%), then hold the remaining to closer to expiration for a bigger target. This helps lock in a profit, yet gives you room for a bigger winner.

GIVING A DYING TRADE CPR

I do not like to adjust or rollover trades, especially losers. There are many traders who do this, and it may work, but to me trying to figure out ways to revive a lost trade is more work than it's worth. Converting a trade to a calendar spread or ratio spread or rolling it back a month, or up two strikes, is not going to help turn the market around. Unlike volatility, prices aren't mean reverting. A stock can go from $100 to $10 and stay there for decades. If you keep adjusting, trying to get back to even, you could be doing so for years, spending a lot in commissions and taking up a lot of your time. You will also be using up buying power on trades that just may never work.

My view on a losing trade is this: Get out and reevaluate with a fresh mind. This also goes for winners. When you're in a trade for a few weeks, it's easy to convince yourself that anything may happen. Once you reach your win or loss targets, it's time to move on. I trade the same stocks, indices, and ETFs over and over again. But I view these as new trades, not continuations of old trades.

Maybe I was bullish and had sold a credit put spread that wasn't making any money with three weeks to go. I'd rather get out and reevaluate with a fresh mind than move it back a few times. Maybe I will decide that an iron condor is a better idea now. It's easier to do this without a position already on.

FINAL THOUGHT

Don't take the exit lightly. Give it as much or more thought than the entry and then stick with that plan. Keep your emotions from dictating when to get out; try to be systematic about it. It may make the difference between being a winning or losing trader.

CHAPTER 21

And in Conclusion

The Director's Cut

U nfortunately this book must come to an end. Once again, I wrote a book that was deemed too big to publish and was asked to shorten it. As I began the task of removing 20,000 words, I found it easiest to delete the last three chapters plus one trading strategy instead of cutting out bits and pieces throughout the book, as I think the rest of the book flowed together nicely. These three missing chapters—on risk, money management, and trading with a plan— could be considered a standalone subject, so they seemed the most logical to cut.

Since you made it to end, I assume you are one of those who would love to keep reading and get my full intended version of this book. Well don't despair, as an added bonus I have included the missing chapters on my website. I strongly encourage you to read them there if you want to get to the next level of trading.

Though they aren't specifically about trading options, the cut chapters can be what separates winning from losing traders and are critical to a trader's success. Even with a great trading strategy, if you cannot control your risk and money management or do not have a solid plan, you will find it hard to succeed. Here is a brief summary of what I include in these chapters.

Chapter 22
Wow That's a Lot of Risk

This chapter discusses many of the risks involved in not just trading options, but trading in general. It starts with distinguishing between systemic, sector, and company risk and explains how you could mitigate some of those risks. Then I discuss trade selection risk, which includes directional risk, volatility risk, picking the right strategy and time frame, outlier risk, leverage risk, Greek risks, black swans, and more. As the chapter title implies, there is lot of risk involved in trading, much more than I can summarize. You cannot avoid risk, but you can minimize it by trading small, diversifying, and staying close to Delta neutral.

Chapter 23
The Must-Have Money Management Chapter

I would consider money management the most important part of being a successful trader. Apart from sheer luck, having a solid money management plan is the one thing that will keep you from blowing out while also letting your capital grow. This chapter discusses reducing risk by implementing money and risk management strategies before entering a trade. It expands on how to protect yourself from all the risks of the previous chapter, while giving you the steps to make a money management plan.

Chapter 24
Finally, the First Step: Having a Plan

To wrap things up, I discuss the importance of having a trading plan in place before you begin trading. It is not easy to make a solid trading plan until you have a good amount of hands-on trading experience and market knowledge. Even so, a trading plan is an important part of making high probability trades and keeping your emotions out of trading. This chapter includes all the ingredients you need to create a tailored plan that will put you on the road to success.

FINAL THOUGHT

Good luck with your trading! Keep learning, especially from your mistakes. I hope this book has helped. I learned a few things along way myself.

MarcelLink.com
Marcel@MarcelLink.com

Index

Page references followed by *f* or *t* refer to figures and tables, respectively.

About the Author

Marcel Link has been trading options, futures, and/or stock for 35 years. In 1987 he began at the bottom, working as a crude oil options clerk on the floor of New York Mercantile Exchange. It was here that he first started gaining invaluable option experience while learning from grizzled pros. Far from the typical speculative buying of puts and calls, he was learning about things like Delta hedging and how to trade discrepancies in volatility when very few people understood what this meant. He was soon trading OEX and SPX options for himself while still a clerk and within two years was able to make enough money to buy his own seat in the NY Cotton Exchange, trading NYFE, Dollar Index, and Cotton futures and options. Though he made money, it only took one stupid overtrading mistake for him to put a big dent in his account. Learning from his mistake, he borrowed some money, learned to control his trading size, and persevered.

In 1996 he received an MBA in finance from Rutgers School of Business, after which he started an online commodities discount brokerage firm, Link Futures. This was at the onset of online trading, and though successful, it was hard to compete with the multimillion-dollar back clearing firms entering the field, and he eventually sold link futures to the clearing house. Owning the brokerage firm and watching retail traders make countless mistakes was like taking a master class in why people lose money trading.

After selling the Link Futures, Marcel began day trading stocks on a proprietary trading desk for the next decade. It was while here that when comparing the traits of winning and losing traders, he decided to write *High Probability Trading* in 2003, which became a very popular trading book, topping Amazon's list of trading books and receiving great reviews. In 2008 he wrote another book, *Trading Without Gambling*, this time about trading with a plan.

Since 2011 he has been living in East Hampton, New York, where he rekindled his early option experience and began trading options and their volatility extensively. Marcel currently is actively trading options and futures again along with managing several stock portfolios. He has given several trading seminars and has consults traders one-on-one basis.

Upon the completion of this book, Marcel plans to start a website, Link Trading Academy, to help traders with option strategies and technical analysis.